ADVANCE PRAISE

"Already, because of Brooke de Lench's inspiration and dedication, a powerful movement of mothers dedicated to improving youth sports has taken form. This immensely readable book brilliantly assembles the most important lessons she has learned, from parents and children on the edge of danger, as well as respected athletes, educators, physicians, trainers, and coaches. Were every mother of a sports-loving child to read this brilliant assessment of the promise and peril that awaits them and their family, and to listen to her wise and thoughtful voice, I am confident that their bonds of love would be strengthened, and their fields of sport would become happier, safer, and more fulfilling places. Brooke is a trustworthy messenger of essential knowledge for the many adults and children who are concerned to change the dangerous games of childhood. I wish that every pediatrician, school principal, and coach would read this book, too, because from their surprise and consternation at everything they didn't know, and their resolve to do something, would flow a parallel professional groundswell to involve and empower mothers.

—ELI H. NEWBERGER, MD, DEPARTMENT OF PEDIATRICS, HARVARD MEDI-CAL SCHOOL, AND AUTHOR, *THE MEN THEY WILL BECOME: THE NATURE AND NURTURE OF MALE CHARACTER*

Home Team
ADVANTAGE

The Critical Role of Mothers in Youth Sports

Brooke de Lench

Collins

An Imprint of HarperCollinsPublishers

This book is written as a source of information only. The information contained in this book should by no means be considered a substitute for the advice, decisions, or judgment of the reader's physician or other professional advisor.

All efforts have been made to ensure the accuracy of the information contained in this book as of the date published. The author and the publisher expressly disclaim responsibility for any adverse effects arising from the use or application of the information contained herein. Text permissions appear on page 293.

HarperCollins books may be purchased for educational, business, or sales promotional use. For information please write: Special Markets Department, HarperCollins Publishers, Inc., 10 East 53rd Street, New York, NY 10022.

FIRST EDITION

Library of Congress Cataloging-in-Publication Data has been applied for.

ISBN-10: 0-06-088163-1
ISBN-13: 978-0-06-088163-4

06 07 08 09 10   WBC/RRD   10 9 8 7 6 5 4 3 2 1

To my sons,
Taylor, Spencer, and Hunter,
who taught me that collaboration and competition
can go hand in hand

CONTENTS

ACKNOWLEDGMENTS

There is no way that I can ever begin to thank each person who has helped to make this book possible. This is the difficult reality of writing such a book. Each of you who has made a contribution know who you are and should know that I value you. I thank all of the mothers who are silently working for change as much as I thank the loudest voices demanding that our kids are kept out of harm's way. I have changed the names of most of the people in this book to protect their privacy or where revealing their identity may be embarrassing or uncomfortable for them.

The team approach that I used to write this book has been a true collaboration between current and veteran sports mothers and fathers and some of the country's brightest experts in their fields. Because no single child or sports psychologist; Olympic, retired, or current professional athlete; coach; physician; mental health provider; athletic trainer; activist;

or academic researcher can provide the breadth and depth of information needed for a book of this kind, this book reflects the collective wisdom of an entire team of experts. I am truly blessed to be a part of such a community.

My gratitude goes to the millions of visitors to the MomsTeam.com online publication, who over the past six years have taken the time to share their darkest moments and happiest memories and to contribute suggestions on ways to make our children's sports years better. Some of the most courageous of all parents I have worked with are those whose children have died in a sports-related accident. Their tears and the stories they have shared have been an inspiration to me. I especially want to acknowledge Karen Acompora, Kelli Colby, Linette Derminer, Maura DiPrete, Anthony Keys, Michelle Tran, Cheryl Lalloo, Rachel Moyer, Joy Lippo, Arista Star, Theresa Smith, and Stew Krug, who turned their deepest sorrows into lessons for us all. Thanks also to all the mothers of Olympic athletes I have spoken with over the years, especially Angela Ruggiero's mom, Karen; Chris Klug's mom, Kathy; Travis Mayer's mom, Lynn; and Shaun White's mom, Cathy. Angela Ruggiero, an incredible athlete and even better person, also deserves special thanks for her support over the years.

Thanks to my agent at ICM, Kate Lee, whose energy, business savvy, determination, and vision helped make this book possible, and to her colleague, Richard Abate.

I am indebted to my editor at HarperCollins, Kathryn Huck-Seymour, for seeing the potential in this book, for her incisive comments, and for keeping me on task during the editing process. I also owe thanks to many others at Collins for their support in this project, including Group President Joe Tessitore; Mary Ellen O'Neill, publisher of Collins Lifestyle and Wellness; Ryu Spaeth, assistant editor; Jean Marie Kelly, Libby Jordan, and Ginger Hawkins in marketing; Paul Olsweski and Michelle Dominguez in publicity; and Marina Padakis in production editorial.

The chapters on abuse and injury prevention reflect important contributions from Eli Newberger, MD; Robert Cantu, MD; David Janda, MD; Linn Goldberg, MD; Diane Elliot, MD; W. Norman Scott, MD;

Jean-Jacques Grimm, MD; Allison Ellison, RN; Maria Pease, MD; Diane Atkins, MD; Steven Horowitz, and Shari Kuchenbecker, PhD; Celia Brackenridge; and David Paulo helped shape my understanding of child rights, child abuse, and child development in youth sports. My Moms-Team colleagues, Keith Wilson, PhD; Shane Murphy, PhD; Suzanne Nelson, Doris Greenberg, PhD; and Jeannette Twoomey, Esq., also made important contributions to the book.

The support and encouragement of Julie Burns, Colleen Superko, Elaine Raakman, Barbara Jones, Carol Anne Beach, Ellen Staurowsky, Nancy Carey, Ilene Lang, Victor Oppenheimer, Suzanne Komorowski, and Gerald Herman all helped make this book possible.

It takes so much more than a village to write a book. Virginia Cargill, my dear friend with one of the most brilliant business minds around, I will forever cherish our friendship and intellectual conversations. And so many thanks go to Sally Bowie for helping me clear numerous emotional, intellectual, and editorial hurdles along the way. You both have helped keep me in the game.

A profound thanks to some of the "village moms" who have supported me during the year I have been writing this book: my neighbor Kathy Jorgensen, for so much, especially with the care of Caleb, my fourteen-year-old golden retriever (best doggie goalie of his day); Margaux Churchill, for her remarkable intuition; Molly Thayer, for knowing just when to zip off an e-mail encouraging me to take a much-needed break; Sandy Alexander, for her wisdom and ability to know just when to bring me a cup of coffee and a laugh; Anne Buxton, who made sure that I was being well fed; and to fellow author and walking pal, Mimi Doe: without her enthusiasm and years of constant encouragement this book may never have been written. And to Lindsey Straus, who offered invaluable advice, support, and encouragement during the long writing process.

Thanks to the following men whose encouragement, personal and professional advice, guidance, and wisdom over the past twenty-five years helped prepare me for the monumental job of writing a book: Dave Stormont, Bruce Button, Rob Walker, and Jim Burness. I will always admire the way that you parent your children and coach your teams, and forever value the friendship you have provided to me and my family.

I am grateful for the staff at MomsTeam, who kept the site running smoothly as I took my writing sabbatical, especially Jackson Tenney, Hubert Chau, Lindsey Barton, David Hubai, Carey Sands-Bohrer, and Jonathan Coles.

Thanks also to the seaside mothers from Duxbury who watched over me and my sisters and all the other neighbor kids as we ran and played, swam and biked, and learned to sort out the rules and play the game our way in the backyards, especially my mother, Missy, and Mary Kaye Gilbert and Mary Fernandes. And, my stepmother Rita for teaching me so much.

And, my never ending thanks to Jean-Jacques Grimm, for teaching me that I can not fight strong winds and waves which go against me; I can only let them fill my sails and carry me in new directions. You have helped make this book a reality.

Finally, I thank my sons, Taylor, Spencer, and Hunter, the most valuable team members in my life. No hat trick in the world could ever replace the one you scored the moment you entered the world together that wonderful summer morning. I have been extraordinarily blessed to have had a front-row seat from which to watch you share, collaborate, and communicate, always without even the hint of sibling rivalry. This book would never have been possible had I not enjoyed such an amazing home team advantage.

INTRODUCTION

The concept of Yin is ever present.
—It is the Mystic
Female from whom the heavens and the earth originate.
Constantly, continuously, enduring always.
Use her!

LAO-TZU, *TAO TE CHING*

America has become a society of excess: super-sized everything. Youth sports are no exception: more of just about everything; practices, games, tournaments, competition, select teams, travel, media coverage, money, burnout, and injuries. The only thing youth sports have less of is kids having fun and just being allowed to be kids. Instead of sheltering them as much as possible from the pressures of the adult world, too many of us introduce our children to those pressures at ever earlier ages; we think that if we don't do everything possible to help them get ahead of their peers, even in preschool, they—and by extension, we—will be branded as failures, as losers, and sent, literally and figuratively, to the sidelines. What is being lost in the process, however, is much more precious: their childhoods.

Look at the statistics. Though 9 out of 10 of all youth sports accidents are preventable, the number of our children suffering unnecessary injuries, and even death, continues to rise. In ever-greater numbers, young athletes are suffering physically, psychologically, and sexually, at the hands of coaches, parents, and sometimes even other players are steadily increasing. Steroid use among high school athletes has grown by 68 percent since 1971, leaving users with severe and lasting physical and psychological problems. Childhood obesity and type II diabetes have reached epidemic levels as more and more children abandon the playground or sports field for the comfort of their couches and Play-Stations.

Several years ago, stories about attacks on referees by coaches, parents, or even young athletes were rare. Now there are a dozen reports of such incidents *each week*. While the blame is usually placed on parents in general, it is the parents who simply reflect the deep structural problems in today's youth sports: a symptom of the disease, not the disease itself. The real problem is much more fundamental: All too often, adult-organized youth sports today is not about kids playing sports, it is about how adults are manipulating the system to serve their own interests: the game within the game.

As mothers feel pressured to pack more and more activities into the lives of their children, even seemingly straightforward tasks, such as registering a child for a sports program and getting them to practices and games—on time, in uniform, properly nourished and equipped—are becoming more difficult and adding to the already stressful lives of the parents and children.

One might think from the papers, the news, or the talk shows in the past decade that the *only* problem with youth sports today is the out-of-control parent. All we have to do, they say, is stick a code of conduct or laundry list of rules under their noses and ask them to sign on the dotted line, initiate "Silent Sundays" (i.e., no cheering at Sunday games), ban them from the stands, and everything will be fine.

But *everyone* involved in youth sports has contributed to the problem.

At a 2006 press conference in Washington, D.C., the Citizenship

Through Sports Alliance issued its inaugural youth sports national report card, giving the following "grades":

Child-Centered Philosophy	D
Coaching	C–
Health and Safety	C+
Officiating	B–
Parental Behavior/Involvement	D

As the Alliance report card shows, almost all aspects of youth sports are getting poor grades. If your child brought home these grades, you would call his teacher and quickly come up with a plan to improve them. This book is that plan.

I am not a child or sports psychologist or former professional athlete, but I have a unique perspective on youth sports. In 2000, with the help of some of the country's most respected experts in the worlds of sports, medicine, psychology, law, technology, business, and marketing, I launched a Web site, MomsTeam.com, to address the needs and concerns of sports mothers everywhere. It is a place where mothers can not only vent, but find ways to change the culture of youth sports. From its inception, MomsTeam's mission has and continues to be to make youth sports "safer, saner, less stressful, and more inclusive."

Thus much of the advice in this book is based on my first-hand experience in the youth sports trenches and from talking to and communicating with thousands of mothers and fathers across the United States, many times in person.

Much of this book is devoted to the practical steps you can take as a mother on a day-to-day basis within your own family—where you have the greatest influence and can have the greatest impact—to provide a better, safer and more balanced youth sports experience for every member of the family, from picking the right sport for your child to gender-specific advice on raising athletic daughters and sons, from ways to get and stay organized, to budgeting your time and money in order to find the balance between sports and family life that works best for your family. I provide detailed advice on steps you can take to keep your child from becoming a victim of abuse—physical, emotional, or sexual—while playing sports, ways you can reduce the chances your child will suffer a serious, catastrophic or fatal sports injury, what to look for in a good youth sports coach, and tips on communicating with coaches, especially to communicating with the majority of coaches, who are men.

Just as importantly, this book is about ways mothers can take advantage of their gifts as women to give youth sports back to our children. It is about the critical role mothers can play, by teaming up with likeminded parents, to help their communities get better grades on their youth sports report cards. It is about mothers shedding the label of "soccer moms" and coming down from the bleachers and into the coach's box and on to boards of directors. It is about challenging the status quo in a new and different way: by creating a balance in youth sports between feminine and masculine, between yin and yang, and, in the process, restoring mothers to their natural role of guardians of children at play for the benefit of all children.

A note from the author:
For convenience, I often write, "boys are like this and girls are like that," or "women are like this and men are like that."

Lest offense be taken, I am only implying that, on average or statistically, "*most* boys/girls or women/men *tend* to be like this or that."

Part 1 The Role of Sports Mothers in the Family

Chapter One

A Mother's Voice
The Missing Piece of the Youth Sports Puzzle

Education commences at the mother's knee, and every word spoken within the hearing of little children tends towards the formation of character.

—HOSEA BALLOU

A CHANCE TO PLAY

One by one, eighteen sixth- and seventh-grade boys entered the gym, barely making eye contact with me or one another. I extended my hand to each as he arrived, and introduced myself. I asked each to find a soccer ball and kick it around until practice started.

As the boys sullenly tossed their sports bag on the gymnasium floor and began to kick the soccer balls, I detected a lot of negative energy. From talking with their mothers, some of their fathers, and their previous soccer coaches, I knew how embarrassed most of them were: embarrassed to have been cut from the travel soccer program in our town because they weren't offered a spot on one of the top three teams, embarrassed because there were supposedly not enough boys or a coach to field a fourth team, and embarrassed that their coach was a mother.

Past coaches and the director of the soccer club had tried their best to dissuade me from coaching. "Don't expect to win any games," they said. Some of the boys have attention issues, they said; several chronically misbehave. Some lack talent or are slow footed. So-and-so's mother is a pain in the you-know-what and will make your life miserable.

To make matters worse, some of the parents, once they learned that I was to be the coach, immediately challenged my ability as a forty-three-year-old mother to coach a team of twelve-year-old boys. One father had called to tell me his son was going to sit out the season rather than play for me: "He deserves better. He deserves a top-level coach," the father said. Most told me not to be surprised if their son quit after the first few practices: "he is angry and embarrassed to be on a team of also-rans, especially one coached by a mother," they told me. The only glimmer of hope they gave me was that their sons loved soccer, and that they thought that they had the potential to be good players.

Instead of scaring me off, however, all the negativity simply strengthened my resolve to turn what everyone expected to be a disastrous season into something special; to give this group of outcasts a season to remember, to give them a reason to keep playing soccer by making it fun again, to show them the very best that sport had to offer, and to teach them lessons through sports that would enrich their lives.

After I let the boys play for twenty minutes (as the mother of three energetic twelve-year-old boys I was well aware of the need for boys this age to burn off steam), free play had turned into a frenetic game of dodgeball. I shouted for the boys to take a break, grab their snacks, and find a seat in the bleachers.

Once they sat down, I introduced myself. Before I began explaining my coaching philosophy, expectations, and goals for the upcoming season, Todd* blurted out the question that seemed to be on most of their minds: "Why don't we have a man for a coach?" Instead of answering, I suggested that they eat their snacks and drink their water while I did the talking, after which I would answer their questions.

*In the interest of privacy, many of the names used in this book have been changed.

"Women are the greatest untapped resource in youth sports. In the countless hours I have spent at youth games, practices and tournaments, I have always been puzzled by the absence of woman coaches. The sidelines seem to be reserved exclusively for men, while women are relegated to bringing the snack, driving the carpool, and sitting in the stands rooting for their kids. To me this is clearly one of the most backward traditions in sports today."

—SCOTT LANCASTER, SENIOR DIRECTOR FOR NFL YOUTH FOOTBALL DEVELOPMENT

No such luck. They bombarded me with questions. Finally, Jared insisted that I answer his question: "Why are you coaching us? What do you know? You are a girl."

After taking a couple of deep breaths, I began again. I had not scripted what I was going to say; instead, I spoke from the heart. "Most of you know that a month ago you didn't have a team to play on. I was the one who asked the men running the program to give you a chance to play. When they told me that no one had volunteered to coach a Division 4 team, I told them I would find someone with a soccer license who was an expert on eleven- and twelve-year-old boys like you, and who loved sports as much as each of you."

The team was finally quiet.

As hard as I tried, I told them, I couldn't find anyone with the credentials, the time, or as much love of the game of soccer as I did to be the coach. "So, guys, I am your coach."

I went on to tell them that during the upcoming season they would learn a lot about soccer and teamwork; that, above all else, they would not only have fun but, by the end of the season, they would be holding their heads up high.

The rest, as they say, is history. A group of angry boys with attention, aggression, communication, and self-esteem issues became a group of boys who respected themselves, one another, and me; a group of boys able to effectively communicate with one another and me; a team that held its own in scrimmages against the town's Division 1 and 2 teams; a team awarded a trophy for sportsmanship at a Memorial Day tournament; a team that went undefeated until the semifinal of the league's postseason tournament; and ultimately, a team I was invited to take to a sportsmanship tournament in St. Andrews, Scotland. One parent later told me that I was the best coach her son had ever had. The director of the soccer club said he had never seen a team play together so well *as a team*.

It was my dream team. I took my wish list of what I felt made a good coach, and what I felt was important to teach boys on the cusp of puberty, and made it come true. I gave the team a safe, nurturing environment in which to do what boys their age want to do most: play, burn off steam, feel safe (at every practice or game I told them I had only one rule: absolutely no teasing or bullying), and have fun.

By the end of the season, I came to realize that essential to the team's successful season—success I measured not so much in the wins and lone loss but in the physical and emotional growth of the players—were my instincts *as a mother* to nurture, encourage emotional openness, value fair play, cooperation, connectedness, and doing one's best over winning, and to provide boys with a healthy outlet for their aggression and competitiveness. It was simply a joy to see the power that sport has in bringing people together.

GUARDIANS OF CHILDREN AT PLAY

Sadly, the joy I experienced as a coach is not being experienced by most mothers. Instead of continuing to serve as the primary guardians of their children at play—hanging out a city window to check on our kids in the street below, or looking into the backyard to monitor a group of ten-year-olds playing touch football—today's sports mothers are more often than not, found sitting in the stands; working behind the concession counter, selling snacks and raffle tickets; working as team administrators; or chauffeuring their kids to and from practice and games. The puzzling absence of women coaches in youth sports, as Scott Lancaster, the director of the National Football League's youth football development program, noted in his book, *Fair Play: Making Organized Sports a Great Experience for Your Kid*, is "clearly one of the most backward traditions in sports today."

The 3:00 a.m. E-mails Many of the e-mails I receive at MomsTeam are from mothers who wake up at 3:00 in the morning worried sick about what sports are doing not only to their kids, but to themselves, and asking for advice about what, if anything, they can do about it. The e-mails suggest that:

❖ While our daughters are participating in athletics in ever-greater numbers, many mothers are struggling to find ways to have their

Many parents believe it is time to challenge the assumption that, for better or worse, competition in youth sports must be defined solely in terms of winning and losing, and displays of power, dominance and control.

Many mothers see
themselves as the
missing piece in
the youth sports
puzzle, that they
believe that the
culture of youth
sports would
improve if it cel-
ebrated the values
of women as much
as men.

voices heard, so that youth sports will reflect not only the values and concerns of men but their own values and concerns as well.

❖ Although more and more mothers have grown up since the 1972 enactment of the Title IX, the federal law mandating that girls be given the same athletic opportunities as boys, many have been told that they don't know enough about sports to warrant moving from the stands to the coaching sidelines or on to a club's board of directors.

❖ Mothers know intuitively that they should be doing everything possible to protect their children from the pressures of the adult world. Taught by many feminists not to value their maternal, nurturing, and intuitive nature, some mothers are afraid to act on those instincts even though they tell them that the current youth sports system too often emphasizes winning and competition over fun and skill development, treats children as young as six as adults, and cruelly and unfairly labels too many as failures before they have even reached puberty. This is *not* the kind of nurturing, caring, and above all, inclusive environment mothers believe their children need to be able to grow into confident, competent, empathetic, and emotionally and psychologically healthy adults.

❖ Many mothers are afraid their children will be ostracized if they criticize the status quo, if they try to protect their children against a runaway youth sports system that injures and unfairly classifies and excludes more and more kids each year.

❖ Many mothers are getting sucked into the crazy vortex of competitive youth sports, where survival virtually requires that they become overly focused on and invested in their children's success in sports. As former *Time* columnist Amy Dickinson wrote in an online article in February 2000, "We sit on lawn chairs yelling helpful instructions to our kids and their coaches. And at night we go to bed wondering if we can pinpoint the moment we became our dads."

What Most Sports Mothers Want What, then, do sports mothers want? From the e-mails I have received at MomsTeam, from my conversations with mothers all across the country, including the mothers of many Olympic athletes, the vast majority of mothers (and many fathers) just want to make youth sports fun again. They want to know that their children will be protected against injury and abuse and given a chance to play until they graduate high school and that the organized sports program in which they enroll their children—the "village"—will protect them and keep them safe while they are entrusted to its care. It isn't just the safety of our own children we care about; as mothers we care about the well-being of *all* children.

Many believe that it is time to challenge the assumption that, for better or worse, competition in youth sports be defined solely in terms of winning and losing, and displays of power, dominance, and control. Instead, many of us want our children to learn that while competition is healthy and necessary (at least after they have developed a mature understanding of what competition means, around age twelve), a successful competition is one where *all* players do their best and respect their teammates, opponents, and the rules.

Many mothers also see themselves as the missing piece in the youth sports puzzle, that they believe that the culture of youth sports would improve if it celebrated the values of women as much as men. As natural communicators and nurturers, mothers inspire coaches, parents, athletic directors, school boards, and local and national youth sports organizations to do more to keep children safe, to balance competition with cooperation, and to think about sports not just as a place to showcase the gifted and talented but as a place where *all* children can begin a love affair with sports and physical exercise lasting a lifetime, instead of ending, as too often is the case, in early adolescence.

MOTHERS: A GREAT UNTAPPED RESOURCE

Women, particularly mothers, as Scott Lancaster noted in *Fair Play,* are "the greatest untapped resource in youth sports." The 42 million mothers of kids in sports represent an incredible resource. In the chapters that follow, there is advice on how to reclaim their natural role as guardians of

"My mother has always been very supportive of me as an athletic female and has allowed me to be my own person. I was one of the first women to wear shorts on center court at Wimbledon. I don't know what would have happened if my mother would have made me wear dresses. I might not have won 10 Grand Slam tennis titles."

—ANNE SMITH

By the Numbers:
* *Number of U.S. women who are moms: 82.5 million*
* *Number of mothers in U.S. with a child participating in at least one youth sport: 42 million*
* *Number of U.S. children ages 4–19 participating in youth sports: 57 million*

our children at play and confidently step onto the out-of-control playground of today's youth sports to assume whatever role they choose, whether it be as parent, coach, team administrator, member of the board of directors of the local youth soccer club, or community activist.

Perhaps then, a new paradigm for youth sports can grow: one that will ensure that our children's sports years are more fun, safer, saner, less stressful, and more inclusive from the first day of T-ball to the last high school game.

Chapter Two

Too Much, Too Soon
Making Sure Your Child's Involvement in Sports Is Developmentally Appropriate

TRUSTING YOUR INTUITION

Many parents question when a child should start playing sports or a specific sport, like football. One mother asked, "How can I get my six-year-old to *stay* interested in playing a sport that he said he wanted to play? After going to the first practice, where he voluntarily sat on the sideline and watched the other kids practice, he has decided that he doesn't want to go back."

How do you decide if your child is ready to play sports? What sports should she play? When is too early? When is too late? What should be your expectations starting out?

In deciding when your child is ready to start playing organized sports and what sport to play, trust your intuition. As Oprah Winfrey told *Newsweek* for its October 24, 2005, cover story on women in power, "The only

You know your child better than anyone. You are the expert for your own child. It is okay to go with your gut about what is in the best interests of your child, whether or not it is what all the other kids are doing.

time I've made a bad business decision is when I didn't follow my instincts." Indeed, researchers at the University of Amsterdam who tested the power of intuition—reported in the February, 17, 2006 issue of *Science*—found that the unconscious mind is *better* at reaching a sound conclusion on complex decisions. As lead author Ap Dijksterhuis told the *Boston Globe,* it "is much better to follow your gut."

If trusting her intuition worked for Oprah Winfrey, it can work for you as well. You know your child better than anyone. Just because most of your child's peers are starting early doesn't necessarily mean your child should, too. It is okay to go with your gut about what is in the best interests of your child, whether or not it is what all the other kids are doing. After all, this is the kind of thing mothers have been doing for eons. Whether it is a decision about when to let your child start sports or try out for a competitive travel team, trusting your intuition is *always* the right choice. You need to have the courage to say no to your kids about sports more often, just as you would say no if your child asked you for candy right before meal time or wanted to stay up way past her bedtime. Don't be scared into saying yes because you fear your child will suffer if you don't.

No Magic Starting Age There is no evidence that an early start gives a child a jump on the competition. While starting early may help your child in some sports, such as swimming, gymnastics, figure skating, and ice hockey, research has not established that an early start makes a difference in most sports. A 1995 survey by Wirthlin worldwide, a Chicago-based research company, found that two out of three American Olympic athletes said they started competing in their sport at age ten or older; slightly more than half didn't start until they were teenagers or young adults. One-fifth didn't start until they were twenty-one or older.

In deciding when your child is ready to start playing organized sports there are a number of factors to consider:

Your child's skills. Assess your child's basic skills (running, throwing, balance, and ability to track objects and judge speeds). An oft-cited study by Northern Kentucky University suggests that half of all children start playing organized sports before they have mastered the basic skills necessary for participation. It is important to start off on the right foot so your child doesn't immediately become discouraged by his lack of skill.

Your child's age. Most children aren't ready to participate in organized sports activities until they are four or five. Even then they should participate on a limited basis (fifteen to twenty minutes of organized activities with thirty minutes of free play). The American Academy of Pediatrics recommends that children not start playing team sports until around age six (girls may be ready a little earlier) and that children wait until middle school to play contact sports such as football. It also recommends against participation in sports such as in-line skating and skateboarding before age five because young children do not have the physical skills and thinking ability needed to perform such activities safely. If you have any doubts about whether your child is ready to play sports, my advice is to wait.

Your child's maturity level. The attention span of six-year-olds, while longer than that of preschoolers, is still limited. Your child is mature enough to play a team sport if she is attentive enough and has enough self-discipline to learn from group instruction. Playing sports can't speed up the maturation process. Be patient and let your child mature at his own rate.

What your child's doctor says. Consult your child's pediatrician before you enroll your child in an athletic program if he has a medical condition (asthma, allergies, or diabetes) that might affect participation.

What you feel. Watching a young child play sports will trigger your natural instinct to protect and nurture. As my MomsTeam colleague, Dr. Shane Murphy, author of *The Cheers and Tears: A Healthy Alternative to the Dark Side of Youth Sports Today,* warns, if you don't think you could control yourself if you were to witness your six-year-old being injured in a game, you may not be ready to handle the stress of your child's participation in sports and should wait until your child is a little older and less fragile. Indeed, no matter how old your child is, you should resist the urge to go to their side if they are injured as this tends to upset most children. If the situation is serious the coach will call for you.

PICKING A SPORT

Once your child is ready to play organized sports, the next question is what sport to play:

Consider your child's interests. As soon as he begins to express his likes and dislikes, let him have a say in deciding what sports to play. Look for clues about what sports he might enjoy in how he spends his free time. Is he always running and jumping, playing ball in the yard, swinging from a jungle gym, or begging you to go for a swim or a bike ride? Does he prefer to play alone (individual sport) or with other children (team sport)?

Think outside the box. Avoid the temptation to simply sign up your child for one of the "big three" (soccer, baseball, or basketball). Your child might enjoy a less popular team sport, individual sport, or an adventure, action, or extreme sport, such as inline skating, skateboarding, indoor and outdoor rock climbing, snowboarding, trail running, lacrosse, water polo, volleyball, field hockey, bowling, or BMX bicycling. For a child with fitness, coordination, and/or confidence issues, consider a martial arts, yoga, or dance program. If your child loves horses, try equestrian sports.

Consider family-focused activities. There are a variety of ways besides organized sports for your child to become and stay physically fit. Family-focused physical activities, such as bike riding, hiking, kayaking, swimming, or golf, can help children stay fit while having fun, and have the added benefit of giving the whole family an activity to enjoy and share.

Match the sport to your child's temperament. Certain personality types are a poor match for particular sports. Kids who are prone to anger if they make mistakes and are hard on themselves when they fail tend to be unhappy in individual sports (remember: even though baseball is a team game, it is similar to individual sports in the sense that the focus is always on individual players, whether they be the pitcher, batter, or fielder) and have temperaments better suited to team sports where they are not always in the spotlight. If your child wants to play a sport that you feel is a bad match for his temperament, let him play, but try to find a low-key recreational program or class where the emphasis is on fun and skill development, not competition and winning.

Consider your child's size. Children who are small for their age face problems playing contact sports: the coach may be reluctant to let them play for fear that they will be injured by bigger kids, so they may spend a lot of time on the bench, which is boring and will turn them off to playing sports. If they do play, they run a significantly greater risk of serious injury. The best choices for small kids are sports in which size may actually work to their advantage—those that emphasize quickness and agility and balance, rather than strength, such as gymnastics and dancing; or endurance sports, such as distance running and swimming. If your child is smaller than his peers but really wants to play a contact sport, find a program where kids are separated not only by age but by size, and if your child agrees, let him play on a team with kids who are younger.

Consider your child's level of commitment. Unless you sense that your child is highly motivated and committed to participating in sports like hockey, ice skating, gymnastics, or swimming, which demand commitment even at an early age, have long seasons, or are practiced almost year-round, such sports are probably not a good match for your child.

Avoid reinforcing gender stereotypes. That certain sports (football, wrestling, martial arts) are considered by some to be masculine and inappropriate for girls or others (dance, yoga) are considered feminine and inappropriate for boys should not be a factor in your decision.

If at first you don't succeed . . . It is a myth that some kids are simply too clumsy or unathletic to play sports. Do what you can to help your child develop a lifelong interest in physical fitness, even if it means exploring a wide range of sports and activities to find one that is right for your child, and even if it takes a couple of false starts.

Consider the cost. The cost of some sports can end up being a budget buster for many families, so it is important to consider the true cost of sports participation before registering your child. (For more on the cost of sports, see chapter 7.)

Only one out of four children who are star athletes in elementary school will be stars when they reach high school.

Consider the program's mission. Since having fun is the most important reason children participate in a sport, find out if the goal of the program is for the kids to have fun and develop as athletes in a safe and friendly environment, or to win the state championship and every tournament it enters. Look for a program that emphasizes having fun, skill development, equal playing time, and fair play, and keeps winning, losing, and competition in proper perspective. A program that allows a player to miss a game or practice to go hiking with his family or attend a family get-together without being penalized, for example, has its priorities straight.

Talk to coaches. Talk to some coaches to be sure their philosophy is the same as yours. (For signs of a good coach, see chapter 10.)

Attend a game. Do you hear laughter and see coaches, players, and parents having fun? Or do you hear yelling and see grim-faced coaches, players, and parents?

Consider *your* goals. What do you hope your child gets out of playing? Hopefully, your goals for your child are to stay or become physically fit, have fun, make new friends, develop skills, start down the road to a lifetime of enjoying physical activity, and to learn valuable life lessons through sports. It is our role as parents to love our children, protect them from harm, and help them realize *their* dreams. It is not to live our lives through them.

DESTINED FOR STARDOM?

It was a glorious autumn Saturday morning in New England: bright sunshine, temperature in the mid-fifties, breezy, and the fall foliage at its brilliant peak. Like millions of mothers across America, I was standing with a group of parents at a local elementary school, coffee mugs in hand, watching our sons and daughters play a coed, short-sided (seven on seven) recreational soccer game.

While I kept my eye on my three sons whenever they were in the game, I couldn't help but notice one of their teammates, a girl named Heather, who was around their age. It was the first time I had seen her play. It was obvious by the way she ran up and down the field, the skill with which she dribbled the ball, and the strength and accuracy of her shots on goal that, at least at age nine, her soccer skills were more advanced than those of my sons and the other players. After Heather scored what must have been her fourth or fifth goal of the day, I turned to my husband and said, "I have no way of knowing, of course, but I am willing to bet right now that Heather is going to be captain of the high school varsity." He said, "Well, a lot can happen between now and then, and it is impossible to predict whether she will still be this good when she is seventeen or eighteen, but if she continues to play like this, I wouldn't want to bet against you."

From that point forward, I made a point of following Heather's athletic career. She continued to shine on the soccer field. Her select club team won the state championship three years in a row; she was a four-time first-team conference all-star and Offensive Player of the Year in her junior and senior years, and team MVP during her senior season. As captain of her high school varsity, she was a four-year starter and a first-team All-State selection. She went on to play soccer in college.

The Guessing Game How did I know that Heather would become a successful high school athlete and play at the collegiate level? I didn't. It was just a lucky guess.

As it turned out, Heather's success as a nine-year-old was due to her natural athletic talent. But for many who experience early athletic success, the reason is that they are so-called early bloomers, children who simply develop ahead of their peers physically and/or psychologically, not that they are gifted athletes.

As a 2004 article in the *Journal of Physical Education, Recreation & Dance* observes, because athletic success involves multiple factors, including genetics, mental attitude, access to training, and money, any attempt to predict future achievement based on how skilled your child is at age nine, ten, or eleven "is likely to be futile." Each child follows his or her own unique developmental timetable. While chronological age provides a rough index of developmental level, differences among children of the same age can be and often are great. In other words, as one expert says, while "development is age related, it is not age *dependent*" (as I can tell you as the mother of triplet sons who were born a minute apart!).

It is also very hard, unless you have a lot of personal experience in a sport, to accurately judge your child's potential. (Even then, your judgment is likely to be clouded by your love for your child.) How well she is doing against her peers is not a very good guide because not only can looks be deceiving, but things can and often do change.

Research suggests that only one in four children who are star athletes in elementary school will still be stars when they reach high school. Predicting whether a preteen athlete will be a good enough high school athlete to land a college scholarship or even influence the admissions process is almost impossible.

Parenting the Early Bloomer The sad but unfortunate fact is that an early bloomer enjoys advantages that can continue long after peers have caught up and, in many cases, passed him in terms of skill proficiency. He tends to receive more positive reinforcement and encouragement from adults; earlier and more extensive socialization into sports; access to better coaching, facilities, and competitive experiences (i.e., places on "select" teams); and benefits from the "residual bias" of being viewed as a talented athlete at an early age.

As a 2004 article in the *Journal of Sports Behavior* observes, "Early selection for elite sport participants [thus] can become a self-fulfilling prophecy for athletes and coaches. Players begin to think of themselves as talented and are thus likely to invest more time and effort into their sport with predictable results. As the identity of previously selected players becomes known to coaches and administrators, they watch those players more closely lest they miss an elite performer."

This is one of the dirtiest little secrets in youth sports.

The Relative Age Factor

Have you ever watched the Little League World Series on television? Ever notice how the players on the teams are almost always much bigger and stronger than the average twelve-year-old and look more like sixteen-year-olds?

What you are seeing is a phenomenon called the relative age factor (RAF) at work. As numerous studies have shown, success in age group competition, as is the rule in soccer, swimming, baseball, ice hockey, and tennis, may simply result from a child being lucky enough to have a birth date early in the selection year.

When young athletes are competing for spots on select teams, a six- to twelve-month developmental advantage can be decisive. Slightly older participants are more likely to be selected because they tend to be more mature physically and psychologically. The relative age factor can and often does have an extremely large impact on success in sports, especially at the elite levels. It is a special problem in sports where height, weight, strength, and power are an advantage.

As the 2004 Journal of Sports Behavior *article argues, "the long-term result of the RAF may be a lowering in the overall quality of the highest competitive team" as talented individuals may be overlooked because they are born late in the selection year.*

Downsides of Being an Early Bloomer While it is clear that numerous advantages are conferred on an early bloomer, if your child experiences early success in sports, such success also has some downsides:

❖ **An early bloomer is able to exploit his or her physical ability without having to work as hard at developing skills as a player.** To stay competitive, less precocious players have to work hard on skill development. When they catch up physically, they may end up being better players.

❖ **An early bloomer often has to try to live up to heightened expectations.** An early bloomer's initial success may lead him to practice and play more than his young body can handle in order to live up to his reputation. Playing under this kind of pressure often leads to burnout and overuse injuries.

❖ **She may be defined or define herself by whether she wins or loses.** If the early bloomer believes and expects that she will always enjoy the kind of athletic success she experiences early in her athletic career, she can fall into the trap of basing her sense of self on always being the best. If she is unable to maintain that success, if that self-image, that identity is shattered, the results can be disastrous and may lead her to quit sports altogether.

❖ **You may be tempted to push her to specialize too early and/or train too hard.** Excessive training too often leads to burnout and/or overuse injuries, some of which don't show up until high school or college but can be traced to excessive training when the player was nine, ten, or eleven. Don't be lulled into valuing short-term success more than your child's long-term interests. If you do, you may be placing your child's physical safety and emotional health at risk (see chapter 8).

Challenges for Parents of Potential Late Bloomers If your child is an average athlete or lags behind his peers, he may be a late bloomer. Late bloomers receive markedly less social support and reinforcement from parents, coaches, and peers.

Worse, the adults charged with the responsibility of evaluating "talent"—most of whom don't understand developmental variability in children—may unfairly nip her athletic career in the bud by concluding that she lacks the potential to play sports at the highest competitive levels. Denied a place on a select, middle school, or high school subvarsity team, the late bloomer is more likely to simply drop out of sports rather than keep playing until she blossoms (that is, achieves her full athletic potential).

The challenge parents of potential late bloomers face is to find ways to give such children the opportunity to stay in sports long enough to give them a *chance* to blossom.

Taking a Balanced Approach The lesson then is not to get too down if your child is not immediately a superstar or too high if he is. The important thing is that he *continues* to play, to develop and learn new skills.

Because there is no way of knowing whether your nine-, ten-, eleven-, or twelve-year-old will be an outstanding player when he is sixteen, seventeen, or eighteen:

❖ Emphasize the process and the journey, not the results achieved.

❖ Avoid praising the outcome and instead praise effort.

❖ Help your child see herself as a whole person, not just as an athlete.

❖ Be realistic about the possible reasons for your child's early athletic success or lack thereof, and make sure your child understands that early success is not a guarantee of future success (and vice versa).

❖ Select a sports program for your child that recognizes the variability in the way children's athletic talent develops by offering all children a chance to play as long as they want to.

Having Realistic Expectations It is critically important that you and your child have realistic expectations about his or her development as an athlete and that you don't confuse your expectations and desires with those of your child. Parents who complain that their child has quit a sport too early may be doing so because he isn't doing what *they* want him to do.

Fun can go out of sports for a youth athlete in a hurry when it stops being what she does just for fun and becomes something she does for an external reason: to get a scholarship, to win a game, to impress a scout, to please a parent. When such reasons for playing take over, the game becomes a chore and burnout becomes more likely.

Whether pressure to participate for external reasons leads to burnout depends on how much control the athlete feels he has over the situation: If he feels in control, if athletic participation is part of his self-development, then sports can be healthy part of the growing up process.

If he feels controlled or feels that he is not making the decisions or developing as an individual, burnout is more likely.

In setting realistic expectations, here are some things to remember:

Respect the phases of athletic development It is generally agreed that there are three distinct phases of athletic development in children, which need to be respected:

❖ The emphasis in the first phase—from ages six through thirteen—should be on having fun, sampling lots of different sports or activities to find the ones a child likes (among the sports my sons tried in this phase were fencing, skiing, swimming, basketball, soccer, baseball, hockey, lacrosse, and football) and developing fundamental skills. It is a time for you to encourage your child's participation and not a time to set expectations or goals, other than having fun and doing one's best. Trying to accelerate the process of developing your child into an elite athlete by skipping this initial phase usually backfires. If your child does not develop a love of the sport and a desire to improve, experts, like Daniel Gould, director of the Michigan States Institute for the Study of Youth Sports, warn, "it is highly unlikely he or she will be able to sustain long-term involvement (although your child may stay involved for a number of years to please [you])."

❖ In the second phase—from ages thirteen to fifteen—your child begins to commit to a sport (or sports) and to focus in a long-term and systematic way, with the help of an experienced coach, on mastering skills and techniques.

❖ In the third phase—beginning at around age fifteen—a child continues to work with a coach to turn technical skills learned in practice into optimal performance in competition, and recognizes the significance of the sport in his or her life.

Practice doesn't necessarily make perfect You can encourage, needle, cajole, or demand that your child practice more, but no matter how passionate you may be and how sure you may be that extra practice will pay off, your passion is no substitute for the passion he needs in order to *want* to put in the extra practice time. You need to help your child value his own developmental process and improvement over time. The focus should be on your child's overall happiness, a balance of fun and development, and the general developmental benefits of involvement in sports. Winning and success should not be the predominant objectives of participation, regardless of which phase your child is in.

Avoid the mind-set that more is better Additional practice may improve your child's performance, hone her skills, and help her become more confident. But it is *not* going to turn her into a star athlete or compensate for a lack of natural athletic talent. There is a fine line between gentle encouragement, with your child feeling that the final decision about whether to practice more is hers, and pushing so hard to persuade your child to practice that she doesn't feel the decision was hers to make. If she ends up giving into your demands, the chances that she will ultimately quit are much higher, as are the chances the extra practice will result in overuse injuries.

Understand that kids have physical limits Parents often forget that children do not have an unlimited capacity for physical exercise. They get tired, just like you, and may not be ready or physically able to handle extra practicing and conditioning.

Avoid the comparison trap There are always going to be kids ahead of or behind your child. It is not how she is doing against friends, a sibling, an older player, or a star athlete that is important. She isn't competing against anyone but herself. The goal is to develop her individual potential to the fullest, not to beat some other young athlete.

UNDERSTANDING CHILD DEVELOPMENT

The explosion of highly competitive sports programs for kids under twelve (e.g., travel soccer, hockey, etc.) would have you believe that your preteen

> "Given the demands of high-performance programs, the greatest threat to children's social development is that adults will over-control the lives of children for the sake of achievement in sport."
>
> —PETER DONNELLY
> *INTENSIVE PARTICIPATION IN CHILDREN'S SPORTS*

is ready, indeed eager for intense competition. But children under the age of eleven or twelve are not always emotionally and cognitively ready to compete because they have not yet developed a mature understanding of the competitive process. They really don't care all that much about winning and losing. As is often said, kids would rather play on a losing team than sit on the bench of a winning team.

The reason kids are competing at an earlier and earlier age isn't that somehow the kids of today are different from the kids of thirty years ago, that they mature that much more quickly. The reason, unfortunately, is that too many *adults* think their kids are ready to compete at an earlier and earlier age. Sometimes it could be to show that they are somehow better parents. In other words, such early competition is a reflection of an *adult-centered,* not a child-centered youth sports culture.

The emphasis at this age should be on developing skills, not competing. Listen to what your own maternal instincts tell you. "Just say no" to programs that place undue emphasis on competing (and, of course, winning).

Puberty: A Developmental Dividing Line In developing realistic expectations for children under the age of twelve, keep in mind that before that age, child development experts say, most children:

❖ Have not yet fully developed a sense of what talent means. Because they tend to think that high effort is an indication of high ability, they tend to define success in terms of learning and effort, and don't understand that someone who tries hard and achieves little likely has less ability than someone who tries little and achieves a lot.

❖ Will often have a difficult time telling you if they are under competitive stress—in other words, if their youth sports experience has stopped being fun. It is therefore important to be on the lookout for signs that your child isn't having fun.

❖ May have difficulty, seeing a team "as made up of a set of interdependent positions whose relationships to one another change as the game is played." For example, typical seven- and eight-year-olds play soccer like an exuberant pack of puppies more interested in falling all over one another (what some call "beehive" soccer), with all the players on both teams chasing the ball without regard to position or assignment, while baseball outfielders all converge on a ball that gets past the infield.

❖ Have difficulty fully understanding and following instructions. All too often parents and coaches speak to kids as if they are adults and fail to adjust the way they communicate to the child's level of development. When adults have unrealistic expectations of children's cognitive abilities, they may erroneously accuse a player of not paying enough attention or not trying hard enough or, worse, get so angry or frustrated that they verbally abuse the child (more about the effects of such abuse in chapter 8). I once heard about a boy who was told by his baseball coach during a game to "go warm up." The little kid, with all the innocence of an eight-year-old, asked, "Why?" The coach, thinking he was being a smart aleck, snapped at him to "forget it, go sit on the bench," when the child was simply wondering whether his big moment had actually come and was really asking, "Why, am I really going to get a chance to pitch?"

❖ Lack the ability to see sports in a larger perspective. As a parent, you need to teach your child that sports have many dimensions; that they aren't just about winning and losing.

❖ May not know to ask for help in becoming technically proficient in a sport (learning to kick a soccer ball correctly, or how to bunt a baseball) because they don't know they are doing it incorrectly.

❖ May not tell you if they have a physical problem (need glasses, knee hurts, shoes don't fit, are wheezing, etc.) that is adversely affecting their performance or enjoyment. Be on the lookout for these kinds of performance issues. If you suspect that your child has a physical problem, ask direct questions like, "Are you seeing the ball clearly?" "Can you hear the coach when he calls out plays from the sideline?"

❖ Are easily hurt if those from whom they seek approval (you and their coach) label them or generalize about them in a negative way ("Stevie doesn't have the speed to be a forward," "Trisha's throwing arm isn't strong enough for her to play third base.")

❖ Will overwhelmingly identify athletic ability as determining social status among their peers (this is true only for boys; girls tend to focus on appearance for peer acceptance). Because sports ability has long been deemed an important factor in a youth's popularity and peer acceptance, especially for boys, coaches who erroneously conclude that a child lacks innate ability—which is then reflected in reduced playing time or, worse, the athlete being cut from the program altogether (more about cutting in chapter 14)—can lead them and their peers to having a low perception of their abilities, which can negatively affect self-esteem.

❖ Are likely, particularly if they are under age ten, to need help understanding how people feel in certain situations. When you take the mystery out of strong emotions, like the jealousy that prompts sibling rivalry, children are reassured that what they are feeling is normal. When they feel understood, they are better able to control their emotions.

❖ Look up to and take their cues from their parents.

❖ Are unable to feel pride purely based on accomplishment and effort, and benefit from receiving external rewards (e.g., trophies) that help trigger positive internal feelings.

❖ Have a difficult time performing multiple skills at the same time (like dribbling a basketball while looking for the open player to whom to pass the ball). This is why the emphasis in this stage should be on learning basic skills, rules, and strategies in a noncompetitive environment and why coaches need to be more educated about child development so as not to place unrealistic expectations on athletes.

❖ Benefit most from coaches who provide the appropriate degree of feedback tailored to the degree of skill acquisition (see chapter 10).

Characteristics of the Over-Twelve Child In setting expectations for the older child, understand that they:

❖ Are better able to handle the pressure of competitive sports because they have more experience handling competition in general, but are also much more inclined to drop out of sports because of the pressure of and emphasis on competition (especially girls).

❖ Crave social acceptance. Peer pressure starts to be more of an issue and can add to the child's stress playing sports.

❖ Are reluctant to ask for help on technical aspects of a sport out of embarrassment.

❖ Are in flux, and performance issues in sports are more likely to have spillover into other areas of their lives (school, peers, home life).

❖ Have an increased capability to self-advocate with their coach (by high school, they should be able to self-advocate without any parental help).

❖ Are better able to base their sense of self-worth on their own efforts and accomplishments instead of on external rewards (e.g., trophies). They are also now able to understand that trophies in sports aren't given to everyone, but are based on accomplishment and given only to the kids who are on the team that wins the championship.

❖ Need extra support to deal with the painful realities of adolescence (changing bodies, awkwardness, peer pressure, etc.).

EARLY SPECIALIZATION AND ELITE TEAMS

One of the most dramatic developments in youth sports over the last ten or fifteen years has been the explosive growth at seemingly ever-earlier ages of the number of highly selective, highly competitive sports teams (the so-called elite, travel, select, premier, and Olympic Development teams) and the related trend toward early specialization (playing a single sport on a year-round basis to the exclusion to all others). Parents, coaches, and kids appear to be searching desperately for an edge in the battle for spots on high school varsities and for college athletic scholarships, an edge which they think select teams and specialization will provide, or at the very least, a way to keep up with their peers.

The emphasis on specialization in today's youth sports may tempt you into buying into the idea—one that many youth sports organizations and coaches actively promote—that your child will be unable to attain success or even make a high school or college team without specializing, playing on a select team, playing year round, and attending special sports camps in the summer; that more (more teams, more practices, more intense and competitive games) and earlier (travel teams at age seven) is better. The fact, however, is that in youth sports the opposite is true: *less* is more.

Many parents are ignoring their own better judgment and intuition, which suggests that early specialization and playing on select travel teams may be unhealthy. The trend, however, toward early specialization is *not* supported by hard scientific evidence. Instead it appears to be driven by folklore, myths, half-truths, a herd mentality, the ever-burgeoning youth sports industry, and by adults too intent on winning.

The reason you may be tempted to enroll your child in a select travel program or allow your child to specialize early in a sport is that you may feel you have no other choice, that it is a matter of competitive survival. Parents erroneously assume that sports are like academics; that because a child who falls behind academically, even in the early grades, may never catch up—a fear that prompts more and more parents to push their children in school, even in the early grades, and hover over them (hence the phrase "helicopter parents")—the same must hold true in sports.

But just as parents who drill their second-grader on questions from the Scholastic Aptitude Test have lost sight of the fact that the best way to prepare a child for college is not to teach by rote but to raise a child who loves to learn, the best way to prepare a child to be a successful high school athlete is to instill a love of sports, not to apply so much pressure on him at an early age by exposing him to the stress of ultracompetitive elite sports programs that he soon sees sports not as fun but as a job and burns out.

If you choose not to allow your child to specialize or play on a select team too early, not only will you be doing your child a huge favor, but if enough of us just say no to select teams and early specialization, we can help create the balanced, child-centered youth sports system our children deserve. Here's why:

Early Specialization and Select Teams Don't Guarantee Athletic Success There is no evidence that an athlete who specializes in one sport before the age of twelve or who participates in a select sports program will end up being a better athlete as a teen or adult. While research shows that elite athletes often start their involvement in their sport at an early age, it also shows that most played a number of other sports when they were young. Indeed, one study showed an advantage to early sport diversification. Other studies suggest that those who specialize at a later age have *more* success. For every successful athlete who specialized at an early age there is one who didn't or who succeeded despite having come to a sport as a teenager or even later.

Playing different sports allows athletes to develop a variety of transferrable motor skills such as jumping, running, and twisting, which ultimately help them become better at their chosen sport. It also exposes athletes to different coaches with different coaching styles, philosophies, and personalities. Focusing on a single activity puts all of a young athlete's eggs in one basket. If kids don't try other sports, how do they know whether or not they might like those sports more or be better at them? There is also an increased risk, if an athlete specializes too early, that he will find out (too late) that he doesn't like the sport in which he has specialized. By postponing specialization and playing a number of different sports, your child will be better able to choose the sports he or she enjoys the most and in which he or she ultimately will have the most success.

Early Specialization Interferes with Healthy Child Development Being on a select team often requires a year-round or near year-round commitment and extensive travel. If you allow your child to participate she can end up socially isolated from her family, peers, and the larger community. The athletic role can become so consuming and controlling that childhood essentially disappears. Early specialization and intense participation on select teams may interfere with normal identity development, increasing the risk that a child will develop what psychologists call a one-dimensional self-concept in which she sees herself solely as an athlete instead of sports being just a part of who she is. There is also an increased risk that academics will take a backseat to athletics.

Many experts believe that if your child waits to play on a select team until sixth grade or later, and waits until high school to specialize in a single sport, he is likely to be better adjusted and happier, have a more balanced identity, and less likely to have an identity crisis when his competitive sports career ends, as it is likely to do after high school. This is because the negative effects of failure in one sport are far less when a child experiences success in other sports or areas of life.

Like early specialization, allowing your child to "play up" if he has skills comparable to the older players—on the theory that moving up the competitive ladder as fast as he can is the best approach—is often not a good idea from a child development standpoint. Oftentimes the child's emotional and social maturity will not match that of the older players. Parents should exercise caution: research has shown that it is usually best for your child to play with kids of the same age rather than push them up the ladder to play with older, more mature players.

Early Specialization Deters Rather Than Promotes Player Development

The emphasis of select teams on winning games and tournaments (the myth that "the more we win, the better we are") may actually *deter* your child's athletic development. True learning doesn't occur during games, where players are often afraid to take risks because a mistake may cost the team the game, but in training, where players have a chance to be spontaneous, creative, try new moves, and take risks. The reason soccer players in Europe and South America are often more skilled than those produced by our soccer system is that their programs emphasize training, skill development, and creativity, and focus less on playing game after game after game, tournament after tournament. Here is good analogy: Your child's math teacher limits her teaching to one day out of the week and gives tests the other four days.

No matter what their mission statements may say, many select programs are purely about competition and have a very cutthroat, win, win, win attitude. Player development can and often does become secondary to winning, with the coach playing the "best" players in order to win and relegating the rest to the bench. Sometimes players who train too much, receive too much coaching, and specialize too early develop bad habits that become harder to fix when they are older.

Before grade six, your child is far better off playing in a low-pressure environment that emphasizes skill development than in an environment that stresses winning and intense competition, which characterize today's select programs.

The Necessary Emotional Maturity May Not Be Fully Developed Until High School A child may be physically ready to specialize in a particular sport and love the sport, yet be too immature emotionally to handle the stress of dealing with teammates (especially if they resent her athletic ability) or how to exhibit good sportsmanship in the cauldron of intense competition. Specializing in a sport can take an emotional toll, both due to the increased stress of competing at a high level and because coaches at this level tend to be more demanding, sometimes to the point of being emotionally abusive (see more about emotional abuse in chapter 8).

Studies show that talent development involves the acquisition of a mature personality during the teenage years—a personality that allows the athlete to cope with all the opportunities and obstacles she will face as an elite athlete. Playing at higher levels is likely to leave very little time for other activities, like family time, religious activities, socializing with friends, or even homework. Until high school, a child may not be emotionally mature enough to appreciate the sacrifices that she will need to make in terms of time and energy.

Select Teams Create an Elitist Atmosphere One of the worst byproducts of the select team system is that it creates groups of haves and have-nots. Too much of a community- or club-based program's resources (best practice times, facilities, coaches) end up being devoted to the select teams, leaving only crumbs to the kids who supposedly aren't good enough to be selected and are relegated to the less prestigious recreational or intramural programs. In addition, less affluent families who cannot afford the cost of expensive travel teams are shut out.

There is no proof that forcing "better" players to play with those who appear at an early age to be less skilled somehow keeps them from developing their "talent." As Michigan State's Daniel Gould observes in a 2004 article, "*all* children need coaches who are trained to be positive and encouraging," and that "[y]oung athletes who play for such positive and encouraging coaches have higher motivation, enhanced self-esteem, lower anxiety and lower dropout rates than children who play for coaches without these qualities."

Nor do the "better" players deserve to play with similarly "gifted" players. At levels below high school varsity, *every* child deserves the chance to play, the best coaching, and to play on the best fields.

Early Specialization Reflects an Adult-, Not a Child-Centered Youth Sports System In order to become an elite athlete, a child needs to be old enough to understand what is involved. Most who specialize early don't know what they are getting themselves into: a cutthroat, high-stakes *business* run by adults.

Before high school, a child is not likely to fully appreciate that if she plays on a select team she may often be practicing or going to bed early, worn out after a hard day of exercise, while her classmates are up late watching TV or socializing, or she may be getting up early, while others are giving their growing bodies the rest they so desperately need by sleeping late.

While some kids choose to specialize because they realize that they have a special talent and want to improve, for many student-athletes, external pressure from parents and coaches steers them in a direction they may or may not want to go. Children who specialize early to please adults fail to develop the critical ability to say no and to know the limitations of their bodies, knowledge that comes only with age and experience (studies show that most elite athletes don't know their bodies, their capabilities, and their limitations, until the *end* of their careers, at about age thirty).

The enthusiasm and passion a child may show for a particular sport is not enough to justify excessive training or participation on a select team. After all, you don't hesitate to limit the amount of time your children spend on other activities they enjoy, e.g., television and video games. Why shouldn't you also place appropriate limits on the amount of time they spend playing ultracompetitive, superorganized sports? Such excessive parental control promotes a youth sports structure reflective of the values and expectations of adults, not of children.

Early Specialization Leads to Overuse Injuries There is no doubt that early specialization and playing on a select team take their toll on a child's growing bones, joints, and muscles. Prior to high school, most children are simply not physically mature enough to handle the stress that playing the same sport on a year-round or nearly year-round basis places on their bodies. According to Safe Kids Worldwide, more than 3.5 million children age fourteen and under get medical treatment for sports injuries each year. Of those, nearly half are overuse injuries, such as Sever's disease (a heel problem often associated with soccer), Osgood-Schlatter disease (knee pain common in male soccer and basketball players), gymnast's wrist, runner's knee, swimmer's shoulder, shin splints (common in soccer players and track athletes), and Little League elbow or shoulder (usually from throwing breaking balls, an ability that professional baseball players and coaches say isn't needed early in a player's career to rise to the professional level).

Twenty-five years ago, only 10 percent of the patients treated by Dr. Lyle Micheli, a pioneer in the field of treating youth sports injuries and director of the sports medicine division at Children's Hospital Boston, were overuse injuries. Now overuse injuries represent 70 percent of the cases he sees.

The surest path to burnout or an overuse injury is to play a sport season after season. Your child will benefit far more in the long run if he takes a season off to play another sport or plays his chosen sport only in alternating seasons.

Early Specialization Leads to Burnout An athlete who specializes early or plays on an ultracompetitive select team is at increased risk of burnout or withdrawal from sport as a result of chronic stress. No matter how athletically gifted your child may seem, if playing sports isn't fun, if your daughter feels pressure to achieve greatness, it won't be long before she quits. If she does, you will always be left to wonder what she could have achieved had she taken a more balanced approach to sports.

Even talented athletes can tire of their sport because of what it takes to win. The boys' swimming program at Greenwich (CT) High School has been hugely successful, losing only one meet in the last twenty-five years. Yet just a handful of the swimmers have gone on to swim in college. After participating in two-a-day practices, morning and night, every day for four years, it's no wonder they were sick of swimming!

Use your intuition to find the right balance, one that helps your child develop his skills but doesn't burn up all of his athletic energy too early.

Chapter Three

Fun, Fun, Fun
How to Put Winning in Its Place

> *The most important thing in the Olympic Games*
> *is not to win but to take part, just as the most important*
> *thing in life is not the triumph but the struggle. The essential*
> *thing is not to have conquered but to have fought well.*
>
> —BARON PIERRE DE COUBERTIN, *FOUNDER OF THE MODERN*
> *OLYMPIC MOVEMENT*

JUST STARTING OUT

My triplet sons were just five when they started T-ball. I can still vividly recall the April night when the head coach called to tell me that they were on the T-ball Red Sox and that the first practice would be held at the high school softball field in two days.

After I hung up I paused a moment to catch my breath. It was a truly exciting time. The first five years of my sons' lives had been a ton of work, but now I felt some of the real fun was about to start. I knew if my sons were anything like me, they would love sports, especially baseball. Mostly, I hoped that the triplets would find a sport or two that they could enjoy playing the rest of their lives.

When we arrived at the first practice, we were greeted by four fathers holding clipboards and wearing Red Sox caps and jackets. The boys were told to pair up and play catch, while the coaches circulated, writing notes on their clipboards. Their stern expressions and lack of jovial banter conveyed the message to parents that they were in charge and this was serious business. We were told we could leave and come back to pick up our sons in an hour.

Some of the veteran parents left. Like a few of the rookies, I stayed to watch. Over the course of the practice, each of my sons checked in with me several times, looking for reassurance. They were the youngest boys on the team, just old enough by age cutoff date to be eligible to play that spring. Some of their teammates were almost a year older, a huge difference developmentally at such a young age (see the discussion of the relative age factor in chapter 2). I kept telling them that everyone, including the coaches, was there to have fun. But I had a tough time believing it. If T-ball was all about having fun, why weren't the coaches smiling? Why weren't they interacting with any of the boys? What could possibly be so important that all four were toting clipboards and stopwatches?

As the season progressed, it became obvious that my sons and a number of other boys on the team were not having fun. During each game and practice, they had the same complaint: the coaches weren't letting them play any of the "fun" positions in the infield, relegating them instead to the outfield, where very few balls were ever hit. The only boys playing the fun spots were the sons of the four coaches! Six boys were never given a chance to play the infield.

I can still remember the sad look on my son Spencer's face as he asked me why he couldn't play the infield. I put my arms around him and whispered, "When your team comes off the field next inning, go up to the coach and tell him you would like to play an infield position. Better yet, tell him *all* the boys who always stand in the outfield want a turn." With a twinkle in his eye that suggested that our plan just might work, he returned to his position in right field.

When the Red Sox came off the field to bat, I saw Spencer approach the coach. He brought along his two brothers for support. "Coach, can we play the fun spots next inning, please?" he asked. How could anyone resist a five-year-old with big smile and a twinkle in his eye?

One of the coaches' sons—who was almost a year older than my sons—blurted out, "You stink. That's why you are out there. *We* are the best."

Spencer began to cry. Between sobs he managed to say, "I don't stink!" No coach came to his defense. Ever-present clipboard in hand, the head coach simply walked away and called off the batting order, leaving it to me to try to console a little boy whose only crime was that he wanted to have fun.

Accentuate the Positive Young athletes are not pint-sized professional athletes. They don't earn performance-based bonuses. They aren't going to be paid a dime more for scoring three goals per game than for scoring three goals in the entire season, or for being on a championship team instead of the team in the cellar. So we need to treat them as kids, not major leaguers.

In an oft-cited 1988 study, the Institute for the Study of Youth Sports at Michigan State University asked ten thousand junior high and high school students to list their twelve top reasons for participating in sports. At the top of the list for both boys and girls was "to have fun." Girls ranked winning as the *least important* reason; boys rated winning eighth.

Ask kids about what they want to get out of sports, and the vast majority will say competitive games in which everyone plays and has fun. Given a choice between fun and winning, most would say having fun. They would rather play on a losing team than sit on the bench of a winning team. Believe it or not, this attitude persists through high school, where you would think that kids would begin to value winning over playing. Three out of four high school athletes, regardless of gender, would *still* prefer to play and lose than sit and win (although twice as many boys than girls said winning was essential for an enjoyable sports experience).

Children aren't born competing; it's something they learn. The best thing we can do for our kids, as parents and coaches, is to keep the

> "The medals don't mean anything and the glory doesn't last. It's all about your happiness. The rewards are going to come, but my happiness is just loving the sport and having fun performing."
>
> —JACKIE JOYNER-KERSEE
> TRACK WORLD CHAMPION

amount of competition in youth sports from becoming excessive, to make having fun and learning the sport as important, if not more important, than winning, especially for younger children. They will have a lifetime of competition soon enough.

As children grow, mature, and improve their skills in playing a particular sport, they begin to see a pattern of successes and failures. Trained coaches call this "self-discovery," and it is a very important part of the learning process. Parents should encourage it. But youth players need the freedom to experiment in practice and games, to take risks, to be creative. If winning is the only measure of "success," such experimentation is stifled and player development stunted. A successful competition is one where *every* player on both teams contributes, does his best, and respects his teammates, his opponents, and the rules.

If you weren't at your child's game or practice, ask, "Tell me about your game" and "Did you and your team have fun today?" instead of "Did you win?" or "How many goals did you score?" Asking your child an open-ended question or whether he had fun invites a response and is more likely to lead to further conversation than asking whether he won because it shows that you are concerned about what matters most to *him*: having fun.

In talking with your son or daughter about the sport they are playing, emphasize the strongest aspect of their game and the new skills they are learning. Recount for them the play in which you saw them demonstrate that new skill. This is the type of positive reinforcement that helps your son or daughter to appreciate the new skills they have learned and how to sharpen them.

Fun: An Essential Ingredient It is a myth that fun has to be sacrificed if a child is to succeed at sports. Indeed, the only way an athlete will continue to play sports—regardless of level of ability—is if he or she is having fun. Athletes have to practice hard to reach an elite level. If it is all work and no play, they simply won't keep playing. Success is determined by the player's own desire to succeed, which comes from a love of the game.

When children are having fun they are more relaxed and better able to learn. A July 2004 Harris Interactive Youth Query of eight- to eighteen-year-olds found that most quit playing at thirteen or fourteen and that the number-one reason they did, cited by four out of ten, was because they stopped having fun. The survey found that the decision to quit had less to do with that boy's or girl's own skills—or lack of skills—than with pressure from adults who acted as if each game was the seventh game of the World Series and the child's need to preserve a positive self-image.

Judging from the number of e-mails I get from parents who are reluctant to let their athletically gifted children quit sports because it isn't fun anymore, a lot of parents have a difficult time with the concept.

REALIZING A LIFELONG DREAM

The Olympic creed was first stated by the founder of the modern Olympic Games, Baron Pierre de Coubertin, and it is as much a cherished ideal today as it was a century ago: "The most important thing in the Olympic Games is not to win but to take part."

For ten glorious days in February 2002, my three sons and I were privileged to be a part of the 2002 Salt Lake City Olympic Games. I truly felt, even though I was only a spectator, that I was also taking part.

So perhaps it was fate that brought me to Salt Lake City on February 15 on a crisp afternoon in the Wasatch Mountains under a brilliant azure sky, far from my home, to celebrate not only my 50th birthday with my sons and numerous friends, but the bronze medal performance of U.S. Olympian snowboarder Chris Klug, who was just as glad to be taking part as I was, no doubt more.

A Life Saved I can only imagine what the day must have felt like for Klug, who was competing less than two years after a lifesaving liver transplant and, fittingly, just one day after National Organ Donor Day. "Without the gift of the donor family, I wouldn't be here today. They're the real heroes," Klug told reporters. While he said he hoped his fame as the first organ transplant recipient to win an Olympic medal would "get

"72% of both [high school] male and female athletes say they would rather play on a team with a losing record than sit on the bench for a winning team."

—FROM CHARACTER COUNTS! COALITION SPORTSMANSHIP SURVEY 2004

families talking about organ donation," he said he never felt any pressure to win to make his ordeal worthwhile. He was just happy to be alive.

"I thought I was going to die waiting," Klug said of the days before his liver donor was found nineteen months earlier. "I was pretty scared. I wasn't thinking about snowboarding or coming back and winning a bronze medal. I was just thinking about hoping to live, hanging out with my family and continuing with life as I know it." Even if he had not medaled, Chris Klug probably would have agreed with de Coubertin that the most important thing in the Olympic Games is not to win but to take part. The same should hold true for youth sports.

Hanging Out A highlight for me while in Utah was to be able to just hang out with my family and all of the new families that I met. What I learned from the parents of Olympic athletes is that they did not push their child into becoming an Olympian, they introduced their child to a number of sports when they were young, and that it was their child's inner passion, the fire within, that drove them to become successful in their sport. In other words, they lived the "just take part" credo Baron de Coubertin so eloquently and succinctly expressed in the Olympic Creed. Karen Ruggiero, mother of three-time Olympic ice hockey medalist and MomsTeam contributing writer, Angela Ruggiero, has told me numerous times that "I never did much to encourage Angela to play hockey; she loved playing the game. There was no need to push her." Angela's younger sister, Pamela, is often asked whether she is jealous of Angela, to which she simply answers, "No, she is doing what she loves. I am only jealous of all of her teammates, who get to see her all of the time."

Lynn Mayer, the mother of freestyle skier Travis Mayer, told me how his love of mogul skiing propelled him to an unexpected silver medal. She said that he told her that when he entered the starting gate at the top of the mountain and saw the sea of spectators below, he beamed with joy because no crowd larger than about a hundred people had ever watched him perform. "I just love mogul skiing so much that I wanted to do the best that I could for myself and my country," he said later.

WHAT TO SAY TO YOUR CHILD AFTER A LOSS

Chances are you've heard the saying "You win some. You lose some. Some get rained out." In a few short sentences, it captures the relaxed attitude parents should have about the youth sports experience. No matter how talented your child may be, there are going to be days when he doesn't play his best or when, despite his best effort, his team loses. How you manage both the ups and the inevitable downs will play a large role in whether your child has a successful youth sports experience.

Here are ten things to keep in mind after your child's team loses or he doesn't perform up to his expectations:

1. Realize that with time, experience, and your **continued support** your child will **improve**.

2. Recognize that youth sports are **not exclusively about winning**. Define success in terms of performance instead of outcomes.

3. Give your child the **respect** he deserves. If achieving athletic success were easy, athletes wouldn't be so admired and respected. Be proud of his persistence.

4. Emphasize the **friends** your child is making through her involvement in sports. Discussing the social aspects of her youth sports experience is preferable to critiquing her performance. Chances are the social aspects, such as the camaraderie of her teammates, are what she wants to talk about after a tough loss. The social aspect of sports is important to both girls and boys, albeit for different reasons.

5. Remember that many times all your child needs is your **love and understanding** and your being there for him. Be sure to validate his feelings. Make your child feel **important and accepted**, no matter whether he wins or loses, plays well or poorly.

6. Accept your child for **who he is**, not for what he has achieved. Acceptance must never be dependent on a good performance or winning.

"It is ethically questionable what well-meaning adults are doing to children in the name of sport, and more specifically in trying to create elite athletes. This culture is justified by the argument that we are giving them every opportunity to 'possibly' become elite athletes and teaching them the values we feel will help them in the adult word. But, when does determination become stubbornness, hard work become obsession, lack of remorse for inflicting pain become pathological, and self-interest become egotistical and narcissistic? Young children need to know that they are loved and appreciated for who they are and not how well they perform."

—ALEXIS PETERS
THE CALGARY HERALD

7. Take a **positive approach**, developing and maintaining **open lines of communication** with your child, even when your points of view on a given subject differ. Talk things out, and give him the benefit of your point of view. Don't simply say yes or no—let the final decision be your child's. Giving your child the right to express his opinions fosters self-reliance, self-responsibility, and ultimately the ability to think for himself.

8. Always take the time to help your child **reevaluate his involvement** (reasons, values, goals, and commitment). This helps your child gain a sense of self-control and self-direction and fosters increased self-motivation. It is important for young players to be praised for their mature and responsible decisions more than their actual playing performance. For example, say "I'm really proud of the way that you got all of your equipment together and made it to your game on time even though some of your friends were having a birthday party. You are showing real maturity."

9. Practice careful listening techniques. Show through your nonverbal communications (posture, facial expressions, and gestures) that you are really paying attention. Employ "active" listening: paraphrase what you feel or understand your child has said. This allows your child to reinterpret if he or she feels that the point has been misunderstood or restate what was said. Use bridges such as "I see," "yes," or "uh-huh" to show that you are listening and understand.

10. Evaluate your involvement periodically and ask for feedback. Every so often, it is a good idea to make sure you haven't become an overinvolved parent, one who places her own needs ahead of her child's. Because it is hard to be objective, ask your spouse or another parent with a child on the team to give you their honest assessment. If they tell you that you are acting less like a supportive parent and more like a critical coach, if they say you appear to always be giving advice or critiquing your child's athletic performance, it is a warning sign that you are becoming overinvolved and need to step back.

SIGNS YOUR CHILD ISN'T HAVING FUN PLAYING SPORTS

Since having fun is so essential to a successful youth sports experience, it is important to be on the lookout for signs that your child isn't enjoying herself. If you see a pattern of any of the following behaviors emerging, it is probably because she is not having fun and, if things don't change, may end up quitting:

❖ **She complains of being sick at practice or game time.** At some time or another, just about every child athlete will tell their parent that they don't feel like going to a game or practice. If, however, your child repeatedly tells you when it's time to go to practice or a game that she doesn't feel like playing because she has a headache or stomachache or is feeling dizzy, she may be telling you indirectly that she doesn't want to play because sports have become too stressful and not fun enough.

❖ **She is slow to return to practice after an injury.** If your child is playing sports for the wrong reasons (e.g., to please you), she may express it by being reluctant to return to play after an injury, even when the injury has fully healed and she has medical clearance to play.

❖ **She is nervous or anxious before, during, or after games.** If your child appears extra nervous, anxious, angry, or sad on the way to, during, or after sports, it may be an indication that she isn't enjoying sports.

❖ **She practices well but plays poorly.** If you notice that your child seems to perform consistently better in practice than in competition it may be because, for a variety of reasons, she isn't having fun competing and is feeling stressed.

❖ **She engages in atypical behavior.** If your even-tempered child suddenly throws a tantrum or hits a teammate or opponent, or your extroverted child suddenly becomes sullen and withdrawn, it may be a sign that your child is no longer having fun in sports.

Oh Henry! Once, before my sons' soccer game, I ran into my friend Lauren who was dropping off her son, Henry, for the same game. As Henry and my sons dashed off to practice, I told her, "I'll wait until you park, and we can walk over to the field together." She looked at me dejectedly. "I won't be staying to watch Henry's game," she said. "He told me in the car on the way over that he didn't want me to come anymore."

Henry was only eight, yet he had strong opinions about who could attend his games. I couldn't understand his reasons, and when I asked Lauren, she was as perplexed as I was. I started ticking off a list of possibilities for Lauren. "You must be one of those moms who yell at him from the sideline," I said half-jokingly, knowing that kids are embarrassed by loud parents. "No, that can't be the reason," she said. "I spend most of my time during the games knitting or chatting with other parents." None of the other possible explanations for Henry's demand seemed to apply either. Thinking that Henry might tell me why he felt the way he did, I volunteered to give him a ride home. Lauren agreed.

In the car after the game, Henry and my three boys were celebrating how well they had played. Henry was a bit sad that his mom hadn't been there to see him play goalie, as he had recorded a shutout. I asked him why she had gone home. "Well, it's a long story," Henry said, "but I don't like her to see me play poorly. In my last game, I gave up five goals. My mom tried to tell me what I did wrong, and I didn't like it. She's never played soccer and doesn't even know the rules."

Kids, especially under twelve, are always seeking their parents' approval. Negative labels and generalizations and criticism can have a devastating emotional impact (see chapter 8). If you critique your child's performance, she will interpret your anger, disapproval, and disappointment as meaning that you don't love her anymore—that your love *is* conditional.

Every child will have good games and bad games. It is important to keep the bad times in perspective. After a loss, your child will most appreciate words of encouragement and a hug. Resist the temptation to hash out every thing that went wrong right after the game or scrimmage on the way home in the car. Just like you after a hard day at work, kids just want to relax after a game or practice; it usually isn't the best time to talk to them. If you want to talk about the game, do it when your child isn't stressed or thinking about the game he just played. Children need to be given the space to process the experience on their own and then move on.

Ignorance Is Bliss As I watched Spencer play indoor lacrosse one Sunday afternoon, I couldn't help but overhear the conversation between two fathers seated directly behind me. "I love watching Dylan's games," said one. "I never played lacrosse and don't have a clue about the rules or what's going on, so I'm not overly invested. It's just great to see them play in a pickup league like this."

The father had hit on the reason he was enjoying his son's games, and his son was enjoying having him at them: The father didn't know anything about indoor lacrosse, so he wasn't in a position to critique the game or his son's performance. Every father I spoke with at lacrosse said the same thing: Their sons *wanted them* to come to games. "It's not that way with his football games," one said.

Unfortunately, most parents who have played the sport that their child is playing or watch it on television think they are experts on how it is played. Many can't resist the temptation to offer a running commentary on the game in progress. Parents who have played the sport have to be extra careful not to put additional psychological stress on their child to follow in their footsteps. (I am reminded of an aphorism: "A little knowledge can be a dangerous thing.") Parents need to show their support just by being at games as spectators, not as judges or commentators.

For a child to ask that his or her parents "not come to my games anymore" is an all too common occurrence. Such announcements seem to come most often after a player has had a bad game or practice. They also seem to come just after pregame warm-ups when the player has missed a number of jump shots or just can't seem to put the puck in the net. The last thing a child needs to hear is a parent giving coaching pointers or putting pressure on him or her to perform from the sidelines. What children want most is unconditional support and encouragement, not criticism. Just knowing that Mom or Dad is in the stands is enough to make a child happy.

Eight out of ten children surveyed in a recent poll said that they wanted their parents at their games. What kids don't like is when their parents make more noise than anyone. Asked what embarrasses them most, *every single child surveyed* listed parents hollering plays or instructions from the sideline or stands. Almost four in ten kids in another survey reported having been embarrassed by the behavior of fans (some of whom may be their parents). Young players need to learn from their mistakes as much as from their successes. Not only do they get confused if parents and coaches are constantly yelling criticism or plays, all that yelling can do long-lasting psychological damage (see chapter 8).

Silence Is Golden Children who have loud and noisy parents are at a disadvantage. Focusing on the game with a screeching parent in the background is next to impossible. A mother is always the first to pick out the voice of her child crying, "Mom, mom!" in a crowded store. It's the same way with kids. It doesn't matter how many fans are yelling, they can always hear their parents through the din.

Don't get lulled into believing that because yelling at players may be tolerated at professional sports contests, it is acceptable to criticize players at youth sports contests. While the intensity and competitiveness of youth sports contests tends to mimic professional contests more and more, resist the temptation to view them the same way.

I remember one time seeing a boy on one of my sons' soccer teams whose dad was yelling instructions at him from the sideline stop in his tracks, look straight at his father, and yell back, "Dad! You're distracting me. Please be quiet! You're making me mess up." It's an embarrassing way for a parent to get the message. Instead of forcing your child to take matters into his own hands by telling everyone that you are keeping him from playing his best, it would be better if you exercised some self-control and kept your mouth shut.

THE OVERINVOLVED PARENT

Does enjoying your Saturday afternoons and evenings depend on whether your daughter won her softball game that morning? Do you find yourself lying awake at three in the morning wondering whether your son will outperform the other players on the team or even make it off the bench? Have you ever brought a pad of paper to the game to keep track of errors your child made so you can have her practice the play when you get home? Are you in a bad mood after your child loses and in seventh heaven after he wins? If you answered yes to any of these questions, then you may be overinvolved.

If you feel as if you are getting too wrapped up in your children's activities you may benefit from playing sports yourself. Better to blow off steam or pent-up stress by leaving the sidelines to take a long walk, participating in a recreational soccer or bowling league, or taking it out on the tennis or swimming pool than to come to your child's game and yell instructions. When I felt myself becoming a bit too involved in my sons' games, I tried to make sure I released the tension by playing squash or taking a vigorous three-mile walk with my dog. When you are calm, you will start to notice your young athlete becoming calm, too.

Enthusiastic parents are vital to all youth sports programs. Being a fan of the team and attending games is, however, only one way for a parent to be involved. If your child needs some space and asks that you refrain from attending her games for a while, or if you know that you just can't resist the urge to yell and scream instructions or, worse yet, criticisms, let her know that you care by volunteering in other ways. Offer to bring water and oranges, organize the carpool or caravan to games or practices. Volunteer to keep score, help the coach with his substitution grid, or be a soccer referee's assistant. Organize a pizza party or other gathering during the season. Your involvement behind the scenes will allow your child to realize that your interest in his program is genuine.

WHO CARES ABOUT THE GAME? I'M HERE TO SEE YOU!

One of my sons was a substitute on his middle school soccer team. I made sure I went to all of his home games and the away games that were close to home. Midway through the season, Hunter came up to me at a home game and said he didn't think he was going to be playing much that game and that I didn't need to stand in the wind and the cold just to see him warm the bench. I told him I came because I wanted to see him and his teammates, not just to see him play. I could tell that my feelings meant the world to him, and that my mere presence eased the pain of not starting.

If your child isn't a star athlete:

❖ Emphasize the *process* of being an athlete, not just winning or losing, goals scored, or minutes played.

❖ Emphasize your child's individual development—how he has improved.

❖ Encourage your child to talk about how she feels about being a sub. Be a good listener. Remind your child that not everyone can be a star, but that *everyone* can contribute to and be a part of the team.

❖ Don't criticize or second-guess the coach in front of your child; it only undermines your child's faith and trust in the coach and his or her decisions. Seek feedback from the coach about ways your child can earn more playing time and how you can help. As your child gets older, encourage him to talk to the coach directly.

❖ Respect your child's feelings; let her know how difficult it is for you to watch from the stands or see the frustration she must feel about not being as skilled as she thinks she should be at the moment. Don't dismiss feelings of being hurt, angry, or bitter, but do help to maintain a healthy perspective on the situation while accentuating the positive feelings which she experiences as well.

❖ Remind her that it is during practices, not games, that she develops her skills.

Cheer for the Team Amy had always been a gifted athlete. She had been the top scorer for her youth soccer team since first grade, and her skills were head and shoulders above her peers. Unfortunately, her parents also stood out. They stood alone on the sidelines, their eyes focused like laser beams on their daughter, cheering only when she made a brilliant move or drove the ball into the back of the net. Not surprisingly, the other parents found their behavior tiresome and self-centered.

Listen to the comments you make at your child's game. Are you singling out your son for the touchdown run but forgetting to praise the guard who made the block that sprang him into the clear? Show support for the entire team. Instead of focusing on your child, choose cheers that compliment the entire team, like, "Good team effort," "Way to go, defense!" or "Great blocking, line!" If you single a player out for praise, spread the wealth. Praise not just your son or daughter but others as well. The players in the game may never hear your words of encouragement, but the ones on the bench will get the message that you are pulling for the entire team, and the parents in the stands or on the sidelines will hear the same thing. Inclusive cheers build team spirit and set a great example for the kids—and other parents—by sending the message that the game is not exclusively about winning and losing but about the overall effort of the team and trying one's best.

Don't Criticize the Players I remember standing with a group of parents after a middle school soccer game one beautiful, crisp New England fall afternoon. Our team had just suffered a heartbreaking loss when a player failed to connect on a pass to a wide-open forward poised to score the tying goal on a breakaway. Mark, the father of the forward—who had scored both of our team's goals in the 3–2 loss—complained that it was "too bad we don't have any players who can score. My son had to play forward instead of shoring up the defense." As the mother of one of the forwards who "couldn't score," I was aghast at the insensitivity of Mark's comment.

No one likes to hear the know-it-all parent providing a play-by-play commentary on the game loud enough for everyone in the stands to hear. It's usually parents like these who, if they could hear themselves make remarks like, "The guard opened a huge hole for the running back. Why didn't he get the first down? We need to try someone else at halfback!"

would ask, "Why the heck did I say that?" If your child has been the target of insensitive comments like these, you know how important it is to keep your criticisms to yourself.

Don't Put Your Child on a Pedestal In lamenting the lack of good forwards, Mark lost sight of why the other parents were at the game. He put his son on a pedestal and, by bragging about his son's athletic prowess, made the other parents feel small. The players knew his son was a strong player. So did the parents. But Mark did not need to insult us or put our children down. If your child overhears you putting her on a pedestal and singing her praises in front of others, she may become afraid to let you down. It's easier for your child not to have you see her do poorly in a game than to be embarrassed in front of all the people that you brag to. Even if she does well, she is being put under unnecessary pressure to perform. When that happens, she isn't having fun.

Besides, as I discussed in chapter 2, children develop at different rates. One day, the shoe might soon be on the other foot. Mark's son might reach a plateau in his athletic development and see other players catch up or even surpass him in ability. Kids need to support one another and play as a team. Parents need to do the same.

Think About How You Are Viewed by Others How do you think your sideline behavior is perceived by other parents, coaches, and players? Imagine what a video playback of your behavior would look like. Would you see youself helping to clean the sidelines after a game or tossing a coffee cup on the ground in disgust after the opposing team has just scored its seventh goal? Would you hear yourself leading a positive cheer, hands clapping with a smile, or see yourself booing and making an obscene gesture at the referee? Would you see yourself stressing out near the player's bench or handing out oranges to players at halftime?

Your child—and all the other players, for that matter—will have the best experience if she knows that you are on the sidelines supporting her and her team, and that you have put the interests of the kids first and left your ego and personal agenda at home. Children learn self-control by watching you display self-control. Like a coach who remains calm and under control in tough situations, parents who exhibit good sideline behavior provide young athletes with an appropriate role model for handling the emotional ups and downs of competition.

Actions speak louder than words. Your efforts to teach self-control will be undermined if your child sees you losing your cool on the sideline and yelling at the officials.

Exhibit Good Sportsmanship Nearly seven in ten nine- to fifteen-year-olds in a recent study said they had seen a fan angrily yell at an official. Three-quarters of the parents and coaches questioned in the same survey said they had witnessed such unacceptable and verbally abusive behavior as well.

Such behavior can negatively affect all the players (see chapter 8 on the effect of yelling). If you are supportive and positive in everything you say and do, it will spill over to all the kids, on both sides of the field. Don't view the other team as the enemy. Talk to parents in the stands from the other team. Congratulate any player who makes a good play. If children see their parents in friendly conversation with parents from the visiting team, they will be getting a very important message: that the game isn't such a life-or-death, kill-or-be-killed affair that parents can't exhibit good sportsmanship. If your kids see you having fun on the sideline, instead of grimly pacing up and down like an NFL coach in the fourth quarter of a playoff game, they will keep the game in perspective and realize that they can be good sports and have fun, too!

Poor sportsmanship should not be encouraged. If a coach goes nuts over a referee's call and is ejected, don't cheer him when he goes into a Bobby Knight-like rage, kicking an equipment bag, and instead of turning the coaching reins over to his assistant coach, leads the entire team off the field or court, forfeiting the game. If we as parents lose our perspective, we can't expect anyone else—least of all our children—to keep theirs. As parents we are our children's last line of defense when it comes to teaching them proper sportsmanship.

Thank the Officials Most youth sports officials regard parent abuse as the most stressful and negative aspect of officiating, one that is driving many to quit officiating. Resist the urge to criticize the officials. Instead, take time at the end of the contest to thank them and compliment them for their hard work.

If you thank the officials, you will be rewarded with a surprised smile and some interesting observations about your child's team. Such expressions of gratitude go a long way to motivating officials to continue officiating and handle the inevitable criticisms by coaches, parents, and players. Remember, most are volunteers and often are young people themselves.

IF YOUR CHILD WANTS TO QUIT

One of the most difficult decisions you and your child will face in youth sports is whether to quit. Once they quit, most kids drop out of sports completely. Many times a child, especially in middle or high school, will tell you of the decision only after she or he has made it. I think that this is unfortunate because sometimes just the right motherly advice might help to sort out the issues and perhaps lead to a different decision.

It is a complex problem, and while there are many reasons for kids to quit, I want to focus here on just two, where, if you were asked for your input first, you might be able to do something that could change your child's mind. Remember, of course, that the decision is ultimately up to your child.

Teammates are bullying and teasing. Studies consistently show "lack of enjoyment" as the number one reason kids quit sports. One of the principal reasons a child is not having fun could be because he is being bullied or teased, either by his teammates or the coach (the others are that the child isn't having fun because he doesn't think he is good enough or because the coach isn't creating an enjoyable experience).

While I know of no formal studies to back this up, I have seen firsthand how kids can eliminate their competition by bullying other kids into not trying out or quitting. I also have an enormous amount of anecdotal evidence (in the form of hundreds of e-mails that I have kept in a "quitting" folder on my computer desktop) to support the idea that it is teasing and bullying that drive many kids from sports because, more than anything else, a child, in order to play well and have fun, needs the respect and encouragement of his teammates.

If you see your child being teased or bullied, or if he tells you it is occurring, talk to the coach and tell her or him that you do not tolerate abuse and ask her or him to put a stop to it. Perhaps you can offer to volunteer at practices to keep an eye on what is going on.

Lack of playing time. No child likes to sit on the bench (although after age twelve, when a child begins to understand that talent is not based on effort alone, he may be willing to sit on the bench just to be part of the team; this is especially true for boys). If you were ever chosen last in a neighborhood pickup game you know the feeling of not being considered one of the better players. This is how a child feels if she is forced to sit on the bench for long periods of time. At the developmental level (the level below high school varsity), every child should get equal or at least significant playing time. If this was the rule rather than the exception, I am convinced that far fewer children would quit sports.

Even if your child is getting less playing time than he thinks he deserves, there are situations where sticking it out and continuing to play is a good idea and may pay huge dividends, such as where he is a bench player on an all-star team. Some years back, Chris Cardone was a bench player for Toms River, New Jersey, during the Little League World Series. Chris was upset about not being able to play more and actually begged his parents to let him come home. His mother told him to write down his thoughts as a way to take his mind off the tough situation he was in. His father told him to "gut it out."

In the top of the fifth inning of the championship game, Chris was inserted into the lineup. In his first at bat he hit a home run, equaling his total for the season. In Toms River's final at bat, he walloped a two-run homer to give his team a 10–8 lead they would not relinquish.

"This must be the ultimate Little League moment," his mom, Lucy, told *Sports Illustrated*. "My son is a bench player, but we kept telling him, 'Sit tight, your chance will come.' What an inspiration this is for every kid who is just sitting there waiting and all he needs is one chance to do something that might change his life."

Listing Pros and Cons If your child is thinking of quitting, help her draft a list of pros and cons of continuing to play a sport. The list will give each of you a better understanding of what is driving her desire to quit. If your child is tempted to quit midseason, ask her to consider the effect her quitting will have on her teammates, what she would think if one of her friends quit, how quitting might affect her future ability to play for this club or organization. Armed with the list, you may be able to give your child a number of options other than quitting.

When you and your child have talked the decision over with the coach and understand that this is the best choice for your child, it is important to help your child quickly find another physical activity.

If the reason your child quits is because of the coach, be sure to write a letter or send an e-mail to the coach—with a copy to the club's board of directors or the school athletic director—documenting the reasons he is quitting, because you may not be asked to evaluate the coach at the end of the season like other parents.

Chapter Four

Not Bad for a Girl
A Mother's Role in Raising an Athletic Daughter

This is my Game. This is my future. Watch me play.

—U.S. WOMEN'S WORLD CUP SLOGAN 1999

On June 19, 1999, I was privileged to witness a truly magical happening—the opening ceremonies and games of the 1999 Women's World Cup. From my seat on the fifty-yard line at a sold-out Giants Stadium, I was one of 78,972 fans comprising, to that point, the largest crowd in the history of women's sports and of Giants Stadium.

Many in the crowd couldn't wait for this special moment, arriving the night before in their vans and motor homes or early on game day to tailgate in the parking lot on a hot, sunny day in the New Jersey Meadowlands. What I remember most were all of the young girls in the stands, especially the large throng of GU14 (girls under fourteen) soccer players sporting Mia Hamm jerseys and smiles full of braces—girls dreaming of one day playing for their country.

The opening ceremonies and the games that followed (a 6–0 blowout by Brazil over Mexico followed by the main event—a stellar 3–0 victory by the United States over Denmark), were especially poignant for one group of fans: women and mothers who, like me, grew up in the days before 1972, the year the passage of Title IX ushered in a new era for women's sports by mandating that girls and young women be given the same opportunity to play sports as boys. We were women who, at best, were offered three or four sports to play in high school or, if we weren't so lucky, were all competing for eight spots on the cheerleading squad. We were the women who went to women's colleges just so we could play the sports we were never given a chance to play in high school (like lacrosse, squash, and soccer); the women who, having been denied the opportunity to play sports when we were young, were now working hard to make sure our daughters were given the same chance as our sons to play sports.

I shed tears of joy during the playing of the national anthem and at the introduction of Donna de Varona, who as co-chairperson of the World Cup, two-time Olympic gold-medal-winning swimmer, pioneering woman sportscaster, and cofounder of the Women's Sports Foundation had done so much to advance the cause of women's sports over the years. When Mia Hamm and the American team paused before the game to applaud *us*, the pre-Title IX athletic women, it gave me chills.

The noise and the enthusiasm on that brilliant June day were sensational. As I watched the American women win their first game—a game that ten years before would probably have been played on high school football field—I knew the tournament represented a sea change in women's sports.

Yet, as soccer players representing each of the sixteen participating nations stood at the center of the field and in strong, clear voices proudly recited in their native languages the World Cup's slogan, I knew that as far as girls and women had come in sports since 1972, many challenges remained.

Most girls drop out of sports when they reach puberty. Gender stereotyping of female athletes as unfeminine continues. The media still underreports female athletes and sports teams. There are still too few women coaches, female athletic role models, and mentors. The increased opportunities for girls to play youth sports seem to have come at a cost: instead of being able to play sports the way they are naturally inclined to play—in a process-oriented, collective, inclusive, and supportive way emphasizing relationships and responsibilities—girls play under the same hypercompetitive, highly commercialized model that evolved in boys' sports. Benefits can far outweigh the challenges, and there are many things you can do as a parent to make your daughter's sports experience a valuable and rewarding one.

BENEFITS FOR GIRLS IN SPORTS

It is well known that sports are good for girls. Sports teach girls commitment, respect for others, how to relax, concentrate under stress, set and achieve goals, accept responsibility and failure, and be gracious winners.

Extensive research shows that physical activity and sport can enhance the mental, psychological, and spiritual health of American girls and young women:

Better Physical Health The health benefits of playing sports for girls are numerous:

❖ **Fewer chronic illnesses.** Girls who play sports have stronger immune systems and run a reduced risk of chronic illnesses later in life such as heart disease, high blood pressure, diabetes, and endometrial, colon, and breast cancers.

❖ **Reduced risk of obesity.** In 1970, one out of every twenty-one girls was overweight; today that number is one in six. Health experts estimate that obesity and sedentary lifestyles are responsible for over 400,000 deaths per year in America, and that inactivity and obesity in the current generation of girls is likely to result in significant health problems later in life. Girls who play sports run less risk of being obese adults.

❖ **Healthier menstruation.** Girls who play sports have lighter and more regular periods and experience less cramping and discomfort. (See, however, the discussion of the female athlete triad in chapter 9).

❖ **Stronger bones and reduced risk of osteoporosis.** Again, a note of caution regarding the female athlete triad. See chapter 9.

❖ **Reduced cigarette and illicit drug use, and less sexual activity.** Two national studies found that female school or community athletes are significantly less likely to use marijuana, cocaine, or most other illicit drugs. The protective effect of sports in this regard is particularly true for Caucasian girls.

Better Grades in School

❖ **Better at organizing, setting priorities, and budgeting time.** Playing sports adds to—not detracts from—a girl's time, energy, and commitment to schoolwork.

❖ **Perform better in science.** A study reported in the April 1998 *Journal of Sociology of Education* found a strong and positive correlation between a girls participation in high school sports and success and higher grades in science (at least for Caucasian girls).

Better Social Life

❖ **Entry into an achievement-based social network.** Sports provide girls a core of buddies, integrating them, as researchers at Catholic University argue, into male-type "networks that are larger, less intimate, and more based on achievement" than the small, intense friendship groups based on building and maintaining relationships to which girls are naturally drawn. This type of network may give female athletes an edge in other areas of achievement as well.

❖ **Greater popularity among peers.** Like male athletes, today's female athletes are more popular. Sports can gain girls entry into the often complex social hierarchies of high school.

Better Emotional and Psychological Health

❖ **Higher self-esteem.** Teenage girls experience a self-esteem crisis during adolescence far more serious than boys. Girls playing sports have higher self-esteem and look less to relationships with boys to build self-esteem. They say that sports give them more confidence.

❖ **Better self-image.** Female athletes obsess less about their attractiveness.

❖ **More self-confidence.** Teenage girls suffer from a lack of self-confidence far more than boys. Studies have consistently shown that girls who are physically active perceive their academic and athletic ability more positively.

❖ **Lower rates of depression.** Two studies found that women and girls who regularly participate in exercise suffer lower rates of depression.

❖ **Lower risk of suicide.** A 2004 study found that the odds that female high school athletes, especially those on three or more teams, will consider or plan a suicide attempt are lower.

Career Boost The path to the boardroom may well go through the girl's locker room:

❖ **Sports help girls develop leadership skills, self-reliance, and self-discipline.** According to researchers at Catholic University, women who are athletes are more achievement oriented, independent, self-confident, and inner-controlled. Nearly nine out of ten women executives in a recent survey by mutual fund giant Oppenheimer said sports helped them be more disciplined. Nearly seven out of ten said sports helped them to develop leadership skills that contributed to their professional success.

❖ **Sports enhance girls' ability to function as part of a team.** Four out of five women executives in the Oppenheimer study said sports helped them to function better as part of a team.

"Many strong girls have found protected space in which they could grow. There are various ways to find that space. For example, athletics can be protective. Girls in sports are often emotionally healthy. They see their bodies as functional, not decorative. They have developed discipline in the pursuit of excellence. They have learned to win and lose, to cooperate, to handle stress and pressure."

—MARY PIPHER
REVIVING OPHELIA

❖ **Sports may provide a key to the executive washroom.** Four out of five executive women in the Oppenheimer study played sports between junior high and college and still participate in some sort of physical activity, sports, or exercise, and two-thirds of those at least three times a week. As Donna Lopiano, CEO of the Women's Sports Foundation, observes, "Sports is nothing more than organizing a group for high performance. And that's what businesses do."

❖ **Sports give girls the ability to speak sports vernacular.** Surprisingly, the Oppenheimer study suggests that sports are used far less to exclude women from conversations and opportunities at work than previously believed: only one in five women executives surveyed said they were ever excluded from a business opportunity because they didn't participate in a particular sport. The study found that women were familiar if not comfortable with sports vernacular. "When it comes to sports talk, we got game," said one female executive.

The bottom line is that while sports are not a magic potion, they do help girls get through the trials of adolescence.

BENEFITS TO SOCIETY

In addition to the benefits girls get from playing sports, society itself clearly benefits from the spirit of cooperation women and girls bring to sports. A comprehensive survey of high school athletes by the nonprofit Josephson Institute of Ethics found that girls are about twice as likely as boys to model good sportsmanship.

Girls in sports argue and communicate anger less than males: instead of being confrontational, when in-group disagreements arise, girls tend to discuss things more rationally and constructively than males (this is something boys can be taught how to do). Team hugs and hand piles are displays overwhelmingly common to female athletes.

A great example of what women bring to sports that can teach and, hopefully, inspire everyone is the story of tae kwon do athlete Esther

Kim. When her best friend of thirteen years, Kay Poe, dislocated her knee before their match for a berth on the 2000 U.S. Olympic team, Kim forfeited her match and trip to Sydney to Poe. She explained that she "couldn't bear to see myself accomplish my only dream by an unfair match. . . . I knew it was the right decision. . . . I've competed throughout my entire life, and through all the matches and all of the training, for the first time in my life, that day and every day, I feel like a champion."

Female athletes, like the recently retired stars of U.S. women's soccer, Mia Hamm, Joy Fawcett, Brandi Chastain, and Julie Foudy, provide the best kind of athletic role models: real women, with kids, husbands, and lives, some of them pushing or in their thirties, that women—and men—can relate to. They are women at their best. They showed how athletes can handle pressure—and winning and losing—with grace and class. Just as importantly, they demonstrated how to be self-effacing and share the spotlight and not hog the glory for themselves (as Mia Hamm exhibited in the recent HBO special on the odyssey of the U.S. women's soccer team, during which she refused to accept the fact that she carried the team; she said *they* carried *her*).

DROPPING OUT

While participation by girls in sports has increased at all levels—Olympic, professional, college, and high school—and society is now more accepting than ever of female athleticism, the fact that girls continue to drop out of sports at six times the rate of boys is an indication that we still have a long way to go as a society in reaching the goal of gender equality in sports. Not only are girls less likely to participate in sports once they reach adolescence but, worse, they are more likely to become sedentary. With such inactivity comes an increased risk of obesity and other health problems.

The statistics from the Centers for Disease Control are sobering: only *one-quarter* of girls in their senior year of high school engage in regular exercise compared to one-half of boys. The percentage of children involved in vigorous physical exercise dropped by half, from 66 percent to 33 percent, between 1984 and 1990. Only one-fifth of the nation's girls have daily physical education, and only one state (Illinois) requires it by law.

Why do so many girls drop out of sports at the cusp of adolescence when they need sports the most? There are a number of reasons:

❖ **With adolescence comes a greater desire for cooperation and connectedness over competition.** Soaring estrogen levels as girls enter puberty prompt a shift in *attitude* by many girls away from competition and toward relationships and connectedness. This turns them off to sports, which become increasingly competitive at the middle school and high school level. As Anne Driscoll, author of *Girl to Girl: Sports and You!*, observed in a 2000 article in *The Boston Sunday Globe*, "Girls . . . by their very nature are relational. . . . [T]he primary aim of girls is to relate to others, to be in relationships with others. Many athletic girls struggle with the fact that competition is not about connecting. It's about vanquishing the other. And vanquishing is not nice." Girls are also more likely to drop out of sports than boys because they feel more pressure to perform well.

❖ **Girls are less tolerant of poor sports behavior.** The values that female athletes seem to naturally embrace—playing a sport not just to win but to have fun, considering the team's success as important as their own, playing hard but playing fair, and above all, being good sports—clash with the winner-take-all mentality and abusive behavior by athletes, coaches, and fans that increasingly characterize today's youth sports, especially at the middle and high school levels. The concern is that such philosophy will threaten the growth of women's sports by turning girls and women off to sports. Many of the girls who continue to play sports persist only because of the social and more emotional aspects (i.e., they feel connected to teammates and coaches).

❖ **Teenage girls experience a crisis of confidence.** Studies confirm what we as women know from our own experiences as teenagers: that girls suffer a severe crisis in confidence and larger drop in self-esteem during adolescence than boys (who *gain* self-confidence as they mature). As a result, girls are more likely than boys to quit sports and other challenging activities because they don't view themselves as being good enough.

❖ **Poor coaching.** Of the eleven reasons cited by girls in a 1988 study as to why they dropped out of sports, the fourth highest was that the coach was a poor teacher; number nine was that the coach played favorites. Coaches who berate and belittle girls turn sports into such a hurtful, harmful experience that dropping out becomes for many a way to avoid further damage to their self-esteem.

❖ **Teenage girls still think sports are unfeminine.** Back when I was in high school it was not real cool for a girl to be a jock. That is why I didn't go out for basketball my senior year even though it was one of my best sports. Sadly, it is still mostly true today. High school girls interviewed by Rosalind Wiseman for her best-selling book *Queen Bees and Wannabes* said girls can be athletic and have high social status but only if they have thin, "feminine" bodies, and that a large, "masculine" build was unacceptable (which is why many excellent female athletes worry about getting bulky if they lift weights).

❖ **Middle school and high school sports are about winning, not participation.** Girls are hardwired to desire connection, cooperation, and collaboration and to resist overt competition. Unlike boys, who are more willing to sit on the bench because it allows them to connect socially with other boys, girls who go out for a sports team expect to play. Many girls quit sports as they enter their teen years because they know that the only way to keep playing is to play sports *like boys* in a hypercompetitive, winner-take-all environment where only the most skilled girls play.

❖ **Girls sometimes don't receive the support they need from their family.** The primary place where girls learn about gender roles is the family. Some families still tend to engage, perhaps unconsciously, in gender stereotyping, conveying the message that girls are inherently less athletic than boys, and that sports are less important for girls than they are for boys.

THE CRITICAL ROLE OF MOTHERS IN THEIR DAUGHTERS' ATHLETIC SUCCESS

As a mother you can have an enormous influence on your daughter's life-long pursuit of physical fitness or sports. Here are some tips on how to help your daughter develop a love of sports and get the most out of her sports experience:

Plant the athletic seed early. The trait of athleticism shouldn't be assigned just to boys. Girls who become elite athletes often report being inspired and motivated to play sports early in life. Starting your daughter out in sports when the time is right (notice I didn't say *organized* sports; as was explained in chapter 2, you don't need to start your daughter in *team* sports until she is six or seven) is important because studies show that if you don't get your daughter involved in sports before age ten, there is only one chance in ten she will be participating in sports when she is twenty-five.

Mold sports awareness and build fundamental skills in preschool. Girls who play sports without basic skills are more likely than boys to feel like failures and give up. Use the preschool years to mold your daughter's awareness of sports and begin developing fundamental skills (kicking, overhand throwing, catching, and running). Use a Koosh ball, which is easy and safe to throw and catch, or a Frisbee, to develop these skills. It is a myth that girls can't throw overhand just like boys.

Encourage your husband to roughhouse with her more. Rough-and-tumble play and other forms of physical play, as well as physical aggression, are three to six times less common among girls than boys, a sex difference that continues through childhood and adolescence. Studies show that fathers tend to engage in more active play with their sons than with their daughters. Encourage your husband to engage in more active play with your daughter.

Talk with your daughter about *your* sports participation. A 2004 study by researchers at the University of Southern California suggests that if you play or played organized sports, your daughter is more likely to play. If your daughter doesn't know you were an athlete because you aren't currently playing sports or don't display your trophies or show her your scrapbooks, she is more likely to think that boys are inherently more athletic than girls. It's never too late for your daughter to know about your sports history; it can change your daughter's perception of where she acquired her athleticism.

Make sure you are a role model for your daughter. Don't unconsciously minimize or restrict your daughter's involvement if you weren't an athlete growing up. If you *were* an athlete growing up, make sure that you talk to your daughter about your involvement and the historical discrimination women faced to their sports participation both in terms of access and gender stereotyping (fulfilling obligations of "women's work" and being relegated to playing feminized versions of male sports). Don't downplay—or let your husband downplay—your athletic accomplishments.

Learning about your participation can also help your daughter overcome conflicts about her own participation that might arise because people have labeled her a tomboy, implying that she is inappropriately masculine.

Make fitness and physical exercise a part of your family's everyday life. Your daughter is more likely to play sports if you are physically active. Instead of just watching your daughter play soccer, join an adult team. Like the soccer-playing mothers in Escondido, California, who call themselves "A Bunch of Moms," you can show your daughter, as one mom told her local paper, that playing sports is more than fun for kids, it is "something they can do for their whole lives to stay healthy."

"My ultimate goal is to be a mom. I think all other accomplishments pale compared to being a mom. I can't wait. I'm going to be like any of those other moms taking their kids to soccer practice. My kids aren't going to care if I was an Olympic gold medalist or not, and that's what's important to me. They are going to care what type of mom I am, what type of role model I am, and about the lessons I can teach them."

— TARA NOTT, OLYMPIC GOLD MEDAL WEIGHTLIFTER PROFILED IN *SUPERWOMEN*

Be an involved parent. Nearly half of female athletes in one study listed parental involvement as the factor that gave them the most encouragement in athletic activities. We need to change the culture in which fathers are the parents responsible for the athletic training of children. It used to be that fathers had more experience in sports than mothers, but in the post–Title IX world of the past thirty-plus years, this is rapidly becoming a thing of the past.

Don't leave it to your daughter's father be the one more involved in supporting her participation in sports. The fact that you may be more involved in other aspects of a child's life than your husband also shouldn't prevent you from having time for your daughter's sports (or your own, for that matter). If you only occasionally play sports with your daughter, she is more likely to view you as less interested in sports than you actually are.

There are lots of ways for you to be directly involved: as a coach, referee, fan, chauffeur, or team administrator (or what used to be called "team mom"). Try to get to as many of her games and practices as you reasonably can.

Take girls' sports as seriously as boys'. While nearly nine out of ten parents now agree that sports are equally important for girls as boys, this means that there are still some who think sports aren't as important for girls. A girl dropping out of sports when she becomes a teenager may simply be having a delayed reaction to messages she got when she was younger that sports aren't for girls (although studies now suggest that the different levels of interest in sports between girls and boys—both in terms of participation and watching sports—is due at least in part to hard-wired differences). In other words, it becomes easier to stop playing sports because society *expects her to stop.* Imagine your daughter growing up to be an athlete; otherwise, not becoming one may be a self-fulfilling prophecy.

Watch and attend girls' and women's sports contests with your daughter. Unfortunately, a bias in media coverage persists that reinforces gender stereotypes and deprives girls and women of appropriate athletic role models. Give your daughter female athletic role models to emulate by watching women's sports on television and attending girls' and women's sports contests. The reason the women's professional soccer league folded after three seasons was due in part to the failure of fans to do what the 1999 World Cup slogan implored them to do: Watch them play. Look for evenhanded sports coverage. Make a point of following with your daughter the careers of girls who have become hometown or regional sports heroes.

Offer extra encouragement. Studies show that adults tend to encourage boys but not girls in sports to be independent and competitive. As a result, girls tend to view themselves as less athletically skilled than they actually are (remember, a lack of confidence is one of the main reasons girls drop out of sports when they reach adolescence). It is therefore critically important that both you and your husband give your athletic daughter extra encouragement by telling her you value her as a female athlete, by letting her know that she has the same capacity as a boy for coping with intense sports competition, and that she is just as tough as any boy. Like Karen Ruggiero, the mother of my friend and three-time Olympic women's ice hockey medalist, Angela Ruggiero, you may not know all of the rules, but what is important is that your daughter knows that you support her every inch of the way. We also need to get to the point that fathers take as much pride in their daughter's athletic accomplishments as they would their son's. Because adolescent girls tend to be highly critical of themselves, try to help increase your daughter's confidence with gentle words of encouragement.

Teach her that being an athlete and being feminine are not mutually exclusive. Because girls grow up in a world where they are still conditioned by the culture and the media into thinking that sports are unfeminine, we all need to work hard to celebrate girls as female athletes and avoid reinforcing culturally based stereotypes. Show your daughter that you are comfortable with the sports she plays, especially if she plays hard, aggressive contact sports like hockey, basketball, soccer, football, or wrestling, and that you appreciate the values girls bring to sports.

Take a long, hard look at how you view sports for girls, beginning with

"All of us love being role models. My role models growing up weren't women athletes. We didn't have them."

—SASKIA WEBBER
U.S. WOMEN'S SOCCER
TEAM GOALKEEPER,
PROFILED IN *SUPERWOMEN*

what sports meant to you growing up, and make sure that any sexist attitudes aren't reflected in your comments and reactions to your daughter's involvement in athletics. Don't show discomfort if she beats a boy in an athletic contest, becomes obsessed with a sport, or wants to begin lifting weights. As my MomsTeam colleague Doreen Greenberg says, "let her know from your reactions and words that sweating and being powerful, muscular, and athletic are 'feminine'." Playing sports does not compromise her femininity. Try to dispel the myth that many adolescents still believe that "masculine" and "feminine" behaviors are mutually exclusive. Teach your daughter that a girl can be interested in stereotypically feminine activities, like keeping scrapbooks and collecting dolls or figurines, and yet also be interested in athletics.

Define competition in a way that resonates with girls. Girls tend to view competition negatively because it is defined by the youth sports culture in terms of winning and losing, and losing results in someone's feelings being hurt. One way to keep your daughter interested in playing sports through adolescence is to help her define competition more in terms of doing one's best (internal competition) instead of beating her opponent (external competition). Tony DiCicco and Colleen Hacker, head coach and sports psychology consultant, respectively, to the 1996 Olympic gold medal and 1999 World Cup champion U.S. women's soccer team, advise parents in *Catching Them Being Good: Everything You Need to Know to Successfully Coach Girls,* that they "teach girls and young women that just because they're competing on the field doesn't mean that this competition is going to hurt their friendships and relationships off the field."

Understand that aggression does not come naturally to most girls. As Dr. Leonard Sax notes in his book, *Why Gender Matters*, aggression between girls doesn't build friendships, it destroys them. So don't criticize your daughter if she doesn't seem to be as aggressive or competitive as you or her dad thinks she should be. But do talk to her about the important difference between aggressiveness and assertiveness.

Emphasize achievement, not attractiveness. Help your daughter avoid defining herself on the basis of her attractiveness and appeal to boys. Emphasize her achievements instead, how good she is at sports, and that her social status can be enhanced by her athletic ability. Teach her that what her body can do is what is important, not how she looks. After all, boys grow up thinking this way.

Teach her to exhibit good sportsmanship. Teach your daughter the importance of continuing to model good sportsmanship.

Let her play on a boys' high school team if that's what she wants. Like my friend Angela Ruggiero, many elite female athletes who reach the Olympic or professional level trained and competed with and against boys, who pushed them to reach their full potential, forced them to prove their worthiness, and helped them gain a sense of competence in their skills and develop self-assuredness in their risk-taking ability.

While you may be personally opposed to your daughter playing on a boys' team, teenagers these days seem increasingly accepting and even supportive of teammates and opponents of the opposite sex. In deciding whether it makes sense for your daughter, discuss your feelings with her and consider practical realities such as her skill level, changing in separate locker rooms, the possibility of being taunted by fans or opposing parents, and the increased risk of injury (especially in contact sports where girls are playing against bigger, stronger, and more aggressive opponents). You should tell your child not to expect special favors, that initial resistance is possible, that boys may experience potential "shame" if they are beaten by girl and see it as a tough blow to their self-esteem. Make sure to talk to your daughter's doctor first to rule out any potential medical reasons she shouldn't play on a boys' team.

Remember that an all-girls team is likely to offer your daughter a very different experience, one that is likely to be less intimidating. Overcoming the gender barrier may not be the athletic role she wants to take on. Being on an all-girls team may make it easier to take the initiative as a leader and build her sports skill level.

"[D]efinitions of femininity have become progressively more complicated. Look at soccer star Mia Hamm or tennis champions Venus and Serena Williams. Women who are strong, aggressive and competitive athletes are now 'allowed' to be considered feminine. But look deeper. On the field, Mia Hamm . . . is intense, fearless. . . . But once she's off the field (as her shampoo advertisements show) she becomes the pretty girl with the beautiful bouncing hair. All of this means that we still haven't gotten beyond girls valuing their place in society by how closely their body comes to society's current ideal image of femininity."

—ROSALIND WISEMAN
QUEEN BEES AND WANNABES

Teach her the importance of athletics for success as an adult. Let her know that she may learn lessons in sports that she may not be able to learn anywhere else, lessons critical to later success in the adult world (e.g., the military, politics, and business). Like the mother of Maria Burton Nelson, author of *Embracing Victory: Life Lessons in Competition and Compassion,* teach your daughters "from an early age that competition in sports is a bridge to understanding competition in other aspects of life, like the business world." Remember that as a woman you are in a unique position to teach a *balanced* approach to sports: that an athlete can compete and care at the same time; she can care about her own ambition but care about opponents as well because they challenge her to do her best. On the other hand, let her know that she can learn about winning and competition in ways other than by playing competitive sports: it can come from extracurricular activities like music, drama, dance, the debate team or other hobbies.

Keep her active in her teen years. Instead of allowing her to give up sports altogether when she reaches adolescence and doesn't want to participate in organized sports, encourage your daughter to stay physically active by helping her find a sport to play on a recreational level. Teach her that there is nothing wrong with participating in sports that emphasize beauty and grace but also require speed, agility, and strength, or sports with no clear winners and losers and with no physical contact between competitors (such as competitive dance, synchronized swimming, and cheerleading, where some girls have taken to wearing T-shirts proclaiming, "I *am* a girl; I *am* an athlete; CHEERLEADING IS MY sport!").

Be intolerant of discrimination. Unfortunately, as far as we have come since enactment of Title IX in 1972, girls still don't have equal participation opportunities. Parks and recreation departments continue to serve more boys than girls, an inequity that prompted the State of California in 2005 to enact a first-of-its-kind law expanding Title IX rules to require cities, towns and recreation districts to ensure gender equity in youth programs they operate and in the use of their facilities by independent groups. As noted in The Women's Sports Foundation report, *Her*

Life Depends On It, "Advocates for girls' programs . . . often have to compete with politically entrenched male administrators of boys' programs for a share of available courts, swimming pools and fields." Girls still get offered fewer sports to play; smaller locker rooms; inferior equipment; less glamorous fields; less convenient practice times; less publicity; less qualified game officials; less attractive game times (i.e. games on school nights leading to smaller crowds, while boys' games are scheduled on weekends); less school support (i.e. pep rallies for boys' teams but not girls'); less community support (i.e. buses for fans to attend away games for boys, but not for girls); and fewer opportunities to play for teams of women coaches or in programs run by women. When you see girls getting the short end of the stick in terms of facilities, equipment, coaching, or game times, fight for fairness, either behind the scenes or, if necessary, in public forums (best to do this as part of a group of like-minded parents; see more on this in chapter 15).

Support programs that put winning in its place. Enroll your daughter in and only support sports programs that emphasize skill development, positive reinforcement, equal playing time, a chance to play all the positions, and that don't place undue emphasis on winning and competition, that treat boys and girls equally, give them equal chances in all aspects of the athletic experience, don't tolerate sexist comments from coaches, or coaches that coddle girls or give them special treatment. (Listen on the sidelines: do you hear the sound of laughter as in a pickup game or yelling and screaming as in pro sports contests?)

Address and support diversity in all its forms. Teach your daughter that to be on a team is to be accepting of players with different backgrounds and personalities, clothes, hairstyles, even sexual orientation. If she learns these lessons early in life, then she will have an easier time in her adult life.

Chapter Five

Letting Boys Be Boys
A Mother's Role in Raising An Athletic Son

The best way to raise your son to be a man who is caring and nurturing is let him first be a boy.

—DR. LEONARD SAX, *WHY GENDER MATTERS*

A LETTER TO THE COACH

One night in the spring of my sons' freshman year in high school, my son Spencer sat on the couch in the family room in front of the fire, pen in hand, writing on white-lined paper on a clipboard. Nothing unusual in that; the cozy room was where our family spent countless hours playing games or reading, and where Spencer and his brothers often did their homework in a "study group," collaborative fashion.

This night was different, however. Instead of lying stretched out on the couch, Spencer was sitting upright smack dab in the middle. He would write a few words, then pull the paper from the clipboard in frustration, crumple it into a ball, and toss it into the fireplace. It was unusual for him to struggle so much to get his thoughts down on paper. After watching a number of crumpled pieces of paper being tossed into the fire, I asked whether I could help. He told me he was trying to write a letter to his freshman lacrosse coach because he couldn't take the yelling and screaming anymore and the team was falling apart. He told me that it was hard to find words to express his anger and frustration, but that he had to write the letter himself.

I was acutely aware of the problem with Spencer's coach, and having talked with many of the players' mothers, I knew that they, too, were having a very difficult season and that something needed to be done. My initial intent was to sit back and observe in the hopes that Spencer and his teammates would be able to work things out without any outside help.

A Close-Knit Group I had reason to be optimistic, at least at the beginning. Spencer and his teammates were a large but close-knit group. Most had played freshman football together that fall; many had been playing club lacrosse together since fifth grade, were coming off an undefeated outdoor club season in eighth grade, and had tuned up for their first year of interscholastic lacrosse by playing indoor lacrosse that winter.

The indoor lacrosse experience had been a very positive one. Each Sunday afternoon, the boys would practice for thirty minutes and then play a game. While they had a coach providing some instruction, the practices and games were organized and run largely by the players themselves.

Spencer had taken the initiative to organize the team, inviting all the players who had played club lacrosse the previous spring to join, along with most of his buddies from the freshman football team who had never played. He collected money from each player and signed the team up for both of the two six-week sessions. During games, everyone got equal playing time, and they all had a ton of fun. No pressure. No yelling. Just a bunch of kids playing a game they loved. It was as close to a group of kids in the neighborhood getting together to play a pickup game that one could get.

Maturity and Leadership An hour and lots of crumpled pieces of paper later, Spencer got up and announced with a look both of relief and satisfaction that he had finished the letter, that he "did it!" I asked if he wanted to read me the letter, but he demurred.

After cleaning up the mess, I carefully unfolded the crumpled-up draft Spencer had left on the coffee table. "Dear Coach," it began. "I have tried to talk to you so many times before, but you would not listen. Your way of talking to me is by yelling at me. When you scream at me, I don't hear anything you say so I am writing this letter. . . ."

I thought the letter demonstrated real maturity and leadership on Spencer's part. It spoke about the way the coach was mistreating all the players, not just about the way he was abusing Spencer with his constant yelling and stream of criticisms.

Writing the letter had clearly been a cathartic experience for Spencer, but unlike letters all of us have written at one time or another—letters we wrote just to express on paper emotions bottled up deep inside, but never intended to send to the person who had caused us so much pain—Spencer was brave enough to actually deliver his letter to his coach, a letter expressing thoughts and feelings that he wasn't able to deliver face-to-face. Spencer told me he saw his coach read it, but that afterward he had nothing to say.

Coach-, Not Child-, Centered Two days went by, then three, without the coach saying anything to Spencer. On the fifth day, Spencer approached the coach and asked him when they could talk about the problems the team was having. The coach laughed, smirked, and asked, "What problems? There aren't any."

After talking with Spencer, we agreed that I would talk to the coach myself. I had so many things to ask him, but most of all I wanted to know why he had refused to acknowledge, much less address, the problems Spencer had raised in his letter. He replied that all the boys had mistakenly thought they knew how to play lacrosse so he had to "knock them down" a few pegs, "tear them apart and start from scratch as if they had never held a lacrosse stick."

I did my best to listen, but none of what he said made any sense to me. He wasn't interested in what I or any other parent had to say or in resolving the problems that were tearing the close team apart.

I took my concerns to the high school's athletic director, which got me nowhere as well. Unfortunately Spencer and many of his teammates had a difficult time recovering from their freshman lacrosse experience. Most of what could have been a remarkable team of boys once they got to the varsity had become so discouraged by the way they were verbally abused that they dropped out or switched schools. What had seemed like a promising high school athletic career for many strong and happy freshmen ended with a whimper instead of a bang. It didn't have to end that way. If our youth sports system was child- instead of adult-centered, if coaches were more sensitive to the fact that a successful sports experience is critical to a boy's emotional and social development, perhaps the outcome for Spencer would have been different.

HARDWIRED TO COMPETE AND WIN

The rough-and-tumble play many boys are so fond of, which experts say begins around age three and peaks between ages eight and ten, also contributes to the formation of dominance hierarchies in boys' groups. A male's greater acceptance of—indeed attraction to—risk taking may also explain why boys, more than girls, are attracted to extreme sports (skateboarding, snowboarding, rock climbing, BMX bikes, etc.).

An interesting 1987 study of boys attending summer camp found that boys, once assigned to cabins, organized themselves into teams led by the strongest, most athletic boys, and that once formed, the teams resulted in reduced conflict and led to an increase in sports competition with boys from other cabins. By the end of summer, the dominant boys were almost always spending time with their cabin mates and spending most of their free time directing the group in competitive athletic activities.

This evolutionary perspective may explain why boys on sports teams, more than girls, are able to figure out who should play what position and who should be captain without the help of the coach. It may also explain why boys seem to be more comfortable than girls in unequal relationships, even if they are the one who is low man on the totem pole. A third-string linebacker is able to be the star quarterback's best buddy

"The macho risk-taking culture that surrounds competitive sports in high school and college leads them to ignore pain, to drink and binge on alcohol, and to act in sexist, disrespectful and sometimes violent ways towards women and others."

—EMILY SENAY, MD
FROM BOYS TO MEN

because he doesn't resent the quarterback's higher status. As Dr. Leonard Sax observes, "This male characteristic has roots that go very deep. If you know the stories of Jesse [sic] and Jonathan son of Saul, or for that matter Don Quixote and Sancho Panza, then you've heard this story before. Those friendships were not less strong because of the difference in status between the friends. On the contrary, the hierarchical character of the relationship defined and even ennobled the friendship." Because boys, like their ancestors, recognize the importance of strong coalitions to their individual and collective survival unlike girls, they prefer to have the best players on their team, not necessarily their friends.

Learning Skills for Adulthood A 2003 article in *Developmental Review* suggests that one of the functions of team sports for boys is to help them develop the social skills needed to form competitive groups or coalitions in adulthood, such as business organizations. Evolutionary biologists theorize that many of these developmental activities also mirror and provide practice for specific behavioral skills which were once associated with primitive warfare, such as throwing projectiles and tracking their trajectory. This might explain why fathers seem so intent on spending so much time with their sons practicing throwing and catching—they are hardwired to pass these skills on to their sons.

The relation between physical aggression and social dominance becomes more obvious and serious in late childhood and early adolescence. Between ages eight and ten, bullying by boys increases at the beginning of each school year and decreases later in ye ar after the social pecking order is established. By grade school, boys' games are more competitive, longer in duration, with more rules and interdependence between players, and with clear winners and losers. By contrast, girls avoid games where winning means someone must lose; they like turn-taking games like hopscotch, where competition is less direct. A 2002 study of fourth- and six-graders showed that during free time boys competed with boys half the time, while only *1 percent* of the girls used recess to compete against other girls.

BENEFITS OF SPORTS FOR BOYS

Like girls, boys enjoy enormous benefits from sports and competition.

❖ Sports help keep boys active and physically fit.

❖ Sports provide boys a healthy way to channel their intense physicality and aggression and feel strong.

❖ Sports help boys develop self-control.

❖ Sports help boys develop self-confidence.

❖ Sports provide a place in which boys can form friendships with other boys. Indeed, sports are central to boys' social relationships.

❖ Sports provide boys with increased social status. Research shows that male athletes across all sports are significantly more popular than nonathletic male peers, with the most popular group being those boys who play both contact and noncontact sports.

❖ Participation in sports makes it less likely that a boy will smoke cigarettes, use drugs, or think about or commit suicide (the suicide rate has almost tripled over the past forty years and is now the third leading cause of death among adolescents fifteen to twenty-four, with the rate for boys higher than for girls).

❖ Boys who play sports in high school get better grades and do better on standardized tests.

Pressure to Conform While sports clearly benefit boys, participation in sports by boys is accompanied by a number of problems. As William Pollack, author of *Real Boys' Voices,* observes, the "[p]ressure on boys to fulfill traditional rules about masculinity can often feel overwhelming. It can lead him to tease, bully or abuse others. It can cause him to make mistakes in how he treats girls. . . . It can prod him toward depression . . . it may even lead him to frightful, sometimes lethal acts of aggression and violence. In almost all cases it makes him want to limit the range of his personal expression or silence his genuine inner voice entirely." Team sports encourage boys to conform to masculine stereotypes and traits such as aggression and toughness, playing in pain, and stoicism. "A failure to display aggressiveness and self-abandonment desired by coaches and teammates subjects adolescent [male] athletes frequently to suggestions that they are feminine or homosexual," notes Eli Newberger, MD, in his book, *The Men They Will Become.* "Without doubt," Newberger argues, "this denigration of the feminine contributes to the potential for male athletes to be manipulative and exploitative in their relationships with real women."

The masculine, heterosexual culture of most athletic programs—particularly in contact sports like football, hockey, and lacrosse—may teach boys to view off-the-field violence as an acceptable means of maintaining their identities as athletes. This same culture can lead male athletes to abuse alcohol and routinely violate no-drinking rules. Because the "jock culture" at most high schools affords male athletes special status—not only among their peers but in the wider school and local community—they often develop an attitude that they are above the rules (see below). Rigid and confining social expectations about masculine and feminine behavior and homophobia also work in tandem to create a climate in which boys may feel compelled to participate in sometimes violent and often demeaning and sexually degrading hazing rituals.

Supporting a Jock Culture

Our sports culture all too frequently extends privileges to athletes because of their presumed special status. Student athletes are given preferential treatment for a number of reasons, including the fact that such treatment is given to professional athletes, on whose world youth sports have become increasingly modeled. It also stems from the emphasis placed on winning, which makes a coach reluctant to suspend a player before the "big game."

Clearly, many high schools support such a jock culture. A 1999 story in the Washington Post *highlighted the jock culture at Columbine High School as indicative of high schools around the country:*

✓ *A state wrestling champ was allowed to park his $100,000 Hummer all day in a fifteen-minute space.*

✓ *A football player was allowed to tease a girl about her breasts without fear of retribution from the teacher, who happened to be his coach.*

✓ *Sports trophies were displayed in the front hall, artwork down the back corridor.*

✓ *Sports pages in the yearbook were in color, while other extracurricular photos were in black and white.*

✓ *Hazing rituals were condoned, with upper class wrestlers allowed to twist the nipples of freshman wrestlers until they turned purple.*

✓ *Those who weren't athletes were considered outcasts, easy targets for bullying and body slams.*

Columbine High School is perhaps no different than thousands of other high schools in glorifying athletes. In a survey of fourteen- to seventeen-year-olds and parents of students conducted in 2000, more than three-quarters of the teens surveyed believed that some students or groups of students were "above the rules." Some parents and students suggested after the Columbine massacre that the way the school indulged jocks—their criminal convictions, physical abuse, sexual and racial bullying—intensified the feelings of powerlessness of Eric Harris and Dylan Klebold and their preoccupation in gaining vengeance against jocks ("All the jocks stand up." "Anybody with a white hat or a shirt with a sports emblem on it is dead.").

"Channeling your young son's aggressive impulses into football and soccer may be a better choice—just in terms of his physical health—than almost any indoor recreational activity you can name."

—LEONARD SAX, MD
WHY GENDER MATTERS

THE ROLE OF MOTHERS IN PARENTING BOYS

The solution to the problems your son is likely to face in sports is obviously not to keep him from playing, but to avoid reinforcing unhealthy gender stereotypes while providing him healthy ways through sports to channel his aggressive impulses. If you have a son, here are some specific steps that you should take:

Encourage sports participation as a socially acceptable outlet for his aggressive impulses. One of the most effective ways for a boy to channel his aggression is by participating in sports. If you have an aggressive, competitive son, encourage him to play a contact sport like football, ice hockey, wrestling, or lacrosse.

Lacrosse: Changing Lives

A classic example of how sports can provide boys a healthy outlet for their aggressive tendencies and turn their lives around is the story of the lacrosse program in the remote Canadian artic circle hamlet of Kugluktuk. Like many indigenous people in the Northwest Territories, the Inuit of Kugluktuk struggle with alcoholism, unemployment, and a high suicide rate. In the decade between 1986 and 1996, twelve school-age children had committed suicide, ten of them boys. Then Russ Sheppard, a recent graduate of the University of Saskatchewan, arrived, bringing with him a vehicle for change: sports, and more specifically, lacrosse—Canada's "other" national game. "I don't think we have a lot of troubled youth," Sheppard told the Baltimore Sun *in 2003. "Like teenagers anywhere, they get lonely, they wonder what people think of them. If they have a chance to do something socially with their peer group and do well with it, their outlook is going to dramatically improve."*

In order to participate, Sheppard required athletes to have an 80 percent attendance rate and do well in school. Thus, athletics have greatly improved attendance, which had been between 60 and 70 percent, and is likely to dramatically improve a poor graduation rate. The number of kids with 80 percent school attendance doubled. The kids quickly took to lacrosse, drawn to its combination of finesse and roughness. The number of players increased from sixteen in the first season to nearly seventy-five years later.

By providing kids an alternative to crime, lacrosse has become the community's lifeline and turned around lives. Nathan Hokanak is living proof of the program's success. In the year before he joined the program, he was arrested three times for breaking and entering to steal money to buy drugs. "I used to always be so angry," admitted Hokanak, "and [when I] started playing lacrosse, [I would] shoot the ball as hard as I could to take out as much anger as I could." Now he has become one of the school's top students and lacrosse players. At the 2006 U.S. Lacrosse National Convention, Russ Sheppard proudly reported that there has not been one teen suicide since he began his program.

Work to eliminate the double standard in coaching. The "assumption that all male athletes benefit from a certain (i.e., male) coaching style is as ridiculous as the notion that all females respond better to a kinder, gentler, nicer coaching style," says Ellen Staurowsky, Associate Professor of Sports Studies at Ithaca College and a former college Director of Athletics and men's soccer coach. "Different athletes respond in different ways depending on who they are, what their goals are, and what motivates them. And good coaches know how to tap into those differences and adjust accordingly."

Coaches of girls' teams generally provide lots of positive encouragement, avoid insulting players when they make mistakes, compliment them when they do well and try their best, are more inclined to de-emphasize winning, believe sports are all about having fun, making friends, and being nurturing. Yet most of boys' teams don't do the same thing. As a fourteen-year-old girl told a California newspaper, it is a myth that all boys "are 'macho' enough to handle criticism, whereas girls might 'break down and cry' . . . [B]oys only act macho because . . . [w]e raise them to be 'real men,' to 'suck it up,' and not show emotion. It is such a shame that we do not let them live up to their potential for growing into sensitive, caring men" by reinforcing gender stereotypes in the way they are coached.

Teach healthy masculinity. At the same time let your son know that he does not need to play sports, particularly aggressive, contact sports, in order to prove his masculinity and heterosexuality. He needs to know that he shouldn't let a sense of honor and duty to the team lead him to do harmful things to himself (like playing through pain, using performance-enhancing drugs, or participating in violent hazing rituals).

As Dan Kindlon and Michael Thompson note in their book, *Raising Cain,* "Very few boys or men are tall, handsome, athletic, successful with women, endlessly virile, and physically fearless. . . . Boys suffer from a too-narrow definition of masculinity, and it is time to reexamine that message. . . . We have to teach boys that there are many ways to become a man; that there are many ways to be brave, to be a good father, to be loving and strong and successful. We need to celebrate the natural creativity and risk taking of boys, their energy, their boldness. There are many ways for a boy to make a contribution in this life."

Because the competitive drive of a male athlete is more likely than a girl's to be expressed in confrontational ways, teach your son healthy ways to deal with physical and emotional pain, to respect his body, limit risk taking, and learn appropriate ways to resolve conflicts in a nonviolent way. Teach your son that on-the-field aggression does not excuse off-the-field aggression.

Break the code of silence. If your son violates no-drinking rules, don't condone such behavior by looking the other way because you believe that being on the team is important to his self-esteem and suspension is too high a price to pay. Whatever you do, don't promote alcohol abuse by letting your son and his friends drink at your home, rationalizing that it will keep him from drinking and driving.

Avoid reinforcing the jock culture. If you have a son (or daughter, for that matter) who is excelling athletically, don't allow his school to treat him differently, such as by lowering academic standards to enable him to participate, or by bending or ignoring team or league rules. Have the courage to uphold your own values, even if the school is willing to look the other way. If the school won't suspend him, you should.

Teach your son to respect girls. Boys need to be able to play with girls and respect them as athletes in order to develop nonsexist attitudes they can carry into adulthood. Instead of being afraid if you let your son compete against girls that he might lose, you should be teaching a different lesson: girls and boys can and should be as equal in sports as they are in other areas of life. You should help your son overcome the feeling that the aggression of female athletes is threatening: it is threatening only because it threatens gender stereotypes.

Ask your son's father to relax. Much of the pressure to conform to a hypermasculine gender stereotype undoubtedly comes from fathers, who, as a general rule, are more likely than mothers to go too far with pushing their children, particularly their sons. Unlike his grades in school, which are private, your son's success or failure in sports is public and on display for all to see.

Observes Harvard Medical School's Dr. Roberto Olivardia, coauthor of *The Adonis Complex: The Secret Crisis of Male Body Obsession.* "I think a lot of fathers are threatened that if their sons aren't doing well, it's somehow a poor reflection on them. They'll say, 'Don't be a wimp.' 'Hit the ball.' Or—and I've heard fathers say this many times at baseball games—'You throw like a girl.' And that is the most shaming thing that a boy can be told." My high school English teacher and longtime *Boston Globe* sportswriter, Tony Chamberlain recently wrote, "Fathers of young children often get so intense about their children acquiring sports skills of dubious future value that they often lose the big picture. . . . Whether it's throwing a baseball, stopping a pond hockey puck, taking a jump shot, or making a slalom turn through the gates, fathers can't resist going at it much too early." Even Tony fell victim to the male propensity for being so intense about teaching their children about sports that they go overboard, admitting that, in teaching his son fishing and sailing, he was a "little obnoxious," to the point where he would drill his son about things that he would most likely have picked up "naturally when they go fishing a few times." As Tony wryly observed, "[L]eave it to a dad to turn everything fun into a drill."

Help your husband keep his ego or hormones from getting the better of him. You don't want him to be like the father who, after attending his twelve-year-old son's first hockey game (a one-goal loss), charged into the locker room, yanked his son up off the bench, and yelled, "You fucking son of a bitch. If you'd hit that guy against the wall you wouldn't have lost the game."

Don't be part of the problem. Boys these days pretty much expect to hear men screaming and hollering at them. They don't expect it from moms, whom they expect to nurture and protect them.

Don't make the mistake of putting too much pressure on your son. As Olympic snowboarding gold medalist Shaun White told the *Washington Post* before the Turin games, "The reason I stopped playing soccer was because of soccer moms. I showed up late for a game, and this mom snapped [at] me. She screamed, 'You go out there and score!' Someone else's mom screams at you, you're eleven. It's pretty intimidating."

Make a point, like Shaun's mom, Cathy, of not putting pressure on your son. As Cathy told me several years ago, "I don't want to push him. If anything, I hold him back because I don't want him to get hurt."

Chapter Six

Ready, Set, Go!
How to Get Organized and Stay That Way

We cannot do great things on this earth
We can only do small things with great love

—MOTHER TERESA

BETTER LATE THAN NEVER

The spring travel soccer season was well under way, with the sixth game scheduled for a town thirty- to forty-minutes from home (depending on traffic). Because I had driven there many times, I knew where the soccer fields were and the quickest way to get there. On this particular Saturday, however, Janice, the mother of Hunter's best friend and teammate, Nicholas, wanted to drive the boys to the game. Since Taylor's soccer game that day was in the opposite direction from Winchester, I was only too happy to oblige Janice's request.

When we had received the game schedules earlier that spring my husband and I had divvied up the driving chores. Every other Saturday, if it was an away game, I would drive. There were ten Saturday games, five home, five away. Because Hunter and Taylor were on different teams, that meant ten away games, ten home games that season.

So that we both got to see Hunter and Taylor play, and so one of us would always be at each of their games, we planned to each attend one of our sons' games each week and switch off the next week. Because the parents of our sons' teammates knew that we always attended their games, we usually ended up driving a mini-van full of players to away games.

I was looking forward to having a Saturday free to do something other than go to a soccer game, which, when all was said and done, usually gobbled up a 3½ hour chunk of the day for an away game, an hour less for a home game, assuming everything went smoothly, which wasn't always the case. Sometimes games started late because the previous game ran late, or the referee didn't show up on time or at all.

Hunter and Nicholas needed to be to the field to loosen up and practice at 12:30 p.m. for the 1:00 p.m. game start. This meant Janice needed to pick up Hunter no later than 11:30 a.m., which would give her an extra ten minutes cushion if there was traffic. I confirmed the plan with Janice on the Wednesday before the game.

Game day came and, at 11:30 a.m., Hunter was outside in his uniform kicking the ball against a wall. When I looked outside at 11:40, he was still there. As noon approached, Hunter became a bit concerned. I told him not to worry; that Janice and Nicholas would be pulling in the driveway any minute.

Hunter had been on time for every game and practice so far that season. With good reason: his coach made late-arriving players run two laps around the field and sit out most of the first half as punishment. At 12:00 p.m. I called Janice at home, hoping that she wouldn't answer because she was already on her way. No answer. Fifteen minutes later, with Janice nowhere in sight, Hunter and I had become concerned. Had there been an accident? I told Hunter we would wait 15 more minutes and, if she didn't show up, I would drive him.

At exactly 12:30, my porch bell rang. It was Janice. She was in a panic. She asked whether I had a pair of size seven soccer shoes, because

Nicholas couldn't find his anywhere. "I ran up to his school but the door was locked," she said. I told her that I probably had a pair up in the attic, but it would take a few minutes to find them. I looked at my watch and then at Janice's car. Nicholas wasn't in it! I asked why. She said that he had already left for the game with his dad so he could at least show up on time and warm up until she got him some shoes.

I said, "Janice, do you know that the game is in Winchester, forty to fifty minutes away, and that Hunter should have left with you guys fifty minutes ago?" She gave me a look as if to say, "What the heck are you talking about? Was I supposed to drive the boys???" Suddenly realizing that she had agreed to drive Hunter, she turned bright red and, trying to save face, said, "Oh, if I hurry, we can still get there before it starts."

I knew that wasn't going to happen. I told her to take it easy on the way; that it wasn't worth getting into an accident. She pulled out of the driveway and drove off. Dazed, confused and *without the shoes* she had asked me to find! Five minutes later, she pulled back into the driveway, flung open the car door and ran up to the porch to tell me what I already knew: that she had forgotten the shoes. Since I kept all of the boys' old soccer shoes in their original boxes (they barely get broken in) in the attic, I was able to quickly retrieve a pair of size seven shoes and hand them off to her like a runner handing off a baton in a relay race. As she ran towards the open door of her car, I called out, "Janice, don't rush! He can be late!" She gave me a wave that said that she would be okay.

Hunter *was* late. He arrived midway through the first half. After running *three* laps around the field, he was relegated to the bench for the rest of the half. Nicholas was on time, didn't have to run laps, and was allowed to play as soon as he laced up our spare pair of soccer shoes.

SPORTS MOMS: WEARING MANY HATS

At no other time have parents needed to choreograph their lives to the split second as they do today. We try to keep track of our busy lives and those of our kids by any and all means possible: desk calendars, PDAs, BlackBerrys, 16 × 20 wall calendars, sticky notes, three-ring binders, and computers. Just thinking about getting our kids to all their activities can be exhausting, unless you learn how to organize, prioritize, and plan ahead.

When you stop to think about it, it's amazing how many different hats a youth sports mom wears:

chauffeur

short order cook and nutritionist

athletic trainer

personal shopper

laundress

child advocate

child psychologist

nurse

cheerleader

chief financial officer

chief operating officer

politician

equipment manager

As a parent of a child participating in sports you need to be prepared and willing to adjust the family schedule to meet the needs of your child's athletic schedule. You should be prepared to give up some of your Saturdays and Sundays, and expect that as a child gets older and moves up the competitive ladder in his or her sport, even three-day holiday weekends (*especially* three-day weekends) and school vacations are likely to get swallowed up by tournaments, clinics, private lessons, etc.

The problem is, of course, more challenging for families with two or more children, each playing a different sport, in a different league, on a different day, at a different time and place. Parents with several children often find that taking their children to lessons or practices is a full-time job. Single or divorced parents have an even bigger challenge.

To keep from going crazy and becoming a burned-out parent (yes, parents can burn out, too), the first key is organization (the second, as will be discussed in chapter 7, is to find the appropriate balance between sports and family life that works best for you and your family).

What Does Being Organized Mean?

You are organized when:

✓ *You give yourself enough time to get somewhere so that you arrive on schedule.*

✓ *You can find what you want quickly and without getting stressed (i.e., without having to search up and down and all around the house; if when you find something you end up saying, "Finally!" you know you aren't as organized as you could be).*

✓ *You know where important information is and can lay your hands on it quickly.*

✓ *You don't agree to do something you can't do, and you fulfill the promises you do make so that you don't leave someone else in the lurch.*

Here are some tips for staying organized—and saving time—to keep from becoming overwhelmed when your child is playing sports:

PLANNING AND ORGANIZING

1. **Plan ahead.**

❖ **Registration.** Registration for youth sports programs usually takes place several months before the beginning of the season, so you need to be on the lookout for registration information in the mail, at school, in the newspaper, online, from your town's recreation or parks department, or youth sports organizations or leagues, and stay on top of those deadlines. When you send in the registration form, include a stamped, self-addressed postcard that can be sent back to you so you know the form was received. If you register online, do not assume that your child has been accepted into the program until you receive an e-mail confirmation. Print out this form and keep it handy for the first practice.

❖ **Health forms.** Completing health forms that may be required for participation will usually necessitate a visit to your child's pediatrician (see the discussion in chapter 9 about the importance of preparticipation evaluations). Since most pediatricians are booked for "well" visits months in advance, don't wait until the last minute to schedule an appointment; you might be out of luck.

❖ **Buying equipment.** Shopping for the right equipment also should be done well in advance of the start of the season. Make sure you know what gear is approved for a particular sport (for instance, Little League rules prohibit a fielder's glove from being more than 12 inches long or $7\,^3/_4$ inches wide; bats can't be more than $2\,^1/_4$ inches in diameter and 33 inches long). If you wait until the last minute, the store may be sold out of what your child needs, forcing you to waste a lot of time running from store to store, trying to find the right equipment.

2. Use the power of the Internet. You can use the Internet to do such things as research and buy sports equipment, get directions to away game and tournaments, confirm schedules, book hotels, and make airplane reservations. If the team on which your child plays has a Web site, be sure that you have it bookmarked so you don't have to waste time trying to find the URL via Google or another search engine.

3. Use e-mail. More and more youth sports organizations use e-mail to keep parents informed of practice schedules, game times, sign-up dates, forms due, tournament dates, directions to games, etc. (Be sure to print out directions no later than the night before an away game; you don't want to leave it to the last minute.) E-mail is also a great way to communicate with other parents and the coach.

4. Use three-ring binders. Put information about each child's activities into a three-ring binder, with a section for each child, and keep it updated with schedules for sports, music lessons, Scouts, notices about school activities, team rosters, and phone numbers, etc.

5. Keep a good calendar.

❖ **Data entry.** Enter every practice, game, and meeting, both start time and finish time (allocate much more time than you think it will take), onto whatever kind of calendar or planner works best for your family (paper calendar or whiteboard, wall planner with moveable magnets, etc.). Display the calendar where everyone can see it. Use different color pens for each member of the family. Assign someone (it will usually end up being you) to be the keeper of the master schedule, the one who checks with family members periodically (preferably every day) to see if events need to be added or deleted.

❖ **Coordinate calendars.** If you use a PDA, be sure to enter the events into it as well, and synchronize the PDA with your computerized calendar, both at home and at work. (Using the reminder feature on a PDA and in most computer calendars, like Microsoft Outlook, is a great way to avoid being late to pick up your son after practice or to get him to the game or practice on time.) Check with your local recreation and parks department to see if a master calendar of events exists. If not, offer to help create one to reduce scheduling overlap and give you and your children time to get to the next event. Perhaps you can team up with other parents to sell your calendar as a fundraiser. Be sure to put your own work schedule on the calendar so everyone in the family can see how their activities fit—or don't fit—in. Block off chunks of time where nothing is scheduled. Just because the time is shown as free, doesn't mean it needs to be filled up with an activity; there should be plenty of free time. If there isn't, you are overscheduling. (See more on this topic in chapter 7.)

6. Use cell phones. With all the family plans offered by cell phone companies, equipping your kids with cell phones is a great idea for busy families. Some cell phone companies are now offering a plan where you can get cell phones for your younger children with up to four preprogrammed numbers and a button to push in case of emergencies. If your child can get rides back from games and practices and calls to let you know, a lot of time (and expensive gas) can be saved.

7. Hold a weekly family planning meeting. Once a week, hold a family meeting to review what happened—good and bad—in the week, just ended and what is coming up in the week ahead. That way everyone knows what everyone else is up to, priorities can be set, and scheduling conflicts identified. (It is amazing how many families get stressed out because they ignore the basic fact that we cannot be in two places at the same time!) If you can't find time to schedule a meeting at home, hold one whenever the entire family is together, such as in a restaurant, or in the car.

8. Teach your kids to stay organized and manage their own schedules. As your kids get older, they can shoulder more and more of the responsibility of keeping track of their own calendar and reminding you when you need to drive them to practice or to a game.

9. Keep track of everything.
   ❖ **Use identification tags.** Put a name tag or write your child's first name in permanent marker on *everything* (shoes, balls, bags, water bottles, etc.) along with your home phone number. Better yet, as soon as your child is old enough, have *him* write his name on his equipment and uniform (a child who writes his name or initials on his uniform and equipment is more likely to make sure they don't get lost). Your child's name should also be on the sports bag to make it easy to iden-

tify in a sea of bags. I recall the time one of my players had a severe asthma attack on the field and needed his inhaler. I turned to the row of eighteen identical blue-and-white bags. It took five extra minutes for parents to rifle through all of the bags just to find the one that was his.

❖ **Keep everything in its place.** Give your child a chance to shoulder some or all of the responsibility for making sure that her equipment and uniform are where they should be. Have your child keep all of her equipment together in the same place, preferably in a sports bag, which is easy to fill, store, and grab. Of course, you, too, need to keep everything where you can find it when you need it (car keys, directions, wallet or purse, cell phone, sunglasses, etc.).

10. Get help with the laundry. Make it your child's job to put her dirty uniform in the laundry room or the hamper. You shouldn't have to rummage around in her room to find the uniform under a sea of dirty clothes. (Teenagers really hate you going into their room when they aren't there; come to think of it, they don't like you coming in even when they are there.) To avoid the hassle of trying to get your child's uniform washed and dried in time for the next practice or game, it may be worth buying an extra uniform. Remember that the laundry isn't done until the uniform, jockstrap or sports bra, and socks are back in the drawer, closet, or sports bag where your son or daughter can easily find them. Remember also that some uniforms are not technically complete if the correct socks are not worn, which may result in disqualification.

11. Game and Practice Days
Keep a large plastic box in the trunk of your car or minivan, containing the following:

❖ **Rain gear.** (raincoats or ponchos, umbrella)

❖ **Extra clothes.** Always bring along extra clothing for your child to change into after playing in muddy or rainy conditions. (The last thing you need is a sick child who has to stay home from school.) Be sure to replace any item your child uses so he always has a full set of dry, clean clothes in the car to change into.

❖ **Extra equipment.** (baseball, soccer ball, glove, tennis balls, etc.)

❖ **Extra socks.** If your child has been playing in the rain, having a pair of dry socks for him to wear after the same will be much appreciated. For the reason mentioned above, having an extra pair of game socks is also a good idea. I lost count of the number of times an extra pair helped prevent one of my sons' teammates from being disqualified.

❖ **Mini first-aid kit.** (see below)

~~~~~~

First-Aid Kit

(You should also have these supplies in your home.)

✓ *Adhesive bandages, sterile gauze pads in a variety of shapes and sizes, and medical tape for cuts and scrapes*

✓ *Pretreated alcohol swabs*

✓ *Butterfly closures for cuts too big for bandages*

✓ *Triple antibiotic ointment (Neosporin or generic equivalent)*

✓ *Nontoxic surfactant (used instead of soapy water)*

✓ *Q-tips*

✓ *Moleskin (don't pop blisters)*

✓ *Chemical ice packs*

✓ *Nonsteroidal anti-inflammatory pain medications (Advil, Motrin, Aleve, or generic equivalent, not Tylenol, which doesn't treat inflammation)*

✓ *Sunblock with SPF of 15 to 25 (anything with a higher SPF is overkill)*

✓ *Insect repellent*

✓ *Anti-itch (cortisone) cream (ammonia diluted with water also does the trick)*

✓ *Synthetic gloves, triangle sling and finger splints, eyewash, antiseptic towelettes, scissors, and tweezers*

✓ *Extra asthma inhalers*

12. Sports Mom Essentials

❖ **Portable lawn or beach chair.** Look for one that is a combination chair and backpack with shoulder straps. They allow you to keep your hands free to carry other stuff to the field (like a cooler), and have pockets to store other essentials.

❖ **Cell phone.** Be sure the battery is charged. A charger for the car is a good idea.

❖ **Rain gear and umbrella.**

❖ **Laminated emergency first-aid cards.** You can find out where your child's team or league can purchase cards on the Internet

❖ **Essential information:**

Game or practice schedules, directions

Cell phone numbers for the coach and other parents

❖ **Street map.** Most leagues provide a map and directions for each venue once you get to their town. Best to have a detailed map of the county in which you live.

13. Planning and Organizing

❖ **Keep coolers in the car.** Keep two coolers: one big, one small. The large one (with wheels) can double as an extra seat; keep ice packs in self-closing plastic bags or buy a supply of chemical ice packs.

❖ **Do an equipment sweep after games.** Do a sweep of the area around the bench or dugout for your child's equipment before leaving a practice or game.

❖ **Join a car pool.** Other parents are running in the same direction as you, so offer to pick up their kid for practice if they'll bring yours home afterward.

～～～～～～～～～～～～～～～～～

Car Pools

Here are some tips about car pools:

✓ **Be on time.** *You should be prepared for problems and traffic.*

✓ **Take your turn.** *If it is your turn to drive, it is your responsibility to drive, no matter if your child is going to the practice or game that day or not.*

✓ **Be responsible.** *A car pool is a cooperative endeavor, and you have responsibility to other members. Talk to the coach or team administrator of your child's team about setting up a carpooling schedule. At the preseason meeting (see chapter 11), sign up other parents and ask them to agree in writing to obey traffic laws. Instead of coming right out and saying to a parent, "Please make sure my child wears a seat belt," I asked, "Do you have enough seat belts for my son?"*

✓ **Expect occasional problems**. *Realize that sooner or later everyone will have a conflict with a car pool. It's best to confirm the night before.*

✓ **Make rules and follow them.** *Stick with them or get out of the pool.*

✓ **Establish and enforce behavioral guidelines.** *Create guidelines and rules about allowable child behavior in the car. Be consistent in discipline.*

✓ **Communicate clearly.** *Be certain to tell each child exactly where to be for pickup, and emphasize the importance of being ready.*

✓ **Establish a foul weather policy.** *After years of wringing my hands and wondering if a game would be canceled because of rain (or a threat of rain), I learned to proceed as if the game would not be called off. This way we were always on time. There were a number of times that my entire team showed up and the other team falsely assumed the game would be canceled and did not show.*

❖ **Call for backup.** When you can't get to a game, ask family and friends to fill in for you.

❖ **Multitask.** It is amazing how much time you will end up spending at youth sports events, especially away games and tournaments, just sitting or standing around, usually talking with other parents who also have nothing to do. Fill the time by getting other things done. Keep a list of small tasks you can accomplish during the downtime, such as paying bills, balancing your checkbook, taking a walk, even doing work (consider taking a portable office with you, including a small file box and laptop computer). On cool days, Caleb, the family dog and an amazing soccer goalie, always came along to take a walk or play with the other team mascots.

❖ **Precook meals.** On busy days, put supper in a crock pot in the morning before work or keep quick meals in the freezer.

Food on the Go

One of the biggest nutritional challenges parents of youth athletes face is seeing that they eat properly away from home. But whether you are traveling to an all-day soccer tournament across town or a two-week tournament in a foreign country, your child's nutritional needs don't have to suffer. There are plenty of ways you can ensure that your child will eat the kind of high-carbohydrate, moderate-protein, and low-fat foods that studies show is necessary for optimal performance. Here are some strategies my MomsTeam colleague, nutritionist Suzanne Nelson, suggests you use in making healthy choices at fast-food, family-style, and ethnic restaurants, and grocery and convenience stores.

Fast Food Strategies

When you are away from home with your child at a tournament or all-day event, time is usually at a premium. But convenience and a shortage of time doesn't mean your child can't continue to eat right, even at fast-food restaurants. Not only do they provide quick service and are easily accessible, but they increasingly offer low-fat, nutritious choices such as salad bars, prepared salads, healthy soups, grilled or baked meat, fish, or chicken or turkey, baked potatoes, and low-fat frozen yogurt or ice cream.

Planning Food for the Road

✓ **Locate and pick restaurants in advance.** *Determine beforehand where the team will eat to assure that a high-carbohydrate meal will be available.*

✓ **Call ahead.** *If they know ahead of time, restaurant managers will generally accommodate large groups like sports teams with special nutritional needs and in a time crunch.*

✓ **Arrange for meals.** *When staying in a hotel that offers food service, contact the catering manager to arrange for high-carbohydrate, low-fat meals within the team's budget.*

If you are having trouble finding a high-carbohydrate, low-fat item on the menu, remember that most restaurants are willing to accommodate special requests.

Grocery and Convenience Stores

At all-day events or tournaments, stopping at a grocery or convenience store is usually a better bet than the concession stand, which typically offers foods that are high in fat (e.g., nacho chips and cheese, fries, and hot dogs) and are expensive. Many supermarkets offer a soup and salad bar with a variety of healthy foods. With guidance from parents and coaches, young athletes can find high-carbohydrate, low-fat foods in most aisles of the store.

It takes planning and practice to find nutritious foods at fast-food restaurants, family-style restaurants, and grocery stores, but it can be done!

14. Road Trips

❖ **Packing.** Don't wait until the last minute to pack for an overnight trip to a tournament. Work from a packing list. This way you avoid overpacking because you don't know what to take, or forget something important and have to waste time and money replacing it in an unfamiliar town.

❖ **Chaperones.** Make sure that your child's team follows the "two-adult rule" on road trips (see chapter 8).

Chapter Seven

High-Wire Act
Balancing Sports with Family

When I was growing up in a seaside New England village, the only sport that my mother—a former world-class synchronized swimmer—insisted that my sisters and I learn was swimming because, as she would tell us, it was the only one that could potentially save our lives. She never had to push us into playing any other sports—our interest in them came naturally. It was a different story when we visited my father and stepmother in Vermont. My father and stepmother were the ultimate outdoors folk, and sports were paramount and always a family activity. From sunrise to sunset they had us outdoors skiing, horseback riding, sailing, canoeing, hiking, fishing, ice skating, golfing, and playing tennis or paddle tennis. We learned to love—and I still enjoy—every single one of those sports. The sports and outdoor activities we did together as a family kept us close.

The balance between family time and sports time is different for each family, of course, but when my husband and I were raising our sons, we made a point of exposing them to a lot of different sports. At one point or another, they took fencing lessons; were members of a swim team; played youth basketball; played lacrosse; learned how to ice skate; played squash with me or their father; played badminton and tennis; ran track; went on family skiing and snowboarding trips; played football, soccer, and baseball; went fishing and on bicycling trips; and engaged in mountain and rock climbing. You name it, they played it.

We enjoyed being with our kids, spending time with them, not just turning them over to coaches. We wanted their character to be developed at home as well as on the fields and courts. They enjoyed spending time with us. They played select soccer, but only when they got to the U12 level. Before that they played recreational soccer and Little League baseball. Taylor stopped playing baseball while in sixth grade. Spencer and Hunter tried Babe Ruth baseball for one season, but as the youngest players by almost a year, they got tired of the politics and sitting on the bench. They all eventually switched to track and lacrosse. One summer, my husband and I took them and a team of boys to Scotland for a soccer tournament, but the goal was to have fun, not to win. We lost every game—some by lopsided scores—but it didn't matter a bit: We had fun, and got to see and play against some superb youth soccer teams.

PARENTING SHOULDN'T BE A COMPETITIVE SPORT

This balance is hard to achieve in any family. Parents feel pressure to help their kids succeed and to keep up with other parents. (It is ironic that parents worry about the effect of peer pressure on their kids but fail to appreciate the effect such pressure is having on *them*.) We have become a nation of "helicopter" parents, hovering over our kids, trying to enrich every second of their lives with activities and feeling guilty if we don't.

Some parents these days seem to take pride in how busy, how stressed their lives and the lives of their kids are, as if that is a measure of how

"A hundred years from now it will not matter what my bank account was, the sort of house I lived in, or the kind of car I drove . . . but the world may be different because I was important in the life of a child."

—FOREST WHITCRAFT

successful they are and how successful they must be in raising their kids. On the one hand, a recent *Self* magazine survey reported that women, while they "see their lives as very full and busy, don't see their lives as disjointed or unmanageable, and say that they easily move among their different roles, aren't exceptionally stressed out, and are pleased with how well they are coping."

On the other, as my friend and parenting author Mimi Doe observes, "It's almost a badge of achievement for some parents to breathlessly describe their 'on the run' lives—as if they're giving their kids a leg up by being on two travel sports teams, the school's team, and a little strength training on the side. Describing their busy schedules seems to validate parents' efforts and suggest that they are giving their children stellar advantages."

The overscheduling of children mirrors their parents' lives: one expert called it "hyper-parenting," that is, raising kids stuck in a "rug-rat race." A spate of recent books, like Judith Warner's *Perfect Madness*, address the stressed-out lives of today's young mothers and describe lives completely out of balance—what one reviewer described as an "endless sea of child-enriching activities, a soul-sucking swirl that leads many mothers into a well of despair," and another termed the "modern American mommy rat race."

Not surprisingly, studies show that the time families spend together has declined in direct proportion to the increased time children are playing organized sports. A study by the University of Michigan's Institute for Social Research found that between 1981 and 1997:

❖ structured sports time doubled

❖ kids lost twelve hours a week of free time, from 40 percent of the day in 1981 to 25 percent two decades later

❖ unstructured outdoor activities declined 50 percent

❖ household conversations became far less frequent

❖ family dinners declined by one-third

❖ family vacations went down by 28 percent

Such research is supported by plenty of anecdotal evidence of an unhealthy imbalance. Writing in *The Toronto Star* about youth hockey in Canada, Jim Coyle described how most "teams now demand commitment worthy of the Marine Corps. Nothing short of a death in the family can justify missing a game or practice. Christmas is often taken over by tournaments. Weekends are swallowed whole. Family dinners are disrupted. It can be an all-consuming commitment."

Consider just a few examples of how far things have gotten out of hand:

❖ A child was benched because he skipped the team's practice to be with his family *on Christmas Eve*.

❖ When one mom, fed up with the grueling schedule her son's football coach set for her son (including weekends), asked the coach, "What about church?" He replied, "Football *is* church."

❖ One twelve-year-old hockey player trained three hundred days a year, attended seven summer hockey camps, and traveled 4,500 miles a year to compete, while his parents spent $6,000 per year on equipment, ice time, and hotels.

❖ A survey of participants at an elite youth tennis tournament in Miami, Florida, found that seven in ten of the parents were spending more than $5,000 per year on tennis practices, and a third were spending over $10,000 per year.

❖ One Texas mother spent $15,000 annually on cheerleading training for her eight-year-old daughter.

❖ A Connecticut mother in the midst of a divorce took out a second mortgage to buy her seventeen-year-old daughter a horse and have it flown from New Zealand to the United States, and reported spending $50,000 annually for her daughter to compete in equestrian events.

Is this the kind of life *our kids* want? A 1997 survey in the *Boston Globe* found that seven out of ten girls between the ages of nine and

sixteen said they preferred playing sports with friends on the playground
to organized sports. A slight majority of boys felt the same way. Other
studies show that parents spend eleven hours less a week (about ninety
minutes a day) with their teenagers, that the average mother spends less
than a half hour per day talking with her teens. Only six in ten fifteen-
and sixteen-year-olds regularly eat dinner with their parents. Yet in survey after survey, adolescents lament the lack of parental attention and
say they want to spend *more* time with their parents, not less.

It isn't even the kind of life *we* want: more than eight in ten mothers in
one recent national survey said they wanted more time to spend on personal and family relationships.

RECOGNIZING THE WARNING SIGNS

How do you know if your child is overscheduled? Here are some clues:

1. **She tells you.** Sometimes your child may simply tell you she is
overextended and wants to cut back.

2. **She exhibits physical and/or psychological signs** (see chapter 2).

3. *You* **are suffering from:**

❖ **Stress.** Do you think life is too hectic, too "crazy"? Don't just shrug
your shoulders and chalk it up to life in the new millennium. Being
competitive shouldn't be what being a mother is all about; moms need
to avoid getting sucked into unhealthy peer pressure with other moms
to push their kids into more and more activities. You can be concerned
about your kids and at the same time take care of your own needs. We
need to resist the Supermomma syndrome. You don't need to put your
kids into a travel program just because everyone else is doing it. Don't
wear your stress as a badge of honor. It isn't really something to be
proud of! Make changes before *you* burn out. As Oprah Winfrey
recently told *Newsweek*, "I tell women all the time that you have to

fill yourself up so you have enough to give to other people. Running around on empty does not serve you or your family or your work."

❖ **Worry.** Do you worry that you are going to burn out? That your marriage is suffering because you have no time alone with your spouse? That your kids are going to burn out?

❖ **Resentment.** Do you secretly resent all the time and money you have invested in your child's sports activities and wish that you and your family could spend more time together, or take a family vacation to someplace other than a soccer/softball/baseball/hockey tournament?

4. Your calendar tells the story. If your children are overscheduled, a look at the calendar may provide all the proof you need. If you don't see *any* or very few blank days on the calendar, if the calendar is a jumble of entries, that means too little free time for:

❖ **Your kids.** Does your child, when asked by a friend to come over to her house to hang out or even to spend an afternoon with you clothes shopping, have to look at her PDA first to see if she can fit it into her schedule?

❖ **Your family.** If there aren't any family events on the calendar, if you and your family never spend any time together, or the only time you spend together is getting to the next event or game, something is out of whack.

❖ **You and your spouse.** It is important for couples to have alone time. You may need to go to the extent of making a date with your spouse, actually scheduling some time together, and putting it on the calendar.

❖ **Scheduling conflicts.** It's a simple fact that you can't be in two places at once. Too many scheduling conflicts create stress and are a sure sign of overscheduling.

The Importance of Unstructured Play

Consider all the nonsporting events and family time you are giving up for sports. Do you consider it your job as a parent to fill every nook and cranny of your child's day with an event or enriching activity? Mimi Doe, author of Busy But Balanced, says parents these days are "busy parents micro-managing busy kids" when "what their [kids'] souls crave much more than another winning game is the loving presence of an adult who listens and cares deeply. They need less pressure to perform and more open-ended time to ponder. Rather than being a project their parents strategically plan, with achievements measured on a corporate-like timeline, kids yearn for a relationship with their mom and dad."

A University of Michigan study showed that only 30 percent of the days of school-age youngsters are free time, to use as they wish. The other 70 percent is packed with classes, part-time jobs after school, homework, and extracurricular activities, like sports.

Free, unstructured time is important because:

✓ Play is, as Williams College professor Susan Engel notes in her book, Real Kids, "a central and vital process during childhood. It is not merely that children need time to unwind or have fun. Rather, without play they will be much less likely to develop just the kinds of thinking we feel are so vital to a productive and intelligent adult life."

✓ It is needed for creativity. Believe it or not, boredom is actually good: in moderation, it stimulates kids to think and create.

✓ It provides opportunities for real parent-child communication.

✓ Quiet time is good. The irony is that weekends, the time families used to spend relaxing from the work and school week, are now filled to the brim with sports activities. Try to set aside some time on the weekends to rest and recharge your batteries for the week ahead.

That our culture seems to increasingly devalue free time doesn't mean you should. Kids need to grow up feeling comfortable with silence.

Your intuition tells you how important free time is. It tells you not to interfere with a child's play unless someone is about to or is being hurt. A mother who would rather have her six-year-old play with friends on a swing, in a backyard tree house, or in an attic full of toys than take them to the park or an indoor arcade is trusting her instincts that it is better for her child's development at this age to provide opportunities for unstructured, child-directed play. As is often the case, too much of a good thing isn't good for your child. The more kids are programmed, the more they need to be programmed and expect excitement to be created for them.

We need to resist the Supermom syndrome. You don't need to put your kids into a travel program just because everyone else is doing it.

SPORTS, BALANCE, AND THE FAMILY BUDGET

Participation in youth sports can be, and often is, expensive. Gone are the days when you paid $25 for a whole season of Little League or recreation soccer, and school sports were free. One mother estimated her family's expenses for her three children at $100,000 over a ten-year period. As a child moves up the competitive ladder, the costs of participating can begin to outpace or, at the very least, strain the financial capability of most families. It can get to the point where the annual cost may be the third biggest item in the family's budget, after the mortgage and car payments. Some of the costs may be covered by fund-raising, but fund-raising does only so much.

Parents often do not realize before enrolling their child in a youth sports program what it is going to cost for that season and, more importantly, beyond (see page 106). They fail to realize all of the hidden costs, only to find out, after it is too late, that they are in too deep to do anything but shell out the dough and sacrifice in other areas. "It kind of sneaks up on you," says Barbara Carlson, president and cofounder of Putting Family First, a Minnesota organization trying to restore balance between organized youth sports and family life. This can lead parents to resent their child's participation, creating tension within the family as a greater and greater portion of the family's income is sucked into the seemingly bottomless hole of youth sports.

One of the best ways to avoid imbalance later on is to get a handle on the costs of youth sports *before* you sign your child up and get yourself in too deep to turn back. (You can calculate sports expenses with a form that is on the MomsTeam Web site.) If you can't afford to have your child play a particular sport because of the expense, don't be afraid to say no. Don't take on more debt or a second job: just be honest with your child as to why he can't play.

In estimating the costs of a particular sport, you need to consider the following categories of expenses:

Registration fees. These can range from less than fifty dollars up into the thousands of dollars. Here is a sampling:

❖ AAU (Amateur Athletic Union) basketball: $150 to $600 base fees per season

❖ Elite swimming: $500 to $3,000 per year

❖ Elite gymnastics: $1,000 to $2,000 base tuition per year

❖ Select soccer: $125 to $550 per season

❖ Fall baseball: $115 to $450

❖ Elite volleyball: $400 to $775 per year

Be sure to ask your child's coach or club what the registration fee covers, especially whether it includes the cost of registering your child's team for tournaments.

Equipment. Be sure to include not only the cost of equipment (shoes, pads, glove, helmet, bat, etc.) but how often particular equipment will need to be replaced, due either to the child's growth or normal wear and tear (for instance, buying a new softball bat every year can run between $250 and $300).

Transportation. With the cost of gasoline now costing 3 or more dollars a gallon (for good, it now seems), travel expenses, even to away games within an hour or so of where you live, can be significant. Be sure to include the cost of oil changes; scheduled maintenance; travel to practices, games, tournaments, summer camps; and airplane fare for distant tournaments.

Food. Dinners at nice restaurants with teammates' families after games and restaurant meals at away games and tournaments will take their toll on your pocketbook, not to mention your waistline.

Lodging. With a night of lodging at even the least expensive motels costing anywhere from $50 to $100 per night, just a couple of tournaments per year in far-away places can cost a family a fortune.

Clinics, private instruction, private academies. Private coaches charge as much as the market will bear. Expect to pay between $20 and $100 per hour. Private academies can run as much as $30,000 per year. Memberships at one of the sports training and conditioning and performance centers that are sprouting up all over the country can run $75 per month, not including the cost of private coaching.

Tournaments. Even split among all the players' parents, the costs to enter tournaments, which can cost $200 to $300 per team, can mount up very quickly.

Summer sports camps. A three-week basketball camp can cost $2,500.

Instructional aids. Books, videos, and equipment like baseball bounce backs or soccer or lacrosse gear can be expensive.

Gifts and mementos. Remember to budget for your share of the cost of the coaches' end-of-season gifts, team photos, and other mementos.

When all is said and done, expect to pay more than $6,000 *per child* per year for club sports, personal training, travel, and equipment beyond the fees for high school sports. Ask yourself whether the money might be better spent on a family ski vacation or a new set of bikes.

Add It Up

The costs of participating in youth sports can be daunting. Consider these examples:

User fees. *More and more public schools, beset with budget woes, are charging as much as $150 per child per sport.*

Professional coaches. *Some parents are paying professional coaches (often ex-pro players) between $60 and $100 per month to coach their child. One club charges $2,500, but if they find someone better than your kid (they are always recruiting), will cut your kid and prorate your money and leave it up to you to explain to your child why he or she is no longer on the team.*

Travel clubs. *Here are some random examples:*

✓ *A club soccer team in Tucson, Arizona: $300 per month*

✓ *Club volleyball: $600 per season for local teams, $3,000+ for travel teams*

✓ *$10,000 a year for travel baseball*

✓ *$3,000 for travel softball*

✓ *$1,500 per season for travel soccer (travel and other expenses not included)*

FINDING THE TIME FOR SPORTS

Not only do youth sports cost a lot of money, they also soak up an incredible amount of time—both yours and your child's. While there are a lot of advantages to sports participation, you need to gauge your level of commitment *before* getting your child seriously involved. Before you sign your five-year-old daughter up for gymnastics or figure skating classes, honestly assess whether you will be willing and/or able to make both the time and money commitment that will be required five and even ten years down the road. You don't want to be put in a situation where you either have to pull the plug on their sports career or end up being resentful.

Before you allow your child to play a particular sport or on a particular team, consider the amount of travel time to practices and games, your work schedule and your spouse's, your child's school schedule and homework demands, car pool availability, and the needs of other family members. You should consider what you and your family will have to give up as a result (Friday night pizza, allowances, church on Sunday, etc.). Sit down with your child before each school semester and ask her what sports she wants to play. Let her establish priorities. It will teach her a valuable lesson about time management and get her in the habit of setting priorities. All too often kids seem to get the message from society and their parents that they can have it all. Setting priorities and understanding that you have only so many hours in the day and only so much money is something every child has to learn, sooner or later. It might as well be sooner.

If you are like most mothers, you want your children to grow and have new experiences, but you want that balanced with a home life, with the family as the center of their lives.

LEARNING TO JUST SAY NO

Despite research showing that parents intuitively know how to balance their child's development, more and more mothers seem to be ignoring their own intuition and overschedule, and overstress their child.

Parents too often feel that if they don't do everything for their child, they are bad parents. It is a myth that the more you do for your child the better. What is good for Mom and Dad is not necessarily best for the child as well. As Mimi Doe says, "[J]ust because our own lives might be frenetic with work, family, and the endless tasks of daily life, doesn't mean that we should program our kids into that rhythm."

Pollsters Celinda Lake and Kellyanne Conway argue in their book, *What Women Really Want*, that "Today's time-pressed woman is trying to learn to say 'No,' in contrast to the 'Yes' woman of previous generations of wives, mothers, workers, and managers." Lake and Conway predict that in the future, "Women will reclaim face-time with their families, workplaces, and communities, pushing for techno-etiquette (no iPods at the dinner table, no cell phones at cocktail parties and weddings, no BlackBerries on vacation)," and that "'Just say no' will become the mantra of the overscheduled, guilt-trapped yeah sayers, as women who chronically *do* choose to *do-not*."

Have the courage to say no. Be honest with yourself and your children, and if you and/or your child are overextended, recognize the toll sports is taking on you and your family instead of feeling guilty and worrying that if you don't do everything possible, don't go the extra mile, your kids will suffer, will be deprived, or will fall behind their peers.

Sometimes the best thing a parent can do for a child is nothing. Children are not miniature adults—there will be plenty of time for them to be stressed and overworked when they actually *are* adults. Trust your instincts, just let your kid be a kid, and say no to:

❖ **Your child:** If your child asks whether he can play a certain sport or join another team, get a private coach etc., don't say yes immediately; tell him you need time to think before making a decision. Ask him to use the extra time to really think about whether it makes sense for him. If your child is invited to try out for a select team before grade six, politely decline the invitation. Instead of automatically writing checks, be more selective about what sports and other activities you pay for.

❖ **You:** Give yourself permission to miss a game or two. It is healthy for your child to understand that the family doesn't revolve around her and that there is a limit to what you will do for her. Parents who never miss a practice or game may actually be doing more harm than good by demonstrating a level of commitment to their child that is higher than what is appropriate for the child's healthy growth and development.

❖ **The coach:** If you feel your child is overscheduled, if you think it is more important for your son to attend a family wedding or cultural event, have the courage to say no to the coach, even if it means that your child will be penalized. Again, trust your instincts. You know what is best for your child and family.

Remember, though, if you say no, you will probably have a lot of explaining to do to your child. She might think you are sending her mixed signals: on the one hand telling her that playing sports teaches her valuable life lessons, especially commitment and sacrifice, but on the other hand telling her that, because you have decided to go on a family vacation during spring break, she won't be able to join her soccer team for a tournament.

SETTING LIMITS AND FINDING BALANCE

If you feel that sports are taking too much of your family's time and money, if you are ready to exclaim, "Stop the world, I want to get off!" you need to restore some sanity.

As Dr. Alvin Rosenfeld, author of *The Over-Scheduled Child: Avoiding the Hyper-Parenting Trap*, observes, "Today's parents need more than pressured athletics; they need time with each other as husband and wife, and time with their children with no goal in mind beyond the pleasure of spending time. On walks, shooting hoops, playing Monopoly, whatever! Somehow many of us are insecure and doubt we ourselves have what it takes to raise our kids well. So we entrust them to 'experts,' coaches and tutors. Yet, what our children really need is *us*, just quiet, unstructured, unpressured time with us."

Here are some tips to finding balance:

1. Hold a family meeting. ❄ Before each sports season, hold a family meeting during which you can look at the family calendar. Highlight each child's activities in a different color, and discuss commitments and goals for the upcoming sports season. Don't simply sign your child up automatically—ask her whether she wants to keep playing and make a *joint* decision. Weigh the short- and long-term benefits of an activity against the cost to your family in terms of money, time, and energy.

2. Set limits that fit your family. ❊ Find the level of sports participation that works for your child and your family. Take your cues from your child and trust your intuition. For some, one sport and one team per season may be right. Some children may thrive on more intense involvement. One mom registered her sons for house leagues because a traveling team's schedule wouldn't fit into her schedule. A friend limited her daughter to one sport a year, but she sent her to skills clinics and camps in the off-season. Work with your children to set limits; don't impose them on your kids. Make sure that everyone agrees on the limits that are set. If you stay too deeply involved in every detail of your child's life, it prevents her from learning to structure her own schedule and find personal balance between activities and downtime. Some limits to consider:

❖ One season off out of four

❖ No select teams before sixth grade

❖ No specialization in a single sport until high school

❖ One competitive sport per season until grade six

❖ Three one-hour practices per week before age twelve; for ages twelve to sixteen, no more than four $1\frac{1}{2}$-hour practices

3. Find a balance between cooperation and competition. ❊ Find a balance between your instincts to nurture and teach collaboration and cooperation and your competitive instincts.

4. Find a balanced attitude about winning and losing. ❊ Keep them both in perspective, neither getting angry and upset when your child doesn't play well or the team loses, nor too excited if your child does well or the team wins. Never tie special privileges or rewards to winning or withdraw attention, love, or affection when your child loses. Above all, let your child know that your love for him is *unconditional*.

5. Find a balanced sports program. ✳ Look for leagues and clubs that balance sports, family, and school and emphasize just having fun. Candidly address the issue of family and sports balance with the other parents and coaches at the preseason meeting (see chapter 11).

6. Find a balance between sports. ✳ Introduce your child to a sport such as golf, tennis, squash, racquetball, cycling, sailing, windsurfing, indoor rock climbing, jogging, kayaking, rowing, or canoeing that he can enjoy whether or not he plays competitive sports. Encourage your child to engage in sports and activities with you as long as he or she enjoys them.

7. Find a balance between kids. ✳ Focusing too heavily on one child's athletic career often causes the other children in the family to feel resentful and may exacerbate sibling rivalry. Every child's interests and activities should receive an equal amount of your attention.

8. Find a balance between sports and academics. ✳ Schoolwork should *always* come first. Remember that there are thirty times more dollars available for financial aid based on academics than for athletics. Consider instituting a no-TV rule from Sunday night through Friday afternoon, or at least limiting TV and video game use to a certain number of hours per day or week.

9. Find a balance between sports and social life. ✳ Try to make sure your child's sports don't keep him from making and keeping friends except other athletes (see chapter 2).

10. Find the balance between awake and sleep time. ✳ "Parents spend so much time and money optimizing their children's success, yet the one thing they are not doing is making sure their kids get enough sleep," says Judith Owens, MD, past chair of the pediatric section for the American Academy of Sleep Medicine. Researchers at Brown University found that teenagers need about *nine hours* of sleep a night, but most are only getting about seven hours a night. They also found a correlation between the amount of sleep and a teen's grades: those who get the most sleep tend to get the best grades; those who get the least tend to get the worst. "The greatest challenge for parents is the balance between homework, sports, music, and sleep—don't overprogram your kids so that they give up their much needed sleep," adds Dr. Owens.

> "[M]any of the kinds of thinking our culture values in older children and adults have their roots in the kinds of spontaneous play in which children engage, when given half a chance."
>
> —SUSAN ENGEL
> *REAL KIDS*

11. Find a balance between family and individual time. ✳ Parents in the United States spend less time with their children than those in almost any other nation. Set aside some family time. Research has shown that teenagers who ate dinner with their parents five times per week or more were the least likely to be on drugs, depressed, or in trouble with the law, and the most likely to be doing well in school and have a supportive circle of friends. Set aside one night a week or month as family night.

12. Find a balance between active and quiet time. ✳ Set aside some time every evening when all the electronic gadgets (PlayStations, computers, MP3 players, iPods, and PDAs) are turned off and you and your kids just have some peace and quiet to think and dream or go outside and marvel at the night sky.

13. Find one-on-one time for you and your spouse. ✳ One suggestion: establish a rule that your kids need to be in their rooms by a certain time each night.

~~~~~~~~~~~~~~~~~~~~

Communities Fighting for Balance

The Minneapolis area is one place where organized efforts are under way to restore balance to youth sports:

> ✓ A grassroots organization called *Putting Family First*, concerned that crucial connections between parents and children are being lost and that the current preoccupation with competition has diminished the rewards of sports as well as diminishing the quality of family life for many families, is trying

to raise awareness about finding balance in the overscheduled lives of families by, among other things, asking that sports events are scheduled to not interfere with family dinners, holidays, and religious participation.

✓ A group called Time IN for Family is spearheading a Let Kids Be Kids! initiative focusing on less intense youth sports programs and collecting family dinner pledges.

✓ A group called Balance4Success, tired of just talking about the hazards of overscheduled kids, recently called for families in three Minneapolis suburbs to demand that Sundays be off-limits for organized sports. No practices. No games. No tournaments. "A vocal minority of supercompetitive leaders and parents are making the rules, and a silent majority has followed along, fearing they will be ostracized," said Andrea Grazzini Walstrom, a leader of Balance4Success told, the Minneapolis Star Tribune. On June 1, 2006, the group launched a campaign called Taking Back Sunday, a boycott of organized youth sports on Sundays.

Chapter Eight

Preventing Child Abuse in Youth Sports
What Mothers Can Do

STAIRWAY TO ABUSE

"Courtney, knock it off!" the coach admonished. "Stop your crying, and wipe your face! You know my rules. Rule number one is to be at practice on time. Late is late, whether it's thirty seconds or thirty minutes. Because this is your first time, your reminder is to run ten sets of bleacher stairs and do five defensive hustle drills," Courtney's coach screamed with the voice of a marine drill sergeant.

After running the stairs for twenty minutes, Courtney became ill and ran to the bathroom, where she vomited. When she returned to the basketball court—humiliated, scared, and too sick to continue—her coach ordered her to finish her stair running.

Courtney's mother, Sandra, reported in an e-mail that a similar scenario played out with another girl the very next day. This time the girl threw up twice. Sandra told me that parents had lodged numerous complaints about the coach but had gotten nowhere. "We're planning to take this issue up with the school board and possibly file a lawsuit if we can't get positive resolution," said her e-mail, "but I would appreciate any and all guidance you can give."

I suggested that Sandra and her husband meet with the coach and call me if the matter was not satisfactorily resolved. After the meeting, she wrote again: "We did have the meeting, but I feel nothing was accomplished. The principal and the coach actually sat there in the meeting and laughed at my husband and me when we voiced our concern over making a twelve-year-old girl run until she puked. Their response was, 'Well, if she can't take it, she doesn't have to play.'

"They said they wanted a winning basketball team, and that they would do whatever it took to get it. I voiced my concerns over the physical and mental well-being of the girls on the team. They told me I would never change a thing, that I was the minority in my way of thinking."

The next day, Courtney brought home a contract for participation in junior high and high school girls' athletics, including a long list of coach-centered rules that were not only inappropriate for twelve- and thirteen-year-olds but called for punishments of rule infractions that were outright abusive. One required that players who failed to make at least seven out of ten free throws in practice to run up to the top of the bleachers and back down for each free throw missed short of the required seven. The same rules applied to everyone, whether a twelve-year-old seventh-grader or an eighteen-year-old high school senior.

Following the list of the coach's rules and punishments was an eight-paragraph missive on his coaching philosophy, including statements that:

❖ Only girls he felt could "compete and handle the pressure" would get playing time.

❖ He would "always play to win."

❖ Girls would be punished, as he saw fit, for poor defensive play and lack of hustle.

❖ Only girls who had rides to school in the morning could be on the team because practice started before school buses arrived.

❖ All practices were closed to parents.

❖ "Playing is a privilege, not a right."

Of the thousands of phone calls, e-mails, and media stories that Moms-Team has received over the past seven years, the ones I find most distressing are those, like Sandra's, that detail youth athletes suffering at the hands of coaches, other adults, and their teammates. Parents are frustrated because they are told that physical, emotional, and psychological abuse is simply the price their children have to pay to be able to play competitive sports, and that if they complain, like Courtney's mother, they will be dismissed as representing a small minority when, in fact, they represent a silent *majority*.

PREVENTING ABUSE

While many children have wonderful experiences playing youth sports and great relationships with their coaches, protecting your child against physical, emotional, or sexual abuse at the hands of coaches or other adults is often not within your exclusive control (what you can do with other parents to reduce abuse will be discussed in chapter 15). There are steps you can take to protect your child that *are* within your control.

The first is to become educated about the different forms of abuse and to understand the damage they can do to your child. What constitutes abuse? As a general rule, child abuse is any form of physical, emotional, or sexual mistreatment or lack of care that leads to injury or harm. It usually occurs when someone uses his or her power or position of trust to harm your child physically, emotionally, or sexually, either directly or through neglect. The abuser can be anyone: a coach, another player, a parent, a volunteer, a spectator, or an official. Abuse can happen to a child regardless of age, gender, race, or ability.

There are four main types of abuse:

1. Physical abuse.

❖ **Physical violence.** Examples: a parent shaking and cursing his eight-year-old son's teammate, a mother attacking a player on the opposing team during a post-game fight, a thirteen-year-old boy beating a fifteen-year-old boy to death with a baseball bat after he teased him about losing a game, and a youth football coach who became so angry at a ten-year-old boy after he dropped a pass that he picked up the youngster and slammed him into the ground with such force that he broke both of his arms.

❖ **Developmentally inappropriate training.** Examples: Hockey coaches in Michigan requiring a group of twenty teenage hockey players to stand in a semicircle at center ice, and then ordering two players to stand in the circle, shed their helmets and gloves, and engage in a fistfight, or a parent who insists that a nine-year-old girl practice and play soccer two to three hours a day, six or seven days a week to the point that she suffers a stress fracture to her pelvis.

❖ **Using exercise as punishment.** Example: the Oklahoma middle school girl's basketball coach who required Courtney to run bleacher stairs until she became physically ill.

❖ **Requiring an athlete to practice or play hurt.** Example: a father of a Little Leaguer demanding that his son continue pitching when he is in obvious pain.

❖ **Depriving a child of proper rest, nutrition, or hydration.** Example: a football coach who won't let his players interrupt practice to drink water or sports drinks on a 95-degree day.

❖ **Furnishing a child performance-enhancing drugs or encouraging their use.** See chapter 9.

Parents, coaches and administrators need to be educated to the fact that protecting children against emotional injuries, from sexual or verbal abuse or harassment, or being exposed to out-of-control or violent behavior by parents, coaches or other players is just as, if not more important, than protecting them from physical injury.

❖ **Hazing.** Example: A fifteen-year-old soccer player was dropped on her head and suffered a brain injury when teammates tried to dunk her head in a toilet.

2. Emotional abuse. Emotional abuse is any attitude or behavior by any person in a position of power, authority, or trust, such as a parent, coach or official, or another player or someone vying for a position on the same team, that interferes with a child's mental and social health and development, including attacks on a child's self-worth and self-esteem. This form of abuse occurs even if the attack is not intended by the adult to cause harm. It also includes the failure to provide the support necessary for the development of a child's emotional, social, physical, and intellectual well-being, such as a coach giving other players preferential treatment, persistent benching, and failing to abide by the league rules on fair and/or playing time. Unfortunately, emotional abuse is widespread in youth sports (see below).

Emotional Abuse in Youth Sports: How Widespread Is It?

A groundbreaking 2005 study by researchers at the University of Missouri, the University of Minnesota, and the University of Notre Dame reported in the Journal of Research in Character Education *found that emotional abuse in youth sports is widespread:*

✓ *More than four in ten coaches have loudly argued with a referee or sports official following a perceived bad call. (Youth athletes said 48 percent of coaches engaged in this behavior, although only 20 percent of parents said they did so.)*

✓ *Seven out of ten youth athletes have heard a fan angrily yell at an official.*

✓ *One in eight parents have angrily criticized their child's sports performance. (A 2005 study, by Blue Cross/Blue Shield of Minnesota reported that more than 4 in 10 parents had seen a verbal altercation between a parent and his or her child they thought was inappropriate.)*

✓ One-third of coaches have angrily yelled at a player for making a mistake, a high rate "of significant concern" to the study's authors.

✓ One in seven athletes made fun of a less-skilled opponent. About one in ten coaches admitted to making fun of a team member.

✓ More than four in ten youth athletes reported having been teased or yelled at by a fan or seeing a fan angrily yell at or tease another player.

If you find yourself yelling at the officials, coaches, or players, or your own child, keep a journal of what led you to engage in such inappropriate behavior so you can get to the root of the problem and put your energies into preventing the behavior before it occurs again, such as by consulting a mental health professional to find out how and why you let your emotions get out of control.

Like physical abuse, emotional abuse can take many forms:

❖ **Harassing.** Example: Calling an athlete names with sexual connotations.

❖ **Yelling.** Example: Screaming or yelling by coaches or parents at players, officials, or other parents.

❖ **Name calling.** Example: An adult who says to a youth athlete, "Hey, Fatty, you can't run the bases to save your life!"

❖ **Threatening.** Example: A parent who tells his child, "If you don't win, you are going to hear about it from me when you get home!"

❖ **Insulting.** Criticizing, shaming, or ridiculing. Example: Adults who make statements to youth athletes like "You're clumsy," "You're a loser," "bleacher material," "second string," "an embarrassment to the team."

❖ **Intimidating.** Example: A hockey father who yells out to a player on the opposing team, "Watch out, number ten. My son is going to break your nose."

❖ **Teasing, taunting, or bullying.** Deliberate and repeated aggressive and hostile behaviors by an individual or group of individuals intended to humiliate, harm, and/or dominate or control another individual or group of individuals of lesser power or social status. An extreme example was the teasing that led a thirteen-year-old California boy to beat a fifteen-year-old boy to death in April 2005.

❖ **Negative questioning.** Example: A mother who asks her child, "Why did you miss that open shot on goal?" or "How could you let that guy beat you?"

❖ **Shunning or withholding love or affection.** Example: A parent who decides not to speak to, hug, or comfort his child after he plays poorly, his team loses, or who shows obvious signs of disappointment.

❖ **Punishing a child for losing or failing to perform up to adult expectations.** Example: A father who requires a child to perform extra chores after a loss.

3. Sexual abuse. Sexual abuse occurs when a person in a position of power, authority, or trust, including a parent, coach, or another teammate, engages in any sexual act with a child. Because it is the worst form of abuse, a more detailed discussion of sexual abuse in youth sports is included later in this chapter.

4. Neglect. Neglect is a chronic inattention to the basic necessities of life and the failure to provide for a child's physical and emotional needs. An adult, including parents, coaches, and administrators, whose neglect (i.e., failure to act) results in or unnecessarily or unreasonably exposes a child to physical, emotional, or sexual abuse is just as guilty of child abuse as those who directly participate in such abuse.

Neglect in a sports setting may take the following forms:

❖ **Abandonment.** Examples: parents who fail to adequately supervise their child's sports activities, don't obtain medical treatment when the child is injured, or postpone needed surgery so the child can continue to play.

❖ **Unreasonably exposing an athlete to the risk of physical, emotional, or sexual abuse.** Example: Adults who by their inattention allow players, coaches, or spectators to continue participating in or attending youth sports contests despite a documented history of violent behavior; a parent who fails to intervene on behalf of his child in the face of a coach's persistent criticism of the child's ability, weight, or lack of heart in front of the child's friends or teammates or who fails to take reasonable steps to protect his child against a sexual predator, such as by allowing closed coaching sessions, or failing to ensure that overnight trips to tournaments are properly chaperoned.

❖ **Failing to protect an athlete against unreasonable risk of injury.** Adults who permit youth athletes to play on poorly maintained or dangerous fields (such as soccer fields with unanchored goal posts, baseball diamonds without breakaway bases, or pole vault pits without adequate padding, see chapter 9), or to use obviously unsafe equipment, neglect to ensure that coaches receive adequate safety and first-aid training, or neglect to ensure that appropriate safety equipment (first-aid kit, AED, etc.) is present at all practices and games.

❖ **Failing to take reasonable steps to ensure that an athlete does not play hurt.** Examples: Parents, coaches, and other adults who fail to follow appropriate return-to-play guidelines—such as when a player may return to practice and games after suffering a concussion—or who allow a child to play injured. (See chapter 9.)

❖ **Failing to take reasonable steps to ensure that the child has proper rest, nutrition, and hydration, and is properly protected against the elements.** Example: Parents who do not try to make sure their teenage children get the nine hours of sleep a night that experts say they need, coaches who insist that a baseball game continue as a thunderstorm draws close, or refuse to give football players adequate rest and hydration breaks during pre-season practices in 95-degree heat (see chapter 9).

THE DANGERS OF PHYSICAL ABUSE

Studies have shown that among the many long-term effects of physical abuse are depression; anxiety; cognitive and learning difficulties; even a lowering of IQ (especially verbal IQ); disordered sleep; flashbacks; loss of empathy; aggressive behavior; chronically high stress levels, which can lead to chronic health effects such as high blood pressure and increased risk of cardiovascular disease; and the inability to maintain relationships.

Experts, like San Francisco sports and child psychiatrist Dr. Maria Pease, report that children who have been abused become chronically hyperaroused, possibly in order to be prepared for the next dangerous thing that might happen to them. As a result, a child may demonstrate less flexibility in responding to changes in his environment and respond out of anger instead of analyzing the situation more calmly. The brain and mind can become overly sensitized in abuse, making a person respond inappropriately to ordinary stimuli, for example, by flying into a rage over a minor disagreement.

Children who have been seriously abused will often display their own aggressive behavior. This is both learned behavior and an identity the child takes on to protect his fragile psychology and sense of self. Repeated abuse causes such powerful feelings of helplessness that it can destroy a child's capacity to defend against the harm and effectively destroy ego functioning, what one expert called "soul murder."

In general, victims of abuse are more likely to develop self-esteem problems, to marry abusive spouses, and to abuse their own spouses because they have learned that verbal abuse unleashed for a "good cause" is always justified. According to experts, physical abuse and violence against young athletes can also lead to:

❖ Obsessive and compulsive behaviors with regard to excessive training

❖ Eating disorders relating to diets imposed in certain sports

❖ Self-injurious behaviors or risk-taking resulting in accidents and injury

❖ Suicide

WITNESSING ABUSE CAN CAUSE DAMAGE, TOO

Several studies have shown that witnessing abuse can have similarly devastating effects. Children who witness their mother being abused by their husbands, boyfriends, or partners are more likely to abuse their own children, even if they are not actually abused themselves.

In extreme cases, children who have strong reactions to viewing violence or aggression can develop post-traumatic stress disorder, experiencing such symptoms as nightmares or flashbacks, routine avoidance of reminders of the event, increased sleep disturbances, irritability, poor concentration, startle reaction, and regressive behavior.

In the youth sports context, witnessing extreme violence, such as the beating death in California of a fifteen-year-old boy by a thirteen-year-old boy with a baseball bat, has the potential for turning a child off to exercise and participation in sports, prevent the development of a healthy adult lifestyle, adversely affect a child's ability to learn, and increase the likelihood that the child will engage in unhealthy behaviors during adolescence, including suicidal behavior and delinquent and aggressive behavior.

EMOTIONAL ABUSE: THE DAMAGE IS NO LESS REAL

Perhaps because the damage caused by emotional abuse is not obvious, like sexual abuse, or immediately apparent, like a physical injury, its effect is often overlooked and minimized. But, says Dr. Pease, the damage is no less real, and, in fact, may be much more damaging and long-lasting:

❖ Children are deeply affected by negative comments from parents, coaches, and other adults whom they look up to and respect. One comment can turn a child off to sports forever.

❖ Children are much more sensitive to criticism than adults: being yelled at, put down, or embarrassed is much more likely to have negative psychological consequences and to cause the child to feel humiliated, shamed, and degraded, and to damage her feelings of self-worth and self-esteem. In a 2004 study of emotional abuse of elite child athletes in the United Kingdom, for instance, the athletes reported that abuse by their coaches created a climate of fear and made them feel stupid, worthless, or upset, lacking in self-confidence, angry, depressed, humiliated, fearful, and hurt, and left long-lasting emotional scars.

❖ If the abuse becomes chronic, the pattern of negative comments can destroy a child's spirit, motivation, and self-esteem. Over time, the young athlete will begin to believe what adults say about him. Abusive comments, even if intended to improve athletic performance, are likely to have precisely the opposite effect.

❖ Children who experience screaming on a regular basis will react in certain ways to protect or defend themselves. This may be adaptive in the moment to survive the screaming but ultimately maladaptive, and may constrict their ability to be psychologically healthy over time.

❖ A more anxious, sensitive child may be intolerant of screaming very early on, and remove himself from the sport. However, he is also more likely to endure the screaming without telling a parent or responding to the coach directly, out of fear of reprisal. A more sensitive child who stays in this situation may be more affected physiologically with overall heightened arousal levels as discussed above.

❖ A more secure child will likely have the same physiological responses but be less vulnerable to them. He may find a way to tune out the yelling or relative comments, but this may come at the cost of emotional sensitivity. As the child becomes less sensitive to his own fearful feelings, he can become less sensitive to the feelings of others, leading to loss of empathy. He will also become less sensitive to emotions in general, and have a loss of sensitivity to positive emotions as well. He is also likely to resent the coach for putting him in such a psychologically vulnerable position.

NEGATIVE EFFECTS OF HAZING

Hazing practices today continue to reflect their historical roots in military units and universities, and societal norms and expectations around gender, and masculinity, in particular. Hazing practices are surprisingly common among middle/high school athletic teams: According to a 2000 survey on hazing of eleventh and twelfth graders conducted by researchers at Alfred University, *almost half* reported being hazed, and half of those by a sports team. Most students were asked to do humiliating tasks, such as pushing a penny across a school bus floor with their nose, sucking someone's toes, skinny dipping, or drinking foul mixtures such as urine, spoiled milk, and eggs. One in five said they were put in harm's way or asked to break the law.

The psychological scars from hazing can remain for years. Hazing at the high school level is particularly harmful because victims are at a developmental stage where they are more vulnerable because of a strong need to belong, make friends, and find approval in peer groups. That danger is heightened by a lack of awareness and widespread failure of secondary schools to develop and enforce rules against hazing.

Contrary to popular belief, hazing, far from bringing teams closer together, usually does just the opposite:

❖ **Hazing builds hate and distrust.** Players subjected to hazing often end up hating those who initiated the hazing.

❖ **Hazing creates a vicious cycle of escalating violence and/or humiliation.** Individuals who have been violated or humiliated or physically hurt in a hazing ritual are more likely to seek revenge. When

"55% of males and 29% of females said they used racial slurs or insults."

—FROM CHARACTER COUNTS! COALITION SPORTSMANSHIP SURVEY 2004

it is their turn to be the leader or perpetrator, they are more likely to escalate the next ritual to a higher level of violence and humiliation.

❖ **Hazing undermines team performance by creating negative fear.** Younger players become afraid of older players and intimidated from doing their best when they are on the field with them.

WHAT YOU CAN DO TO PREVENT ABUSE

Now that you know the forms abuse can take and the damage it does, here are some steps you can take as a mother to prevent or minimize the risk that your child will be subject to the any of the different forms of abuse in sports:

1. **Be proactive.**

   ❖ **Model appropriate behavior and attitudes.** Teach your child that violence—emotional or physical—is not acceptable in solving personal problems. Make a point of building your child's self-esteem at every opportunity.

   ❖ **Limit training** (practices, games, training at home or with private coaches) to prevent overuse injuries.

   ❖ **Make sure your child gets enough rest.** Children ages ten to seventeen need as much sleep, if not more, as younger children. Don't let your child burn the candle at both ends by getting up early for practice and then staying up late to do homework after long afternoon or evening practices.

   ❖ **Don't let your child play with an injury** or postpone needed medical treatment, and don't allow your child to return to practice before his injury has healed (see the discussion in chapter 9 about return-to-play guidelines after a player suffers a concussion).

   ❖ **Make sure your child is adequately hydrated** before, during, and after sports (see the discussion of heat illness in chapter 9).

❖ **Avoid becoming a statistic** by engaging in any of the myriad forms of emotional abuse discussed above.

2. Request background checks. ❋ Find out if the club requires background checks of coaches and all other adults, paid and volunteer (see below). At a minimum, coaches should have job descriptions that define and limit their authority, references should be checked, and there should be ongoing monitoring and evaluation. In higher risk situations (such as when the coach frequently travels out of town on unsupervised trips with young athletes) more extensive background checks should be performed. Part of keeping children safe is not taking offense when asked about your own background. If you work with children, and are asked to take part in screening, accept this as a positive step to keeping children safe.

Background Checks

It is every parent's nightmare that their child will be a victim of a sexual predator while participating in youth sports. This has become a very high profile issue in sports as well as in other segments of society. Unfortunately, sexual abuse of young players occurs in team sports, as well as in individual sports.

Background Checks: A Powerful Tool

Many sports leagues now require that all adults (paid employees as well as volunteers) involved in youth sports pass a background check. It is a safety measure so important that it should be run on all adults. While there are many different services that perform background checks to choose from, it is up to each sport league to determine the cost and depth of the background check suited best for its needs.

Background checks are effective in the sense that most sexual predators are not willing to have their background checked. The hope is that adults who should be around kids will not apply and thus they will be able to weed out potentially harmful people.

The problem with some background checks is that they don't screen for criminal convictions outside of the individual's state of residence. Indeed, a review of a major youth sports organization's applicants by ChoicePoint, a leading background check service, disclosed that nearly half of the 6,881 criminal convictions it found among 57,053 background screens were for individuals applying outside the state where they lived. It is therefore important that the service your league uses undertakes a comprehensive national search utilizing multiple criminal record sources, including fugitive file, state and county criminal record repositories, prison, parole, and release files from state Departments of Corrections, Administrative Office of Courts, and other state agencies.

Another potential problem with background screening is that many non-profit organizations compensate boards of directors, grounds crew, coaches and other adult members earn a salary or a stipend which technically exempts those adults from these checks. When requiring background checks, the use of the word "volunteer" may be unintentionally providing some individuals a loophole to avoid being screened. The most comprehensive way to conduct background checks is to require background checks for everyone over the age of 17 working with or in the vicinity of children.

Online Information
As a parent it is appropriate to ask the administrators of your sports league if they have done background checks on all adults involved in their program. If the answer is yes, then you know the foundation for safety has been established and the league understands the importance of the issue.

If the answer is no, then help the administration find a company to perform this important service to your league. The sophisticated background screening product offered by ChoicePoint, Volunteer Select Plus (www.volunteerselectplus.com), appears ideal for non-profit youth sports organizations because it taps directly into state and county criminal databases and provides instant criminal search reports without the need for fingerprinting.

3. Ask for institution of a two-adult rule. ❋ Dr. Keith Wilson, a psychotherapist, MomsTeam.com expert and founder of a rape and sexual abuse center in Nashville, Tennessee, says that while there a variety of steps a parent can take to protect their child from sexual predators, by far the most important step is to make sure that a coach is never alone with a child. This may be more difficult in individual sports like tennis and golf but this precaution is vital to the safety of the young player.

A child is vulnerable to sexual abuse by a coach because he or she inherently trusts the coach and may be unable and unwilling to accept an abuse of that trust. If the coach is never alone with a child, the child is protected from being a victim of sexual molestation.

Prohibiting a coach and player from being alone also protects the coach from accusation or innuendo that something could have gone wrong. A coach's career can be destroyed if the accusation of inappropriate behavior is made because the coach has no way of defending himself if he was alone with a child. This is a simple but powerful protection for all people involved. If an opportunity for inappropriate behavior never exists then inappropriate behavior cannot be alleged. Neither is inappropriate behavior likely.

4. Certified coaches. ❋ Ask if the club's coach is certified and a member of a coaching association with a code of ethics. Just as we would never send our children to schools with untrained teachers parents should insist that our coaches have adequate training and are certified in the sport they are coaching and know how to relate to children in a positive and nurturing manner (see more on coaches in chapter 10).

5. Know the warning signs of sexual abuse. ❋ While reliable statistics are not available, what data there is indicates that sexual harassment and abuse by authority figures in sports is widespread, especially among elite athletes. A 1996 Canadian survey of elite and recently retired Olympic athletes reported that 21.8 percent of the

266 respondents had had sexual intercourse with persons in positions of authority in sport. Of this total 8.6 percent reported being raped. 23 were under 16 years old at the time of the sexual assault, while 2.6 percent experienced unwanted sexual touching prior to that age.

It is therefore important as a parent that you know the warning signs of sexual abuse. Experts say that if the answer to any of the following questions is yes, a coach may be sexually abusing a player:

❖ Does your child's coach make her feel that she needs him in order to succeed?

❖ Does your child's coach spend time with you in an attempt to win your trust or try to be a surrogate parent?

❖ Does your child's coach act differently with him when in front of others?

❖ Does your child's coach try to control her—even off the field?

❖ Does your child's coach try to separate him from his teammates or other sources of support, like you or his friends?

❖ Does your child's coach spend a lot more time with her than with other athletes?

❖ Does your child's coach try to be alone with her?

❖ Does your child's coach give him gifts?

Your child may not always tell you there is a problem. You know your child best, so be aware of unexplained behavioral changes such as:

❖ Sudden aggression

❖ Quitting the team or being reluctant to return to the sport activity

❖ Sleep disorders

❖ Emotional disorders

❖ Regression to behavior typical of a young child (clinging etc.)

❖ Sliding grades

❖ Changes in appetite

❖ Fear of washrooms, locker rooms, or closed doors

❖ Running away

❖ Sudden interest in sex disproportionate for the child's age. It is important to note that sexualized behavior in children is usually the *result of* sexual abuse, not its cause.

❖ Reluctance to talk

❖ Frequent vomiting

In some cases, there may be obvious physical signs of abuse, such as:

❖ Bruises

❖ Scratches

❖ Inflammation

❖ Lesions

❖ Bleeding

❖ Genital injuries

❖ Sexually transmitted diseases

❖ Pregnancy

Be vigilant and talk to your child if you see one or more of these signs, but bear in mind that the presence of any of these symptoms does not automatically mean that your child has been physically or sexually abused. If you have reasonable grounds to suspect that a child may be suffering sexual abuse, you must report it immediately to the local child protection agency or police.

6. Speak up. ❋ If you hear abusive language or see abusive conduct, whether from a coach, player, or parent, don't remain silent. Speak to the coach or, where appropriate, *to higher* authorities including the police. If you see a pattern of abuse, start to keep a journal with a timeline of incidents.

7. Know the adults your children are spending time with. ❋ Since the dawn of time, women have been responsible for nurturing and protecting their children from harm. A mother would never leave a child in the care of a total stranger.

❖ Get to know your child's coach. The tendency is to give tremendous license to someone who is a coach. Don't put him or her on a pedestal. Respect is earned.

❖ Go to practices and games periodically to watch the coach in action, and see how she or he interacts with the athletes.

❖ Private or closed practices are a warning sign of sexual abuse. If the coach wants to exclude you from practices, ask why.

❖ Keep an eye out for other children whose parents are unable to attend practices or games.

8. Educate your children. ❋ Families are a place where children learn survival skills and how to solve problems. In caring for and nurturing your children, teach your child:

❖ To let you know whenever abuse in any of its forms has occurred. As I told Courtney's mother, giving a child a cell phone is a good idea because she can use it to call home when abuse is taking place. If you don't answer, but have voice mail or an answering machine, she may able to use these features to document the abuse.

❖ To distinguish between friendly teasing and bullying, flirting, and harassment.

❖ To distinguish between proper and improper touching (see opposite).

The Difference Between Proper and Improper Touching

Here's what experts say you should teach your child about the difference between proper and improper touching:

✓ **Most physical contact is okay.** *It is okay for a coach to touch your child where contact is necessary as part of the instruction process or to provide for his or her safety (such as spotting in gymnastics). Often touching—like hugging or high fives—takes place as part of celebrating: a home run, a big win, a soccer goal. Touching is okay if it is respectful of a person's personal boundaries and comfort level, is done in public, and is nurturing (done to provide comfort, reassurance, and support).*

✓ **Sexualized touching is not okay.** *When a hug becomes fondling, a kiss on the cheek becomes a long kiss on the lips, and a pat on the rear becomes a seductive stroking of a body part, the touching has become sexual. Your child needs to know that he or she may be confused as to whether the line has been crossed into sexualized touching. If so, the child should talk about the touching with you or someone he or she trusts.*

✓ **Any contact with private parts is wrong.** *Make clear to your child that no adult is permitted to touch his or her private parts (penis, vagina, anus, breasts), except for health reasons, and your child should not touch an adult's private parts, even if asked. If confused about whether a touch is okay, your child should ask someone he or she trusts.*

✓ **Improper touching is not the child's fault.** *Your child needs to know that if an adult touches his or her private parts, or asks the child to touch the adult's, it is not the child's fault.*

✓ **Whomever he or she tells will listen.** *Make sure your child knows that, if he or she tells you about improper sexual contact, you will believe what he or she tells you. If he or she doesn't want to tell you, your child should know he or she can talk to any other trusted adult, whether a favorite teacher, the school's guidance counselor, or a minister or rabbi.*

✓ That it's okay to say no if the coach is doing something that makes her uncomfortable in any way.

✓ To be assertive and establish strong personal boundaries.

✓ That ignoring abuse can often lead to a cycle of ongoing harassment or abuse, and victimization. Harassment or abuse needs to be reported when it occurs and not kept secret.

✓ That sexuality is not a taboo subject. If we want our children not to think the topic is off-limits, they need to know about such aspects of sexuality as sexual anatomy (accurate labels for penis, vagina, anus, breasts, and so on), birth control, sexually transmitted diseases, sexual intercourse, homosexuality, masturbation, and abortion. They need to be provided opportunities for conversation, encouraged to ask questions whenever and wherever they surface, and they need to be assured that nothing is off-limits, that there is no such thing as a stupid question, and that if you don't know the answer, you will try to find out.

WHAT TO DO IF YOUR CHILD REPORTS HARASSMENT OR ABUSE

If your child tells you that he or she is being harassed, abused, or neglected, experts say you should:

❖ Take your child somewhere where he or she can talk freely.

❖ Listen and believe.

❖ Never ignore even seemingly trivial calls for help.

❖ Support your child.

❖ Discuss your child's options with him or her.

❖ Help your child to restore a sense of control in his or her life by involving your child in deciding how to deal with the problem.

- ❖ Reassure your child continuously.

- ❖ Speak on a level your child can understand.

What you hear may shock you. No matter what you are told, stay calm and show that you are listening. It is extremely important that your child knows that harassment or abuse is not her fault, nor a reflection on her. Possible responses include, "I believe you," "This is not your fault," "You did not cause this in any way," "You are a victim," "I am going to help you."

Harassment, abuse, and neglect can inflict deep psychological damage on young people. Arrange for counseling to help your child come to terms with what has happened. Other family members may need this support as well.

Your response to eliminate the abuse or harassment should be determined by the nature of the behavior and the age of the victim. Options include talking to the coach, manager, or club president. This can often clear up a simple problem quickly. If you feel that the situation cannot be resolved at this level, other avenues include:

Reporting the harassment, abuse, or neglect to:

- ❖ the club's board of directors;

- ❖ the state organization; and

- ❖ the national sport organization.

Calling

- ❖ Local child protection agency or police.

- ❖ Kids Help Phone: 1-800-668-6868. Trained counselors are available twenty-four hours a day to help children deal with painful situations.

❖ Rape crisis center (sexual abuse only).

❖ Crimestoppers: This allows you to leave an anonymous tip with the police.

Suing. In exteme cases you may sue anyone who had an opportunity to do something about the abuse and didn't. This could include the perpetrator, the employer, the national sport organization, the state sport organization, the club, and so on. Of course, this doesn't erase what happened to your child but it can help the healing process and alert people to take such abuse more seriously.

We all want a safe and nurturing environment for our kids. The best way to prevent your child from becoming a victim of physical, emotional, or sexual abuse while playing sports is by staying involved and keeping your eyes and ears open. The moment you feel uncomfortable because you don't trust the coach or think your child is not safe, you need to either correct the problem or take your child off the team.

Chapter Nine

Player Down!
Protecting Kids from Serious Injury or Death

> *Becoming a mother makes you the mother of all children.*
> *From now on each wounded, abandoned, frightened child is*
> *yours. You live in the suffering mothers of every race and*
> *creed and weep with them. You long to comfort all who are*
> *desolate.*

—CHARLOTTE GRAY

DEADLY STATISTICS

During a break in his game, six-year-old Zachary Tran playfully dangled with some of his teammates from the crossbar of a large, metal soccer goal. His mother, Michelle, told me that when she asked him to stop playing on the goal he got down. She then left to take another child to the bathroom. Several minutes later, while no one was looking, the goal fell on Zach, causing massive head trauma. Paramedics were unable to revive him, and he was pronounced dead at a nearby hospital less than an hour later.

On September 28, 2001, seventeen-year-old Matthew Colby died after sustaining head trauma in a high school football game in California. The young linebacker died from bleeding and swelling in the brain, most likely after suffering repeated blows to the head during two earlier football games.

Matthew's mother, Kelli, told me that Matt had complained to friends of headaches after the two earlier games, and game films showed he delivered and sustained several blows during the course of those contests. At the coaching staff's instruction, Matt saw a doctor and received clearance to play on Sept. 28, although he was held out of contact drills for a week leading up to the game in which he died.

On October 4, 2003, Joseph DiPrete-DiGioia, a fourteen-year-old high school freshman from Belfast, Maine, was running through the woods in a cross-country meet. No one was at checkpoints on the course with walkie-talkies. When Joseph failed to emerge from the woods at the finish line, his mother, Maura, told me she knew something was dangerously wrong. She begged the meet's organizers to mount a search, but for two hours they ignored her pleas, believing that Joseph had simply skipped out of the race. Several hours later, Maura and his coach found her son's body partially hidden in the tall grass beside the running trail, a victim of sudden cardiac arrest. Joe was missing for almost two hours and was found ten minutes after the staff started looking, and the time of his death was about ten minutes before being found, meaning that he was alive in the cold rain for one and a half hours.

These stories are about just three of the hundreds of children who die each year from preventable causes while playing sports.

The number of children injured in sports is staggering:

❖ According to the Safe Kids campaign, 3.5 million kids ages fourteen and younger receive medical treatment for sports-related injuries each year, half of which are overuse injuries.

❖ An estimated 12 million student athletes ages five to twenty-two sustain sports or recreational injuries annually, resulting in a loss of more than 20 million school days and direct medical costs in the billions of dollars.

❖ According to the CPSC, the number of emergency room visits for cheerleading injuries almost doubled from 1994 (15,700) to 2004 (28,400). More than half of catastrophic injuries—those involving severe skull or spinal damage—suffered by female high school and college athletes between 1983 and 2004 were in cheerleading, according to the National Center for Catastrophic Sport Injury Research.

❖ According to the Brain Injury Resource Center, there are an estimated 300,000 sports-related concussions in the United States each year. Concussions are most common, as one would expect, in contact sports, where 10–15 percent of athletes are likely to suffer some sort of concussion in a year, but only comprise about 10 percent of athletic injuries across all sports.

❖ A 2001 study published in the *Journal of Child Neurology* found that around half of all football players at the high school level suffer at least one concussion a season.

Too many of our kids are becoming statistics. And sadly, *nine out of ten youth sports accidents and deaths are preventable.* Set out below are the steps you can take as a mother to reduce the chance that your child will become a statistic.

REDUCING THE RISK OF SUDDEN CARDIAC DEATH

By some estimates, as many as three hundred children die of sudden cardiac death (SCD) from playing sports each year. There are two critically important steps you can take that can significantly reduce the risk to your child.

The first is to have your child undergo a thorough preparticipation evaluation (PPE) every year. Not only can a PPE be an effective tool in identifying athletes who should not be playing sports because they have congenital heart defects or a history of concussions, but it is also useful in identifying other medical problems that may affect sports participation, such as asthma or the female athlete triad (discussed later in this chapter).

The problem with PPEs, however, is that less than one high school in five in this country uses the most up-to-date form containing all the elements, including the cardiac exam developed and recommended by the American Academy of Family Physicians, American Academy of Pediatrics, American College of Sports Medicine, American Medical Society for Sports Medicine, American Orthopaedic Society for Sports Medicine, and the American Osteopathic Academy of Sports Medicine (see sidebar). My advice is to make sure the doctor asks the right questions, even if they aren't required, and uses the current PPE form, even if the school doesn't require it.

Signs That May Indicate a Child Is at Risk of Sudden Cardiac Death (SCD)

Family History

Congenital heart defects run in families. That just one family member died of SCD or has the warning signs may mean other blood relatives are at risk for SCD. Unexplained deaths should prompt comprehensive cardiac screening for all members of the immediate family and may save lives. Unfortunately, doctors sometimes fail to appreciate familial risk. In one case, after a nineteen-year-old Virginia woman died from sudden cardiac arrest while running, no one told the family that the cardiac defect that caused her death can run in families. Two months later, her seventeen-year-old brother also fell dead while running. Because of the importance of family medical history, the surgeon general launched the Family History Initiative in November 2004, which provides a computerized tool to aid in organizing a family history, especially during family gatherings, where multiple family members are present. (An updated version of the tool is available at https://familyhistory.hhs.gov.)

Here are the questions that should be asked about family history during a PPE:

Has anyone in the child's family:

✓ Died for no apparent reason (SIDS, car accidents, drownings)?

✓ Have a heart problem?

✓ Died of heart problems or sudden cardiac arrest before age fifty?

✓ Had syncope (fainting) or presyncope (nearly fainted)?

✓ Had unexplained seizures?

✓ Had significant arrhythmias (irregular heartbeat) or a pacemaker?

✓ Had any of the following genetic disorders:

    ✓ Hypertrophic cardiomyopathy (HCM)

    ✓ Dilated cardiomyopathy (DCM)

    ✓ Marfan syndrome

    ✓ Ehlers-Danlos syndrome

    ✓ Arrythmogenic right ventricular cardiomyopathy

    ✓ Early coronary artery disease

    ✓ Coronary artery anatomical anomalies

    ✓ Brugada syndrome

    ✓ Long QT syndrome (LQTS)

    ✓ Short QT syndrome

    ✓ Primary pulmonary hypertension

    ✓ Rheumatic fever (infection of the heart), hypertension (high blood pressure), or Kawasaki disease?

Personal Medical History

In addition to questions about family medical history, it is important that your child be asked about his or her personal medical history, especially whether he or she has ever experienced:

✓ Chest pain with or without exercise?

✓ Excessive, unexpected, or unexplained fatigue with exercise?

Every youth sports coach should receive training in first aid and sport-specific injury prevention. It is sad, but true, that the majority of coaches, even at the high school level, receive inadequate safety training.

✓ Excessive, unexpected, or unexplained shortness of breath with exercise? (Doctors don't always recognize this as a symptom of congenital heart disease, sometimes mistaking it for exercise-induced asthma. In one case, a fifteen-year-old boy was pulled out of a soccer game because of shortness of breath, and later diagnosed with asthma. A month later he suffered SCD on a soccer field as a result of HCM.)

✓ Heart palpitations (heart races or skips beats during exercise)?

Second, you can work in your community to strengthen the cardiac "chain of survival," the five-step process (early recognition of medical emergency, activation of emergency medical system, early CPR, early defibrillation with an automatic external defibrillator (AED), and early advanced life support by paramedics) developed by the American Heart Association (AHA) for providing treatment to those who experience sudden cardiac arrest (SCA) outside of a hospital setting, such as at a youth sports competition.

While a complete discussion of the chain of survival is beyond the scope of this book (for a more extensive discussion go to the cardiac awareness channel on the MomsTeam Web site), it is well established that quick execution of each and every link can dramatically improve the chances of survival for someone experiencing SCA, either as a result of a congenital heart defect or from an ill-timed blow to the chest, such as from a baseball or lacrosse ball (a condition called commotio cordis; according to a 2005 study reported in the *Journal of Pediatrics*, commercially available chest protectors do not protect against this condition). The chances of survival decrease 7–10 percent with each passing minute. If an AED—and a trained lay operator—are immediately available at a youth sports venue when an athlete goes into sudden cardiac arrest, the chances of survival are 50 percent.

While the introduction of new lightweight, portable, user-friendly AEDs—some of which can now be purchased over-the-counter without a doctor's prescription—more parents, coaches, and athletic trainers certified in CPR (note that the AHA recently revised CPR guidelines to call for thirty hard compressions, instead of fifteen, for every rescue breath), and increased awareness have reduced the risk of SCD to youth athletes and saved lives (see below), more can and should be done. The lack of an AED continues to result in deaths, such as occurred in November 2005 when a seventeen-year-old soccer goalie was hit in the chest and experienced SCA (most likely from commotio cordis) and died when it took paramedics fifteen minutes to arrive.

With fewer school nurses than ever before, often rotating between schools, some schools may be without professional medical coverage for hours or days every week. More and more, it is up to teachers, athletic trainers, coaches, and staff, and even other students to recognize when a student is in cardiac arrest and initiate the chain of survival. Programs to train high school students in CPR and operating an AED, and implementation of a lay rescuer AED program where needed (i.e., where an EMS "call-to-shock interval" of five minutes or less cannot be reliably achieved), may need to be developed. If funds are not available to purchase AEDs, you may wish to raise funds privately (Friends of Athletics, booster clubs, PTA, Rotary, student activities such as bake sales, car washes, etc.).

The Chain of Survival: It Really Works

On June 13, 2001, 13-year-old Sean Morley was struck in the chest by a baseball during a game in Deerfield, Illinois. The ball struck at the most vulnerable time in the cycle between heartbeats, resulting in a condition called commotio cordis. Sean fell to his knees, his head fell forward and hit the ground, and he then slumped over on his side.

Sean's mother, Norma, told me later that a mother of one of the players saw a police car driving down the street and ran in front of the car to flag him down. At the same time the police officer got a call from a father in the stands, who had been asked by the coaches to call 911. The police officer happened to have an AED in the trunk of his cruiser, which a local cardiologist and his wife had donated to the town.

Two fathers in the stands who happened to be doctors began immediate CPR. When the police officer arrived with the AED, it was used to shock Sean's heart so that, by the time paramedics arrived, a normal heart rhythm had been restored, saving Sean's life.

REDUCING THE RISK OF SERIOUS INJURY OR DEATH FROM CONCUSSION

The Danger of Second Impact Syndrome The most serious risk your child faces if he suffers a head concussion is from a condition called second impact syndrome (SIS). SIS occurs when an athlete, like Matt Colby, returns to competition after sustaining a head injury and suffers a second head injury before symptoms associated with the first have cleared, which may take days or even weeks.

Postconcussion Signs and Symptoms

A concussion is a traumatic brain injury resulting from a sudden acceleration, deceleration, or a violent torque of the head that causes an immediate but temporary alteration in brain functions. Contrary to popular belief, your child does not have to experience a loss of consciousness (LOC) to have suffered a concussion. In fact, the vast majority of concussions (more than 90 percent in one study) do not involve LOC.

Experts have learned that LOC does not predict the severity of injury. Severity is now measured primarily by how long it takes for symptoms to clear. Instead of being graded, concussions may be categorized for management purposes, according to the current 2004 Prague guidelines, as either simple—a concussion that progressively resolves without complication over seven to ten days, one in which concussive symptoms persist, including recurrence with exertion, involving concussive convulsions, LOC of one minute or more, prolonged cognitive impairment following injury, or suffered by an athlete who has suffered multiple concussions over time or repeated concussions with progressively less impact force—in which case, additional considerations be-

yond simple return-to-play advice, including neurological testing and multidisciplinary treatment by physicians with specific expertise in managing concussions, is required. New guidelines, however, are about to be issued that do not refer to any concussion as "simple" because, while symptoms may clear in 7 to 10 days, the concussion could lead to a cumulative brain injury.

If your child exhibits any of the following symptoms or problems, she may have suffered a concussion or may not yet have fully recovered from one:

✓ Amnesia (posttraumatic or retrograde)

✓ "Bell rung" (i.e., hears ringing in his ears)

✓ Balance problems

✓ Concussive convulsion/impact seizure

✓ Confusion

✓ Depression

✓ Dizziness

✓ Drowsiness

✓ Excess sleep

✓ Fatigue

✓ Feel "dinged"

✓ Feel "foggy"

✓ Feel "slowed down"

✓ Feel dazed

✓ Feel stunned

✓ Headache or persistent pressure in head

✓ Hearing problems (e.g., ringing in ears, sensitivity to noise)

✓ Inappropriate emotions (e.g., laughing or crying) or personality change

✓ Inappropriate playing behavior (e.g., running the wrong direction)

✓ Irritability or emotional changes

✓ Loss of consciousness/impaired conscious state

✓ Loss of orientation

✓ Memory problems/post-traumatic amnesia

✓ Nausea

✓ Nervousness

✓ Numbness/tingling

✓ Poor balance, coordination, or unsteady gait

✓ Poor concentration, easily distracted

✓ Significantly decreased playing ability

✓ Slurred speech

✓ Slow to answer questions or follow directions

✓ Trouble falling asleep/sleep disturbance

✓ Unaware of period, opposition, score of game

✓ Vacant stare/glassy-eyed

✓ Visual problems (seeing stars or flashing lights; double vision; sensitivity to light)

✓ Vomiting

As my MomsTeam colleague, Dr. Robert Cantu, co-director of the Neurologic Sports Injury Center at Boston's Brigham and Women's Hospital and one of the world's leading concussion experts, explains, the second blow may be unremarkable, perhaps involving only a blow to the chest that jerks the athlete's head and indirectly sends accelerating forces to the brain. Affected athletes may appear stunned but may not suffer LOC, and they often complete the play. They usually remain alert on their feet for fifteen seconds to one minute or so but seem dazed. Often, affected athletes remain on the playing field or walk off under their own power. Usually within seconds to minutes of the second impact, the athlete—conscious but stunned—suddenly collapses to the ground, semiconscious with rapidly dilating (widening) pupils and loss of eye movement, and stops breathing.

Although precise statistics are not available, SIS is more common than previous reports have suggested. According to Dr. Cantu, the center continues to see one to two documented cases of SIS each year but is certain that the condition is under-reported, as the history of the first injury is often not obtained.

Even a single concussion can lead to permanent injury. While SIS is obviously the biggest concern, even a single concussion can impair a child's ability to reach his full cognitive potential, inhibiting his ability to learn and undermine his classroom performance; cause personality changes; behavioral, emotional, and attention deficit disorders; and accelerate the natural process of brain degeneration that accompanies aging. Medical science is only beginning to understand the links between multiple concussions and increased risks for afflictions like Alzheimer's, depression, memory loss, cognitive loss, and dementia. The initial research, however, is alarming: a 2005 study, conducted by University of North Carolina at Chapel Hill researchers and colleagues, found that retired National Football League players faced a 37 percent higher risk of Alzheimer's than other U. S. males of the same age, and the repeated concussions brought on by blows to the head during their playing days significantly boost the chances that retired professional football players will suffer dementia, such as mild cognitive impairment, in later life. The data suggest that a history of recurrent concussions and probably sub-concussive contacts to the head may also be risk factors for late-life memory impairment and mild cognitive impairment. Two recent studies suggest that years of heading a soccer ball may result in the short term in weaker mental performance, including a decline in cognitive function; difficulty in verbal learning, planning, and maintaining attention; and reduced information-processing speed. The long-term effects of heading, however, are less clear. Once an athlete suffers a concussion, the risk of suffering a second concussion is three to four times greater. Usually, the second concussion requires less of a blow and a longer recovery time. The risk of concussion increases with each subsequent concussion. As one mother of a brain-injured athlete said, "I never knew that concussions leave a calling card."

Prevention Is Difficult In deciding whether to keep your child out of contact sports because of the risk of concussion, understand that, contrary to popular belief, football helmets do *not* protect against concussions: they are designed to prevent bleeding in the brain and skull fractures, not to protect against injury to the soft tissue of the brain, such as result from a concussion. According to a study reported in the journal *Neurosurgery* in February 2006, however, changes in helmet design and new helmet technology may reduce the incidence of concussions in high school football players. The concussion rate for players wearing the new "Revolution" helmet made by Riddell was 31 percent less than for those wearing standard helmets. Remember also that while most athletic head injuries occur as a result of direct blows to the head, it is possible to suffer a concussion from a violent hit to the chest that snaps the head forward, or a violent hit to the front of the neck that snaps the head backward. If your child wants to play soccer, a helmet may offer some protection against concussions resulting from player-to-player collisions and ground contact (which cause most of the concussions in soccer), but *not* against the effects of repeated heading.

Education and Following Return-to-Play Guidelines Is Critical If your child does play contact sports, it is important that you be proactive on the subject of concussions. Because concussions are so difficult to diagnose, with the symptoms sometimes not showing up until days after injury; because the only cure for a concussion is rest; and because the consequences of SIS are so catastrophic (the death rate is nearly 50 percent), there are number of important steps to take.

First, as a parent, you should:

❖ Learn to recognize the signs of a concussion (see earlier sidebar)

❖ Seek immediate medical attention (ideally by a medical doctor with head injury training) if signs are present

❖ Monitor your child over time for signs of neurobehavioral abnormalities

❖ Not let him return to play until he has received medical clearance (see sidebar on return-to-play guidelines)

❖ Observe him closely whenever he is playing for signs suggesting brain injury

---

Return-to-Play Guidelines

When a child shows any symptoms or signs of a concussion, experts at the 2nd International Conference on Concussion in Sport held in Prague in 2004 recommend:

✓ The player should not be allowed to return to play in the current game or practice. (This is a much more conservative approach than earlier return-to-play guidelines would have allowed and essentially adheres to the philosophy "When in doubt, sit out.")

✓ The player should not be left alone—regular monitoring for deterioration is essential over the first few hours following injury.

✓ The player should be evaluated by a doctor.

✓ The player should not be allowed to return to play until he has completed the following medically supervised step-wise process:

1. No activity, complete rest. Once symptom free, proceed to step 2.

2. Light aerobic exercise such as walking or stationary cycling; no resistance training.

3. Sport-specific training (i.e., skating in hockey, running in soccer).

4. Noncontact training drills;

5. Full contact training after medical clearance;

6. Game play.

If any postconcussion symptoms recur, drop back to previous asymptomatic level and try to progress again after twenty-four hours.

Because activities that require concentration and attention may exacerbate the symptoms and delay recovery, it is important that your child limit her day-to-day activities and school-related activities until she is symptom-free. In other words, it is important to emphasize to your child the need for physical and cognitive rest in the first few days following an injury (no homework; stay home from school).

Experts strongly recommend that an athlete be held out of play when he suffers multiple concussions, for an extended period of time (around seven days) after symptoms have cleared, especially during the same season. An athlete suffering three mild/simple concussions or two moderate/severe/complex concussions in the same season should not be allowed to play again that season.

Second, because the macho culture of youth sports, particularly in such aggressive contact sports as football, hockey, and lacrosse, puts athletes under significant pressure to "shake off" a concussion or "take it like a man"—pressure that coaches and parents can exacerbate, either directly or subtly, in their desire for team and individual success—emphasize to your child that shaking off a concussion is not a badge of honor and that failing to immediately report or underreporting concussion symptoms may be placing themselves at potentially life-threatening risk of brain injury.

Two recent studies clearly establish that high school football players are significantly underreporting concussions: while trainers say only 3.6 to 4.1 percent of players report concussions during the season, the percentage of players asked after the season whether they had experienced concussion symptoms jumped as high as 47.2 percent depending on the study.

Also, consider pushing for increased training among coaches, officials, and athletic trainers in recognizing concussions and strict adherence to appropriate return-to-play guidelines. An excellent learning tool for anyone concerned about concussions in sport is the CDC's multimedia tool kit, *Heads Up: Concussion in High School Sports*, which can be ordered in kit form or downloaded free of charge from the CDC's Web site at http://www.cdc.gov/ncipc/tbi/coaches_tool_kit.htm. If your child's school has not adopted a single set of return-to-play guidelines, ask it to develop one.

In addition, ask your child's school to conduct neurological tests on all athletes in contact or collision sports before every season to provide a baseline to be used as a benchmark for comparison purposes should an athlete sustain a concussion (there are a number of affordable computerized testing programs now on the market that do this).

PREVENTING HEAT-RELATED ILLNESSES

Heat illness is one of the *most preventable* of all injuries in youth sports.

Deaths from heat stroke occur most in football. Twenty-one high school football players died of heat stroke between 1999 and 2006, the overwhelming majority in the first four days of preseason practice, when players are not acclimatized to heat, intensity and duration of practice, or their uniform. But *any* athlete exercising vigorously in the heat (long-distance runners, tennis and soccer players), especially those with eating disorders, congenital heart disease, diabetes, and those who are obese, are at risk of heat-related illness or death.

Here are some steps you can take to reduce the risk that your child will suffer a serious or catastrophic heat illness in hot and humid weather:

❖ Make sure your child has become *acclimated* to the heat *before* starting preseason practice or vigorous exercise in the heat.

❖ Make sure your child is *properly hydrated* before, during, and after sports (see table). Two out of three children are dehydrated before practice even starts. Because children do not instinctively consume enough fluids to stay hydrated, it is up to you to make sure they get enough to drink. Kids need to drink from their own water bottle *on a schedule* rather than in response to thirst. This is because by the time they say they are thirsty, they are *already* dehydrated. You need to remind your child to drink 5 to 9 ounces (ten to eighteen half-ounce gulps) every twenty minutes during exercise, depending on weight. If you have a younger child, give him a water bottle with marks on the side showing how much he should drink at a time.

❖ Make sure your child recognizes the warning signs of dehydration and heat illnesses (see below) *and* understands just how important it is to speak up if he has any of these symptoms (as with concussions, silence can be deadly).

❖ If your child is playing football, make sure the program is following *new preseason football practice guidelines* issued by the American College of Sports Medicine (see below).

Signs of dehydration:

✓ *Dry lips and tongue*

✓ *Sunken eyes*

✓ *Infrequent urination or small volume*

✓ *Bright-colored/dark urine or urine with a strong odor*

✓ *Apathy or lack of energy*

✓ *Tires easily*

✓ *Irritability*

Signs of impending heat illness:

✓ *Weakness*

✓ *Chills*

✓ Goose bumps on chest and upper arms

✓ Nausea

✓ Headache

✓ Faintness

✓ Disorientation

✓ Muscle cramping

✓ Reduced or cessation of sweating

HYDRATION CHART

AGES 6 TO 12	AGES 13 TO 18
Before Sports	**Before Sports**
Drinking fluids prior to exercise appears to reduce or delay the detrimental effects of dehydration.	Drinking fluids prior to exercise appears to reduce or delay the detrimental effects of dehydration.
• 1 to 2 hours before sports: 4 to 8 ounces of cold water	• 1 to 2 hours before sports: 8 to 16 ounces of water
• 10 to 15 minutes before sports: 4 to 8 ounces of water	• 10 to 15 minutes before sports: 8 to 12 ounces of water
During Sports	**During Sports**
• Every 20 minutes: 5 to 9 ounces of a sports drink, depending on weight (5 ounces for a child weighing 88 pounds, 9 ounces for a child weighing 132 pounds)	• Every 20 minutes: 5 to 10 ounces of a sports drink, depending on weight
After Sports	**After Sports**
• Postexercise hydration should aim to correct any fluid lost during the activity.	• Post-exercise hydration should aim to correct any fluid lost during the practice.
• Within two hours: at least 24 ounces of a sports drink for every pound of weight lost	• Within two hours: at least 24 ounces of a sports drink for every pound of weight lost

Source: MomsTeam.com.

Signs of heat cramps, the mildest form of heat illness:

✓ Thirst

✓ Chills

✓ Clammy skin

✓ Throbbing heart

✓ Muscle pain

✓ Spasms

✓ Nausea

Signs of heat exhaustion, a more serious heat illness, which may require medical attention:

✓ Nausea

✓ Extreme fatigue

✓ Reduced sweating

✓ Headache

✓ Shortness of breath

✓ Weak, rapid pulse

✓ Dry mouth

Signs of heat stroke, a *life-threatening* medical emergency in which the body's temperature-regulating processes cease functioning, requiring immediate action, and which left untreated can result in death:

✓ No sweating

✓ Dry, hot skin

✓ Swollen tongue

✓ Visual disturbances

✓ Rapid pulse

✓ Unsteady gait

✓ Fainting

✓ Low blood pressure

✓ Vomiting

✓ Headache

✓ Loss of consciousness

✓ Shock

✓ Excessive body temperature with an excessively high rectal temperature (over 105.8°F)

Preseason Football Practice Guidelines

To reduce the risk of heat illness in preseason football practice, the American College of Sports Medicine issued new guidelines in 2004 recommending the following:

✓ **Limited practice duration.** Football practices should be a maximum of three hours long for the first week (this is total length of practice, including warm-up and cooldown periods), with the practice length increased gradually over a two-week period to allow players to become acclimatized to heat.

✓ **Weigh-ins.** Players should be weighed before and after practices. Since the volume of sweat loss varies by child, this is the most accurate way to determine how much fluid an individual athlete has lost during practice and needs to replace.

✓ **Lighter clothing.** During the first weeks of practice, players should wear light-colored, lightweight cotton or mesh shorts with helmets and shoulder pads only (not full uniform). Athletes should be given a chance to remove their helmets whenever possible (e.g., during instruction, water and cooldown breaks).

✓ **Frequent fluid breaks.** Players should be given cooldown and fluid breaks in a shaded area at least every thirty to forty-five minutes or more frequently, depending on heat and humidity *level. Each athlete should drink a minimum amount of fluids before returning to practice. Sports (not "energy") drinks are recommended instead of water because they replace electrolytes lost in sweat and contain carbohydrates for energy. Fluids should never be restricted.*

✓ **Close monitoring.** *The staff, including the athletic trainer, should be on the lookout for signs of heat illness. A buddy system should be used, with players monitoring each other. If heat illness is suspected, the player should immediately be removed from practice. If heat stroke is suspected, the player should immediately be cooled down by applying wet towels to the head and neck and hosing him off with cold water until EMS personnel arrive.*

✓ **Rehydration.** *After practice, athletes should be required to rehydrate to replace lost fluids.*

Not only is it important that you monitor the quantity of water or sports drink your child needs to ensure adequate hydration and prevent heat stroke, but that you monitor the *quality* as well. Countless children become seriously ill each year from drinking from the bottle of a teammate infected with a contagious disease such as the flu, mononucleosis, or hepatitis, or from drinking contaminated water or water containing high levels of lead, such as from a hose or school water fountain. Many states ban the practice of providing drinking water from hoses that are not raised above the ground because bacteria from the ground can get into the hose and multiply.

The federal Lead Contamination Control Act of 1988 (LCCA) requires schools to identify, repair, or remove watercoolers or fountains with toxic levels of lead. The LCCA does not require schools to monitor the water from the showers, which are a common place to fill drinking water containers. With the large amounts of water that athletes need to drink it is best to make sure the source of the water is in compliance. In February 2006, the Environmental Protection Agency released a new kit to help schools reduce lead in drinking water, *3Ts for Reducing Lead in Drinking Water in Schools*. (The Ts stand for Training, Testing, and Telling.) The kit provides the information schools need to identify potential sources of lead in their facilities, to monitor school drinking water for elevated lead levels, to resolve problems if elevated lead levels are found, and to communicate about their lead control programs. The kit is available on the Internet at www.epa.gov.

REDUCING INJURIES THROUGH PROPER CONDITIONING

Conditioning-related injuries occur most often at the beginning of a season, when kids are most likely to be out of shape. Such injuries are preventable if, before the start of the season, your child follows a conditioning program designed specifically for the sport he is playing. Don't assume that your child is in shape to play sports simply because she is young, healthy, and appears physically fit.

Although proper conditioning will reduce the risk of injury in all sports, it is particularly important for girls, who are predisposed to instability or dislocation of the kneecap (patella), pain and problems under the kneecap, and noncontact injuries of the anterior cruciate ligament (ACL), especially in sports like soccer and basketball that require twisting and cutting. The ACL injury rate for girls is two to ten times higher than for boys and has reached epidemic proportions. Having suffered a noncontact ACL injury playing lacrosse in college, and a spiral break of the right leg right below the knee playing squash in my twenties, I can personally attest to the seriousness of such injuries; in particular, a torn or ruptured ACL is a serious, life-altering injury often requiring immediate surgery and six to eight months of rehabilitation.

Proper conditioning (especially building up hamstrings and inner quadriceps muscles) has been shown to prevent some of these injuries. Indeed, some experts recommend that elementary school gym classes begin teaching girls how to strengthen their leg muscles as a way of avoiding knee injuries in high school and college. Drills in which girls are taught to pivot, jump, and land with flexed knees and stop with a three-step stop with the knee flexed instead of a one-step stop with the knee extended have also been shown to reduce the risk of noncontact ACL injuries in female athletes.

REDUCING INJURIES BY STRETCHING, WARM-UPS, AND COOLDOWNS

Your child's natural flexibility varies by age. At about age ten, kids start to lose flexibility because their bones are growing faster than their muscles. Flexibility starts to improve again at around age thirteen for girls and fourteen for boys. Because athletes with poor muscle flexibility experience more soreness, tenderness, and pain after exercise, flexibility exercises to stretch tight muscles should be mandatory for young athletes, says the American College of Sports Medicine.

Research shows that cold muscles are more injury prone. While a proper warm-up is important for all youth athletes, it is particularly critical during growth spurts and for girls, who should focus on front-to-back, side-to-side, and circular movements to strengthen and stretch leg muscles to reduce the risk of ACL injuries.

Children should learn at an early age the importance of loosening up before any physical activity and how to warm up and cool down properly so that it becomes second nature. Your child's coach should include both warm-up and cooldown periods during training. Before the first practice, ask the coach for a list of all the exercises that will be used. That way, you can have your child continue training at home, and you can discuss with your child's pediatrician any concerns you might have about the exercises.

REDUCING INJURIES BY USING APPROPRIATE SAFETY EQUIPMENT

Lots of injuries children suffer playing sports could be easily avoided had they simply worn the proper safety equipment, particularly mouth guards, safety goggles, and helmets (see opposite). Also, because extreme sun exposure during childhood and adolescence is one of the leading causes of melanoma, a very serious form of skin cancer, make sure your child applies an SPF-15 sunscreen before playing outdoor sports—even under clothes, as they do not provide protection from the sun's harmful rays.

Eye Protection in Sports

✓ *Eye injuries are the leading cause of blindness in children.*

✓ *As many as 90 percent of all sports-related eye injuries could be prevented by wearing protective eyewear while playing certain sports.*

✓ *Prevent Blindness America recommends sports eye guards for basketball, baseball, football, soccer, and hockey; an additional polycarbonate face guard attached to the helmet for baseball and football; and a wire or polycarbonate face mask for hockey.*

Mouth Protection in Sports

The majority of mouth injuries occur in baseball, basketball, soccer, field hockey, softball, and gymnastics. Most could have been prevented had the athlete worn a mouth guard. Mouth guards protect not only the teeth but the lips, cheeks, and tongue, and reduce the risk of such head and neck injuries as concussions and jaw fractures. While there are three types of mouth guards (stock, boil and bite, and custom) the advantage of a dentist-fabricated mouth guard, according to David Cusanello, DMD, is that they can be used in multiple seasons after the child's mouth has finished growing, are more comfortable, and allow an athlete to speak.

The American Academy of Pediatric Dentistry recommends a sports mouth guard for all youth competition, regardless of sport. The American Dental Association recommends mouth guards in the following sports: acrobatics, basketball, boxing, discus throwing, field hockey, football, gymnastics, handball, ice hockey, lacrosse, martial arts, racquetball, rugby, shot putting, skateboarding, skiing, skydiving, soccer, squash, surfing, volleyball, water polo, weight lifting, and wrestling.

Goal Safety Tips
- *Children should NEVER move goals*
- *Anchor soccer goals at ALL times*
- *Pad soccer goals*
- *When out of use anchor or chain one goal to another and lie in the down position*
- *Remove nets when goals are not in use.*

Helmet Protection in Sports

The Consumer Product Safety Commission estimates bicyclists sustained approximately 151,000 head injuries (defined as injuries to the head, ears, mouth, eyes, or face) in 2004 requiring emergency room treatment, skateboarders about 18,000, horseback riders around 14,000, snowboarders 8,540. There were 52,000 such injuries in football, almost 6,000 in ice hockey, and over 63,000 in baseball. Helmets should be used for all types of wheel sports such as bicycling, scooter riding, and inline skating. Also for horseback riding, rock- and wall-climbing, baseball, softball and T-ball, football, ice hockey, lacrosse, skiing, snowboarding, and sledding. The 2002 death of Penn State pole vaulter Kevin Dare, and two other young pole vaulters that same year, prompted several states and state high school federations to pass laws or rules requiring high school athletes to wear helmets while pole vaulting. In May 2006, ASTM International (formerly the American Society for Testing and Materials) issued a pole vaulting helmet standard.

REDUCING INJURIES FROM FIELDS OR EQUIPMENT

Countless thousands of children are injured each year as a result of unsafe fields and equipment.

According to the Consumer Product Safety Commission, at least twenty-nine fatalities and forty-nine major injuries nationwide during the period 1979–2004 have been linked to unanchored or portable soccer goals, four deaths in 2004 alone. If your child plays soccer, make sure the goals are properly anchored, so your child or any other mother's child doesn't become a statistic like Zachary Tran. In addition, soccer goals should be padded to reduce the risk of injuries, particularly to goalies.

If your child plays baseball, make sure the league uses breakaway bases, which the Little League Baseball organization will mandate as of the 2008 season. According to orthopedic surgeon Dr. David Janda, the use of breakaway bases may prevent or lessen the severity of the 6,600 base-contact sliding injuries that are suffered each year in organized baseball.

If your child plays any outdoor field sports, make sure the field is safe. (One-quarter of all soccer injuries are the result of poor field conditions, for example.) Don't leave it to the referee to check the field for holes, puddles, broken glass, and stones or other debris. Be proactive, setting up a field detail:

❖ **Before the game.** Have a parent check the condition of the field, remove debris, and eliminate any hazards, and check to see that the soccer goals are securely anchored and padded and that there are no jagged edges.

❖ **After the game.** When the game is over, ask the players and parents to make sure that the field is clean and free of debris by removing all litter from the field, sidelines, and around the player benches.

❖ **Set up a schedule.** Assigning field detail to the parent bringing the water and orange slices to the game probably makes the most sense.

❖ **Enlist coaches and players.** Before starting practice or pregame drills, the coach should check the field from corner to corner (including the goals). The players can help, too. That way they will learn how important it is to have a clean and safe playing surface.

❖ **For indoor courts:** Check to make sure all water spills are dried before playing on basketball, squash, etc. courts.

REDUCING WEATHER-RELATED INJURIES

About four hundred children and adults in the United States are struck by lightning each year. Of those, about eighty die, and most of the rest are left with permanent disabilities. While not all of these tragedies occurred during a sports activity, many of those that did could have been prevented. Finishing a youth sports contest is not worth death or crippling injury. Here's what you can do as a parent to protect your child from suffering a weather-related injury:

❖ Learn about lightning and how to prevent being hit.

❖ Ask your child's club or league to establish and enforce a policy for

- *NEVER allow anyone to climb on the net or goal framework.*
- *Apply safety/ warning labels in clear site*
- *Fully disassemble goals for seasonal storage.*
- *Movable soccer goals should only be used on flat fields.*

every practice and game in the event of bad weather. Volunteer to be the "weather watcher."

❖ If the club won't set a policy, suggest to the coach at the first preseason parents' meeting (see chapter 11) that he or she agree to follow a set weather policy.

❖ Educate your kids. You not only need to educate your son's or daughter's coach, club, and league, but your own kids need to understand the policy.

❖ When all else fails, establish your own family weather policy. I educated my sons about the dangers of playing sports during an electrical storm after a thirteen-year-old neighbor was killed by lightning because he did not leave the baseball field soon enough during a thunderstorm. Be sure to explain in advance to your child the circumstances that will prompt you to take him off a playing field out of fear for his safety, even if the coach won't. If you need to take your child off the field, choose your words carefully so as not to insult the coach or embarrass your child. Remember, no matter what, your child's safety is more important than any game. If you can't be at the game, mention your personal policy to another parent or caregiver.

REDUCING OVERUSE INJURIES BY SETTING PARTICIPATION LIMITS

As noted earlier, nearly half of the injuries children suffer each year playing sports are overuse injuries. Some of the blame rests with parents following a "more is better, earlier is better" philosophy. All too often, parents feel that unless they buy into this mind-set their kid will be left in the dust by more ambitious parents.

There are a number of commonsense steps you can take to reduce the risk of overuse injuries. First, before you let your child play on two or even three teams in the same sport at the same time or specialize in a sport, consider that while all those extra practices and games may help her achieve athletic success over the short term, all the extra wear and tear on her body may lead to overuse injuries years later. As a 2004 public service campaign by the National Athletic Trainers' Association and the American Academy of Orthopaedic Surgeons asks parents, "What will they have longer, their trophies or their injuries?"

Second, set limits. Your child is far less likely to suffer an overuse injury if he takes off at least three months a year from sports, and practices and plays no more than twelve hours per week in any one sport or twenty hours per week for multiple sports (because different muscles are used).

ENCOURAGING YOUR CHILD NOT TO PLAY INJURED

Prompted by self- or externally imposed pressure to keep playing so as not to disappoint parents, or a fear that if he admits to an injury, he will lose his place on the team, a youth athlete may keep his injuries to himself, sometimes with tragic consequences.

A sixteen-year-old baseball player who had to undergo so-called Tommy John reconstructive surgery on his elbow after starting *sixty-four* games one summer for a travel baseball team recently told the *New York Times* that his arm hurt for years, but he never went to a doctor: "You know, like they say, you play with pain. If you are a good pitcher on a team of fourteen- or fifteen-year-olds, you're going to be throwing too much." Looking back, he said, "I'm the living example of someone who did too much. I would tell young kids coming up now, 'Don't be such a hero. Take a rest. I look back now at all those games I won when I was fourteen or fifteen. They weren't worth it."

GUARDING AGAINST ANTIBIOTIC-RESISTANT STAPH INFECTIONS

In October 2003, health and sports officials, including the National Federation of State High School Associations, the Centers for Disease Control and Prevention, and the NCAA, all issued warnings about an antibiotic-resistant skin infection once common to hospitals and prisons but now being seen in those playing close-contact sports, such as wrestling and

By the Numbers:

- Number of children ages 14 and under suffering sports injuries serious enough to require medical treatment: 3.5 million per year
- Number of days of school lost by children ages 5–22 sustaining sports injuries: 20 million per year
- Annual cost of health care for children injured playing youth sports: 12 billion
- Percentage of avoidable sports-related injuries in children ages 5–22: 90

football. The contagious staph infection, methicillin-resistant staphylococcus aureus (MRSA), while usually mild, can in advanced cases result in a life-threatening blood or bone infection, as some strains carry a toxin that destroys white blood cells. Treatment with penicillin-related antibiotics is ineffective.

Because the infection often looks like an ordinary skin wound or boil (other signs are fever, pus, swelling, or pain), diagnosis is difficult, and it is important that, as a parent, you are aware that MRSA might be the cause. In addition to steps that can be taken by sports programs and coaches, the CDC says you can help to prevent the spread of staph infections and protect your child from sports-related skin infections by encouraging him to practice good hygiene (no sharing of towels or other personal items, showering and washing with antimicrobial soap after every practice or tournament); laundering uniforms, athletic supporters, and sports bras separately after each use; and for wounds that appear infected, taking your child to a doctor and getting a culture. When you do, make sure to tell your child's doctor that your child plays sports and that you are concerned about CA-MRSA (community-acquired methicillin-resistant staphylococcus aureus).

WATCHING FOR SIGNS OF THE FEMALE ATHLETE TRIAD

In 1992, the American College of Sports Medicine first recognized that girls and women in sports are particularly susceptible to three conditions that have come to be known as the female athlete triad: disordered eating, menstrual irregularity, and osteoporosis.

Disordered eating Contrary to popular belief, eating disorders are not limited to classic eating disorders (anorexia and bulimia), but occur on a spectrum ranging from calorie, protein, and/or fat restriction, and weight control measures (diet pills, laxatives, excessive and compulsive exercise in addition to normal training regimen, self-induced vomiting) to full-blown anorexia and bulimia.

Depending on the survey, eating disorders are thought to affect anywhere from 15 to 62 percent of girls. Among teens and younger children, disordered eating has reached "epidemic levels," according to researchers at the National Association of Anorexia Nervosa and Associated Disorders. A ten-year study revealed that some 7 million U.S. females and 1 million males have eating disorders, and that 10 percent reported that disorders began in elementary school, with some children as young as seven or eight preoccupied and dissatisfied with body image and weight. Indeed, fully 40 percent of nine-year-olds in one Harvard study reported dissatisfaction with body shape and as a remedy turned to dieting.

Anorexia is a condition in which a child's diet does not allow him or her to maintain his or her weight within 15 percent of the mean for children of their age and height. Remember: daily requirements for calories, carbohydrates, and protein are greater for athletes. The warning signs of anorexia are:

❖ Sudden weight loss or gain

❖ Distorted body image

❖ Obsession with weighing oneself

❖ Avoidance of social eating (i.e., a child who likes to eat alone)

❖ Preoccupation with food and dieting and an unreasonable fear of being fat

❖ Hair loss

❖ Intolerance to cold

❖ Obsessive exercising

Bulimia is when a child engages in binge eating (i.e., eating too much uncontrollably in one sitting) and then purging (vomiting, exercising

- *Youth football related deaths in 2004: 17*
- *Number of children under age 20 paralyzed while playing football in 2004: 16*
- *Percentage of injuries occur during practices, not games: 62*
- *Number of states requiring an athletic trainer for each high school: 15*

intensely) to get rid of the food just eaten. The following are warning signs of bulimia:

- ❖ Frequent use of bathroom after eating
- ❖ Fluctuating weight
- ❖ Bloodshot eyes
- ❖ Swollen glands
- ❖ Swollen extremities
- ❖ Discolored teeth (i.e., eroded tooth enamel from frequent vomiting)
- ❖ Feelings of depression, guilt, or shame about eating
- ❖ Suicide attempts
- ❖ Drug use
- ❖ Aches and pains
- ❖ Dramatic fluctuations in athletic performance
- ❖ Loss of concentration in schoolwork and athletics

Disordered eating results in serious health problems, some of which are potentially fatal, including heart problems such as irregular heartbeat, muscle weakness or fatigue, fainting, irreversible bone loss, and electrolyte imbalance. The mortality rate in severe cases can be as high as 10–15 percent from heart failure, hormonal imbalances, or suicide.

Those at risk of disordered eating. Though seen in all sports, those at greatest risk are those engaged in:

- ❖ A single sport on a year-round basis (see chapter 2 for reasons why early specialization is a bad idea)
- ❖ An endurance sport (long-distance running, swimming, cross-country skiing, rowing, kayaking)

- ❖ A sport demanding a thin physical appearance (gymnastics, ice skating, ballet dancing, diving)

- ❖ A sport with weight classifications (wrestling, martial arts, rowing)

The personality of an elite athlete and the personality of one prone to eating disorders have a lot in common: an addictive/compulsive personality, a strong desire to do well/achieve perfection (or have parents who are perfectionists), a high desire to please other people, a desire to push oneself to the limit and to work through pain without letting anyone know. In other words, disordered eating in athletes presents a classic chicken-or-egg question: Do sports create eating disorders or do sports attract girls who are already prone to eating disorders?

Girls are also sent conflicting messages by our culture and, as I discussed in chapter 4, by their peers: that it is acceptable for them to participate in sports, but they also need to maintain the figure of a supermodel. The effect of societal pressure to be thin combined with similar pressures in sports may be a higher incidence of disordered eating behaviors and body-shaping drug use (tobacco, diet pills, diuretics, laxatives, amphetamines, and anabolic steroids) in athletic girls.

Menstrual irregularity, or amenorrhea. Healthy weight is important for normal estrogen levels. When a female athlete's weight drops to an unhealthy level (i.e., when the percentage of body fat falls below 17–18 percent), either through disordered eating and/or intense training, menstruation may not start, may become irregular, or stop altogether. It is a myth that the absence of menses simply proves that a female athlete is training hard, and that amenorrhea is a *positive* adaptation of girls to exercise.

A girl is deemed to have primary amenorrhea if she has not begun to menstruate within four and a half years after onset of breast development (menstruation usually begins between ages twelve and fifteen for nonathletic females and thirteen to fifteen and a half for athletes). A girl who has not gotten her period for three to six months, menstruates irregularly or with very light flow, or at intervals longer than thirty-five days is considered to have secondary amenorrhea.

"I started talking about my experiences, and all of a sudden I just blurted out about my bulimia, which I'd never discussed with anyone else before. I had always felt so ashamed. It was such a relief to finally start talking. I always feel there's a reason things happen, and for me the reason wasn't winning all those medals. It was to be able to share my experiences, the good and the bad, with other people who may be going through what I went through."

—DARA TORRES, WHO OVERCAME BULIMIA IN **2000** TO BECOME THE FIRST U.S. SWIMMER, MALE OR FEMALE, TO SWIM IN FOUR OLYMPICS, PROFILED IN *SUPERWOMEN*

Amenorrhea affects girls competing in all sports, but is most prevalent in competitive female gymnasts, 90 percent of whom get their periods a year or two late. Because a female's body needs estrogen to absorb calcium for strong bones, not enough estrogen can cause bones to lose thickness and strength, resulting in a greater risk of stress fractures and osteoporosis. Research suggests that even minor forms of menstrual dysfunction may adversely effect bone density and lead to at least partially irreversible bone loss, although the silver lining to delayed menstruation is that it may lower a girl's risk of developing certain estrogen-related cancers.

Osteoporosis. A girl's teen years are a critical time for developing normal, strong bones as they are the years in which girls add half of their bone mass. Only 10 percent of bone mass is produced after age twenty. Too much exercise can affect bone mass and density, leaving a female athlete prone to increased risk of stress fractures if a girl is not having regular periods and does not have normal estrogen levels. And later in life, increased chance of ostoeporosis.

Prevention. First and foremost, a proper balance of exercise, body weight, calcium intake (1,500 mg of calcium if irregular periods, 1,200 mg if regular). Vitamin D (400 IUs daily) and estrogen are critical to prevent osteoporosis. If necessary, you should take your daughter to a dietician or nutritionist who works with adolescent athletes.

Second, to screen for the triad, make sure your daughter has a preparticipation evaluation. It is essential that in taking the medical history your daughter's pediatrician asks questions about nutrition, menstruation, evidence of bone mineral loss (stress fractures; dual energy X-ray absorptiometry scan, or DEXA), and body image. An abnormal menstrual history can be a red flag for eating disorders and psychological issues. Your daughter should keep track of her periods.

Third, as a parent you should avoid pressuring your daughter to achieve an unrealistically low body weight, such as by comments about appearance, good or bad foods, dieting and nutrition (this advice holds true for your sons as well, particularly swimmers and wrestlers). You should be wary of coaches who conduct out-of-competition weigh-ins or measurement of body fat, especially public ones, which can highlight for teenage girls the already sensitive issue of their weight. (One prominent Southern California swim club that counts among its alumnae numerous Olympic gold medal winners labeled members with what it deemed too high a body fat ratio as members of the "Blub Club.") Because girls tend to internalize criticism more than boys, if the coach is critical of her weight, he or she can have a negative effect on a female athlete's self-esteem.

Fourth, if you suspect that your daughter exhibits symptoms of one or more elements of the triad, let her know that you want to help but that you can't keep the matter a secret, nor can you solve the problem on your own. If she is found to have disordered eating, experts recommend a multidisciplinary approach to treatment (medical doctor, nutritionist, mental health professional). Above all, be patient.

EDUCATE YOUR CHILD ABOUT THE DANGERS OF ANABOLIC STEROID USE

The federal Centers for Disease Control and Prevention reported in 2003 that 850,000 high school students admitted to using anabolic steroids (not to be confused with benefical steroids such as those used to treat severe asthma attacks). From 1993 to 2006, steroid use among high school students has risen from one in forty-five athletes to one in sixteen. Steroids use is not limited to boys: A recent national study reported that as many as 175,000 high school girls had used steroids at least once in their lives.

While steroid use leads to increased lean body mass, strength, and muscle definition and decreases the recovery time from exercise, it also can have serious long-term side effects, some of which may not be apparent until after a longtime abuser's playing days are over.

Most users simply believe, naively, that they will not suffer any adverse side effects. Others take steroids to improve their self-esteem. Males may use steroids because, like anorexic women who think of themselves as fat even when they are thin, they see themselves as little and weak even if they are very muscular, a phenomenon dubbed by one expert as the "Adonis complex."

If you suspect your child is using—or considering the use—of steroids, explain that not only is such use illegal but it is *very, very dangerous*. Explain to your child that steroids can adversely affect the following:

❖ Liver

  ● Jaundice (yellowing of skin and eyes)

  ● Hepatitis

  ● Liver tumor

  ● Cancer

  ● Peliosis hepatitis (blood-filled cysts in the liver)

❖ Cardiovascular system

  ● Coronary artery disease

  ● Heart arrhythmia

  ● Decreased HDL (good cholesterol)

  ● Increased LDL (bad cholesterol)

  ● Heart attack

  ● Abnormal blood clotting

  ● Hypertension (high blood pressure)

  ● Stroke

❖ Male reproductive system

  ● Decreased testicular size

  ● Sterility

  ● Prostate gland disorders

- Increased breast development (gynecomastia)

- Increased nipple size

- Changes in sex drive (usually up then down)

❖ Female reproductive system

- Amenorrhea (disruption or cessation of menstrual cycle)

- Shrinkage of breast tissue

- Clitoral enlargement (irreversible)

- Deepening of voice (irreversible)

- Excessive hair growth (irreversible)

- Male pattern baldness (irreversible)

❖ Psychological effects

- Aggression

- Anger

- Hostility

- Irritability

- Restlessness

- Violence

- Paranoia

- Hallucinations

- Delusions

- Depression (often accompanied by suicidal thoughts)

- Major mood swings

- Males taking steroids can experience anorexia nervosa

❖ Other ailments

  • Severe acne

  • Kidney tumors (rare)

  • Degeneration of tendons (a common problem due to the tremendous increases in muscle strength and size)

  • Stunting of growth in children and adolescents

  • Increased fluid retention (leading to swelling in the face)

  • Headaches

  • Dizziness

  • Nosebleeds

  • Stomachaches

  • Urinary and bowel problems

  • Hair loss

  • Insomnia

  • Altered thyroid function

  • HIV/AIDS (sharing dirty needles)

  • Weakening of the immune system

  • Death

If you suspect your child is using steroids, here is what to look for:

❖ Large gain of muscle mass over a short period of time (twenty pounds of muscle gained over a summer by a high school athlete is usually not the result of weight training alone)

❖ Increased time spent in the gym and a preoccupation with weight training

❖ Dramatic changes in personality (moodiness, aggression, and hostility, etc.)

❖ Abnormally large breasts in males (gynecomastia)

❖ Stretch marks (cutaneous striae), especially around the breast area

❖ Increased acne, especially on the back, face, and chest

❖ Facial puffiness due to water retention

❖ Needle marks on the buttocks

❖ Increased blood pressure and heart rate

❖ Reference to steroids in conversation (some of the slang words for steroids include "roids," "juice," "sauce," "slop," "product" and "vitamins")

The three main warning signs are acne, gynecomastia, and cutaneous striae. If all three are present, it is highly likely that your child is using steroids.

Help: Safe Alternatives The alternatives to steroid use are proper nutrition, weight and aerobic training, and sports injury care. Athletes need to know that they can achieve tremendous results with these methods. Most athletes have.

Not only should you talk to your child, but you should consider asking your school system to implement the ATLAS (Athletes Training and Learning to Avoid Steroids) and ATHENA (Athletes Targeting Healthy Exercise and Nutrition Alternatives) programs to combat steroid use. National federally funded programs developed at the Oregon Health & Science University in Portland, ATLAS and ATHENA are designed to prevent young high school athletes' disordered eating and body-shaping drug use through peer-led educational workshops. The ATLAS program for boys has been shown to cut new use of anabolic steroids in half and lower the incidence of drinking and driving by 24 percent. Girls in the ATHENA program report less ongoing and new diet pill use and less new use of athletic-enhancing, body shaping substances; significant positive changes in dietary habits; greater self-efficacy for exercise training; better ability to control their mood; less belief in the media and enhanced resistance skills; and reduced intentions for future disordered eating habits and body-shaping drug use. Program participants were also less likely to ride in a car with an alcohol-consuming driver or be sexually active, and more likely to use seat belts. The incidence of sports injuries was also reduced.

ASTHMA

Nearly 5 million children in this country suffer from asthma. Without immediate treatment to keep a child's airways from constricting, asthma can be fatal. Even if only mildly asthmatic, kids can suffer fatal asthma attacks playing sports. A report in the February 2004 issue of the *Journal of Allergy and Clinical Immunology* found that sixty-one confirmed asthma deaths occurred during the seven-and-a-half-year study period; white males between ten and twenty are most at risk; deaths of whites outnumbered blacks by almost two to one; twice as many males died as females; and basketball and track accounted for more asthma deaths than any other sport, but fatalities also occurred in football, swimming, and cheerleading (asthmatics playing any aerobic sport are at risk).

Despite the risks, asthma shouldn't keep your child out of sports. With proper precautions, they can play. Here are some tips:

❖ Make sure your child—or his coach—has his rescue inhaler at all times.

❖ Make sure your child's asthma is stable. If he is up during the night coughing and wheezing, it is probably not a good idea for him to play sports the next day.

❖ If your child needs his rescue medication before a game and once during the game, that's okay. If he needs to use it a third time, do not allow him to continue to play.

Safety Checklist

✓ *Make sport-specific first-aid kits*

✓ *Make sure an emergency medical plan is in place*

✓ *Create a strong chain of survival to protect against SCD, including use of revised CPR guidelines*

✓ *Initiate regular preparticipation evaluations to identify congenital heart problems, neurological abnormalities from multiple concussions, and signs of the female athlete triad*

✓ *Follow return-to-play guidelines to avoid SIS*

✓ *Ensure proper hydration to avoid heat illness*

✓ *Require use of appropriate safety equipment (mouth guard, protective eyewear, helmets, sunscreen)*

✓ *Ensure fields are safe (anchored and padded goalposts, breakaway bases, proper lighting, no debris, etc.)*

✓ *Set participation limits to avoid overuse injuries*

✓ *Require preseason conditioning (especially important for girls)*

✓ *Teach the importance of stretching, warm-ups, and cooldowns*

✓ *Take precautions against staph infections (washing, separate washing of uniforms)*

✓ *Recognize the signs of female athlete triad*

✓ *Teach the dangers of steroid use*

✓ *Take precautions for the asthmatic child*

Part 2

Sports Mothers,
Coaches, and
Other Parents

Chapter Ten

Put Me In, Coach!
The Signs of a Good Youth Sports Coach

To laugh often and much; to win the respect of intelligent people and the affection of children . . . to leave the world a better place . . . to know even one life has breathed easier because you have lived. This is to have succeeded.

—RALPH WALDO EMERSON

WHO WAS THAT GUY, ANYWAY?

Peter was a former high school and college soccer star. After he coached my sons' indoor soccer team one winter, and based on recommendations from other coaches, I asked him to be my assistant coach on a team I had been invited to take to an international sportsmanship tournament in St. Andrews, Scotland, the following summer.

At a tune-up tournament over Memorial Day weekend, Peter exhibited some disturbing behavior, challenging the opposing coach to a fight on the sidelines during one game and getting ejected in another. I also began to see in Peter an emphasis on winning completely at odds with my coaching philosophy and goals for the team. Even though the players' families were paying the kids' way to Scotland and despite my promise that everyone would get roughly equal playing time, Peter informed me that the "best" eleven or twelve players would get the lion's share of the playing time during the tournament and the other six or seven players were likely to see little action and spend most of the time on the bench.

Increasingly worried that I had made a mistake in taking Peter on as an assistant, I finally decided to follow the suggestions of several parents (and my intuition as a mother) and ask around about Peter. I learned about several incidents in Peter's past which raised concerns about his character and whether he was an appropriate role model for the players.

Armed with the information, I pulled Peter aside and asked him if there was anything in his background I should know about. He immediately flew into such a rage that had I not asked the question in the middle of a soccer field with parents and players looking on, I would have feared for my safety. Rather than agree to my request for a copy of his police record, Peter quit the team on the spot.

The next day, Peter told me he had reconsidered and wanted his job back as assistant coach. I told him I would consider reinstating him, but only if he could act like a mature adult, answer my questions about his background, and accept that, whether he liked it or not, I would be following an equal playing time rule, even if it meant we lost every game in Scotland. When he refused to sit in the same room with me to discuss my concerns and coaching philosophy, I knew that as a parent and a coach I could not run the risk that Peter might pose to the psychological health of the players if I allowed him to come to Scotland with us.

Initially impressed with Peter's own high school and college playing record, I had almost fallen victim to the all-too-common myth that a good athlete automatically makes a good coach. Unless they have had coaching training, former athletes tend to teach kids as they were taught at the high school or college level and are often ill-equipped to impart their knowledge to kids in an age-appropriate way.

CRITICAL ROLE OF COACHES

There is no doubt that the people who coach our children's sports team can make the difference between a positive experience, one they will remember fondly for the rest of their lives, and a negative one, one that can leave emotional and psychological scars that don't ever go away and turn them off to sports forever. Coaches have a complex and difficult task, yet a wonderful opportunity to hold a place in a child's heart for that child's lifetime.

WHY COACHES COACH

There are really only a few reasons why coaches coach. Some played the sport and want to give something back to the game they love. Some are natural teachers who enjoy working with children and see coaching as an opportunity to teach life lessons, develop skills, and be a role model. Some are coaching to fulfill a community service obligation imposed by a court or their school. Some coach to make extra money. Some, particularly at the select team level, are professional coaches. But most—some estimates run as high as 85–90 percent—are motivated to coach because they have a child in the program.

Over the thirteen years my sons played sports, they had an assortment of coaches with different personalities, coaching techniques, philosophies, and approaches. Some were child centered, some were coach centered. Some "safety comes first" coaches postponed games at the sound of approaching thunder. Others insisted that kids remain on a baseball diamond while lightning flashed nearby. Some were coaches who developed every player by giving them equal playing time. Some sat out eight-year-olds for most of the game. Some were coaches who had been trained in the sport they were coaching; some coaches did not know all the rules or equipment requirements. A few coaches knew about child development and gender differences. While coaches come in all shapes and sizes, with different types of personalities, a good coach is:

Trained both in coaching youth athletes and the sport he is coaching. He has shown his commitment to coaching in the following ways:

❖ By becoming educated (better yet, certified) in the sports he is coaching and about child development

❖ By keeping his coaching skills current, such as by attending coaching workshops

❖ By acquiring a thorough understanding of the rules of the game so he can teach the sport correctly (remember: the rules may have been modified for children)

❖ By watching and learning from other coaches

Teaches, models, and demands respectful behavior. A recent study revealed that there is a high probability on most teams that one or more of the lesser skilled players will be bullied or teased by a more skilled teammate. Good coaches are alert to the possibility of bullying and proactively seek ways to reduce it. Similarly, a good coach teaches and models respect for the opposing team.

Coaches should also model appropriate behavior toward officials, but more than four in ten admitted in a 2005 study that they had yelled angrily at an official. Coaches should neither yell at officials nor permit their players to do so.

Models fairness. Coaches model fairness by:

❖ Treating every player (including her own child) the same

❖ Employing an equal playing time (through sixth grade) or meaningful minutes (through high school subvarsity) rule

❖ Applying team rules to all players, whether the child is a natural athlete and never shows up for practice or a less talented player who always shows up for practice

❖ Recognizing an obligation to develop the so-called weaker players at least as much if not more than stronger ones

Requires proper sideline behavior by parents. A recent study established what the media has been telling us for years: parents are indeed misbehaving on the sideline. Coaches need to stress not only the importance to parents of attending games, but of appropriate sideline behavior: applauding all players, and not yelling at players, coaches, or officials.

Sets realistic, age-appropriate expectations. All too often coaches do not clearly understand critical child development milestones and that large physical and psychological differences, even among children the same age, are common. A coach shouldn't try to push a child to do something for which he is not developmentally ready, like specializing too early. As Tony DiCicco and Colleen Hacker say in *Catch Them Being Good*, coaches should challenge their players "to stretch them individually and collectively" with the "demands placed on players . . . carefully balanced between their actual skills and abilities."

Understands that coaching girls is different from coaching boys. As Dr. Leonard Sax notes *Why Gender Matters*, the "innate, biologically programmed differences between girls and boys" lead them to take the playing field, "as they enter the classroom with different needs, different abilities, and different goals."

A supportive, nonconfrontational approach usually works better with girls. Studies have shown that stress impairs learning in females, with moderate stress degrading young girls' performance. (This is why, according to Dr. Sax, girls on average don't do quite as well on standardized tests, such as the SAT, as one would expect based on their grades; moderate stress actually *improves* the performance of boys.) Girls' coaches have players help one another relax before the big game.

For many girls, the social and more emotional aspects of sports are more important than skills, and thus girls are more likely than boys to look to their coach as an ally and a friend, particularly at the middle school and high school level, and seek her advice about personal matters totally unrelated to sports. Because girls have a harder time than boys competing against one another, they need to be able to support and get along with their teammates in order for the team to function. Girls need to feel that the other girls on the team don't view themselves as better athletes. The coach doesn't single girls out as stars. She gives girls plenty of opportunities for team camaraderie to allow them to enjoy the social aspects of sports.

When working out a problem, a girls' coach knows to smile and look her player in the eye, which reassures her that she is a good person. She empowers her players by putting herself in her player's place to validate her feelings. Because girls have better hearing than boys, a coach of a girls' team modulates her voice and avoids yelling (of course, a coach shouldn't be yelling at boys either).

Avoids reinforcing culturally based gender stereotypes. A boys' coach doesn't tell the players to suppress their emotions (contrary to Tom Hanks's famous line in *A League of Their Own*, there *is* crying in baseball). Indeed, he encourages emotional openness. He doesn't motivate boys by engaging in gay- or girl-bashing, such as by asking a boy who isn't displaying what he deems the appropriate level of aggression in football, "Do you want to trade in your shoulder pads for a training bra?" He doesn't act like a drill sergeant or treat young athletes like warriors in battle. He doesn't believe that sports is a place for "boys to become men," or push players to be tough and play with an injury.

Is patient, stays calm, and never loses his cool. Patience and self-control are essential in teaching kids new skills, coaching games, and dealing with parents and officials. But while they may be among the most important attributes a coach can have, according to a 2005 study by researchers at the Universities of Missouri-St. Louis, Minnesota, and Notre Dame, they appear to be the ones in the shortest supply among America's youth sports coaches.

One of my sons' soccer coaches was suspended for the rest of the season for threatening a referee after receiving a red card for dissent. Coaches should be able to accept bad calls by umpires, refs, and other sports officials (remember, most of them are volunteers, too) and mistakes by players without a public display of emotion or of dissatisfaction. A coach who makes things tense by his yelling and shouting creates an atmosphere that is not conducive to learning and having fun.

Doesn't intrude on the learning process. The best youth sports coaches don't unnecessarily intrude on the learning process during practices and games. They don't script every moment of practice or micromanage. They aren't running around during practice constantly blowing a whistle or correcting players in a loud voice.

Knows when to teach. The best times for a coach to teach players are at practices, during time-outs, and after games. In general, the worst time to teach is during the competition itself. Instead, the coach should quietly observe his players during competitions and talk to them only during time-outs or breaks in the action, providing feedback using short, informative phrases, cues, or buzzwords to avoid overloading players with information. A coach who is always yelling instructions from the sidelines makes it impossible for the team to focus on playing the game.

Emphasizes the positive. Coaches who constantly point out and correct a player's mistakes end up intimidating players and make them afraid to take chances or be creative. Making a child cry is not the most effective form of motivation. Constructive criticism should be given between positive statements, with specific praise offered for effort and demonstrated improvement (general praise is meaningless, even annoying to players). Anecdotal evidence collected from coaches by the Positive Coaching Alliance demonstrates that team performance improves when coaches drop negative coaching techniques such as intimidation and humiliation and replace them with more positive methods.

Adjusts his coaching style to fit the individual and team. Like a good teacher, the coach gets to know his players as individuals; is sensitive to their needs, both in sports and their personal lives; understands what works and doesn't work to motivate an individual player to do his or her best; and helps them learn new skills. By being child- rather than adult-centered, he allows every player to express his or her individuality and realize his or her full potential.

Makes practices fun. He uses a games-based (i.e., "organized sandlot") approach to practices which deemphasizes structured drills. Because kids get bored easily, he keeps all players involved and busy whenever possible, setting up several stations where players can do drills or games at the same time while always moving (see sidebar).

Teaches that sports are about having fun. He provides a framework, through practices and competition, for a positive sports experience: a fun atmosphere in which athletic skills, meaningful relationships, and social skills (conflict resolution, communication, putting team goals above personal goals) are developed. Athletes should be laughing, even at age eighteen.

~~~~~~~~~~~~~~~~~~~~~~

The Play's the Thing

A litter of wild kittens and their mother were living in a brush pile in the foundation of an old barn behind our garage. Through a window in the garage I watched the kittens play as their mother sat watching on a nearby stone wall. As the days turned to weeks, I couldn't help notice how comfortable and happy the kittens seemed to be. They developed a sense of balance that I had never seen in the dozens of domesticated kittens I have had in my life. I realized that they had become better climbers because their mother had given them the freedom to learn. And what I truly noticed was how relaxed she was as her litter scrambled about. She was calm because her kittens were happy and becoming successful climbers.

It's a lesson that applies to youth sports. Sometimes the best way for a coach to teach is to step back from the field and just let the kids be kids and have fun. Like a kitten, a child has no other "job" than to play. Just as the mother cat was content to watch her kittens play, I have found the most enjoyment coaching when I am able to watch the team laughing, playing, and having fun. If the team is not happy or having fun during practices and games, then what's the point?

Some of the best practices my teams have ever had were those where I followed a "games-based" teaching approach—where I stepped off the field and told the team to take over the practice and do what they wanted, to organize the practice themselves, just so long as they had fun. They would usually decide to play a skill game, one of about twenty-five that I use to develop skills without drilling. The only time I stepped in is when I saw that a certain skill could be taught in order to help the play.

If your child is allowed to have fun, she will be eager to go to practice, not just games. Success in a sport is partly a function of a player's desire to succeed. The motivation to succeed depends on how much the player loves the sport and is able to enjoy it in all its aspects.

Teaches that sports are about sportsmanship and playing fair. Coaches of nine- to fifteen-year-old athletes in the 2005 Missouri-Minnesota-Notre Dame study indicated a very high level of agreement with the statement "Teaching sportsmanship is a major part of a coach's job." They also agreed strongly with the statement "Coaches have a responsibility to help members of their team become better people, not just better athletes."

Yet many coaches appear to be doing a poor job of teaching sportsmanship and moral reasoning. As Michael Josephson, head of the Josephson Institute of Ethics, notes, "Too many youngsters are confused about the meaning of fair play and sportsmanship and . . . have no concept of honorable competition. As a result they engage in illegal conduct and employ doubtful gamesmanship techniques to gain a competitive advantage." In an environment in which winning is paramount, children may internalize the value that it is acceptable to do anything to win, even if it means cheating, bullying teammates, breaking the rules, intentionally injuring an opponent, or faking an injury to get a time-out.

Part of the problem may also be our culture—a society in which too many professional athletes exhibit poor sportsmanship—so it's even more paramount that coaches, parents, officials, and youth sports organizations do a better job of teaching moral behavior to athletes.

As a society we would not find it acceptable if teachers encouraged their students to cheat on tests. Youth sports should be no different. Programs to teach athletes moral ethics and to help coaches teach moral ethics should be instituted or expanded in every community to teach decision making, sportsmanship, competitive integrity, leadership, justice, and competitive responsibility. The programs should include such topics as leadership, fair play, teamwork, respecting opposing players, cheating, and the consequences of off-the-field behavior.

Defines success in sports more broadly than just winning. A good coach keeps winning in perspective and places the emphasis on self-improvement, mastering skills, creating community, and achieving personal and team goals. Instead of viewing competition exclusively as a matter of winning and losing, he understands that opponents are cocreators of a sporting experience and that competition is a process of striving *with*, not *against*, others to do everyone's best. He doesn't play only the "best" players (see below) or exploit loopholes just to win, such as telling his players not to swing the bat in order to draw walks from a wild pitcher. He doesn't forfeit a game just because he doesn't like the way the umpire calls balls and strikes.

Ensuring Equal Playing Time with a Substitution Grid

At the youth level (up to grade six), coaches should put together a grid on a piece of paper before each game to show the players who will start and those who will substitute. Writing out the lineup in advance also makes it easier to move players around so they can play different positions. The grid needs to indicate at what minute or inning subs enter the game and their positions. A substitution grid is great because it allows the coach to concentrate on watching the game instead of trying to simultaneously keep track of how long each child has played.

A preprinted grid can help set up a balanced lineup with a mix of more and less skilled players and ensure that everyone gets to start an equal number of games. Copies can be given to parents so they know when they could take a break to push younger kids on the swings or run to the bathroom.

Following an equal playing time rule creates a win-win situation for:

✓ **The players.** *All the players have more fun and aren't resentful or jealous of one another because they know they are being treated equally. They play together more as a team, are less selfish, and feel less pressure to excel in order to earn more playing time.*

✓ **The parents.** *They know in advance that their child will be getting the same amount of playing time as every other player.*

✓ **The coach.** *An equal playing time rule eliminates two of a coach's major headaches: the pestering from players to "put me in coach. I'm ready to play!" and the complaints from parents that their son or daughter isn't getting enough playing time.*

Looks for team-building opportunities. A good coach looks for chances to help her players bond as an effective and cohesive team by, for example, holding team parties, going to high school games together as a team, team car washes, and encouraging high fives, rally caps, and "dog piles." I used to bring a cooler with Popsicles and other frozen goodies for break time during practices. It is the little things that go such a long way in bringing a group together.

Is sociable, empathetic, and a good communicator. In the ideal world your child's coach will be someone who is a good two-way communicator. He is someone your child feels he can talk to, who is open and friendly (when he talks to her, does he get down on her eye level?), someone with whom your child can connect one-on-one, who doesn't put up barriers to communication, such as clipboards, desks, or assistant coaches. A good coach polls her players to find out what is important to them and how games and practices could be more fun. She doesn't take things too seriously or make winning a matter of life or death; she can laugh at herself, take things in stride, maintain a positive attitude, and just let the kids be kids.

You should feel as a parent that you can talk to the coach about your child or the coach's philosophy and be *taken seriously*.

The coach should communicate frequently with athletes and their parents via meetings, e-mail, handouts, etc. (see a more detailed discussion of this topic in chapter 11); invite input from parents about practice schedules and the number of tournaments the team will enter; hold drop-in meetings for parents; and ask parents and players to complete postseason evaluations (youth sports programs should get this kind of feedback as a matter of course; see discussion on accountability in chapter 15). He is proactive, looking for signs of trouble with athletes or parents and coming up with ways to nip the problem in the bud. He genuinely listens to what players and parents say and tries to meet their needs, if possible. By listening, a good coach can better relate to his players and understand the true reason for a player's behavior, whether it is slacking off during practice or not performing to her ability in games. That way, the coach can come up with a way to motivate the player to perform at his best.

Is organized (but not too organized). A disorganized coach creates chaos, which can make the difference between a successful and an unsuccessful season. I found that three-ring binders with tabs for parent contact information, schedule, directions to away games, team roster, substitution grids, practice plans, notes about each player (allergies, etc.) were the key for staying organized. Before the season, the organized coach provides parents with schedules; directions to away games; e-mail addresses of coaches, players, and parents; and asks a parent to volunteer to be a team administrator, or what used to be called a "team mom" (see more on team administrators in chapter 13).

Is trained in first aid, CPR, use of an AED, and injury prevention and treatment. He refuses to jeopardize the health of an athlete in order to improve the team's chance of winning by asking a player to play while injured, strictly follows return-to-play guidelines for concussions (see chapter 9), avoids exposing athletes to overuse injuries by limiting the duration of practices to what is developmentally appropriate, and reduces the risk of injury by ensuring that athletes engage in warm-up and cool-down exercises.

Is child-centered. He understands that the game belongs to the players, not the coach or parents, and that the players and the game should be the focus, not the coach. A coach needs to periodically ask, whose sport is this? The answer should be the same every time: the athlete's. A coach is there to guide, motivate, help, teach, and inspire, not to control or to gratify his ego.

WARNING SIGNS

Are there coaches out there who meet all the criteria I have just outlined? Of course there are. But there are many coaches who are failing to teach and model ethical behavior and are physically, emotionally, and psychologically abusing children in their care, playing favorites, and placing winning ahead of having fun and skill development.

Some coaches are well-meaning but may not have the skills or personality to be a successful coach. They are easy to spot. But just because a coach appears to know what he is doing doesn't mean that he is a good coach. In particular, there are three kinds of coaches to watch out for:

The drill sergeant. Watch out for coaches who treat young athletes like warriors in battle, think that making a child cry is the most effective form of motivation, who believe sports is a place for "boys to become men," push players to be tough and play through pain and injury ("suck it up,") and never show emotion, or who try to motivate boys by engaging in gay- or girl-bashing.

The entrepreneur. Some coaches, especially at the elite level, are coaching for personal or financial gain and will do just about anything to win and get ahead, even if it means leading your child (and you) into believing that there is a scholarship or Olympic gold medal with his or her name on it if only he practiced more, took this or that nutritional supplement, attended a particular summer camp (usually one where he is an instructor), transferred to the school where he is a coach, or spent an extra year in middle school so he is older and bigger when he gets to high school ("redshirting"). Be on the lookout for coaches who use charm and flattery to make unrealistic claims about your child's talent.

The loose cannon. Be on the lookout for coaches who are constantly yelling or screaming, arguing with officials, exhibit rapid mood swings, are impulsive, have an inflated sense of their own importance, have an unhealthy need for admiration, exhibit an unhealthy lack of empathy, who turn on anyone who disappoints them, try to make you feel inadequate and question your credibility if you question their judgment, or are overly defensive and controlling about even minor matters. Look out for coaches who are constantly jumping from job to job, never staying for more than a season or two. This a sure sign of trouble ahead.

How to avoid bad coaches. The best way to protect your child from a bad coach is, of course, not to let him play for such a coach in the first place. Do whatever you think is reasonably necessary to find out about the coach before the season starts and there is still time, hopefully, to find him a place on another team. Talk to parents of athletes who have played for him. Ask them if you can talk to their children to get their perspective. Find out if any complaints have been filed against him with the club or league or the local police. If the club conducts evaluations of coaches, ask to see them, or, if they won't provide the actual evaluations, ask how he ranks against other coaches. Trust your instincts. Better to be safe than sorry.

Chapter Eleven

Communication Breakdown
How to Communicate Effectively with Your Child's Coach

When You know better
You do better

—MAYA ANGELOU

A MOTHER'S DILEMMA

Not a day goes by at MomsTeam that we don't hear from a parent seeking advice on how to talk to a coach. Typical is an e-mail I recently received from a mother from Georgia desperately looking for advice about what to do about her daughter's abusive softball coach. Intent on winning the state title after getting to the "elite eight" the year before, the coach, a twenty-six-year-old former Minor League baseball player, would punish girls for poor play or rule infractions by forcing them to stand in front of a pitching machine as balls hit them square on their backsides. If someone missed a grounder during infield practice, the coach would take out his anger by hitting balls at them harder than the girls could field. One hit my correspondent's daughter in the throat. She tried to "suck it up," but the pain was too great and she started crying. The coach told her that it was mind over matter, that somehow her throat really *didn't* hurt.

The mother's e-mail went on to say that her son had played for the coach when he first came to town, and the boys had gotten to the point that they simply walked off the field when he started hitting hard grounders that they could not field. "I don't think the girls will do that," the mother wrote. "I know these girls are tougher than a lot of the boys, and I think they will hang in there to prove they can.

"Other parents have tried talking to the coach about these issues, but he does not see anything but his way," the e-mail continued. "Of course, the girls always say, 'Don't say anything because he will take it out on me at practice and make me run more or something like that, do more push-ups. It's like the army has taken them and we can't get them back.'"

A NO-WIN SITUATION

Talking to a coach like this one is often a no-win situation: keep quiet and the abuse continues; speak up and the coach may retaliate against your child. As one mother said after seeing a coach grab an eleven-year-old boy and violently shake him for tossing his baseball helmet after striking out (no doubt imitating what he had seen countless Major League Baseball players do), "I've learned to keep my head down."

If the world were a perfect place, talking to a youth sports coach would be as natural and relatively stress-free as talking to your child's teacher. Coaches often spend more time with our children than any other adult, so we should spend more time communicating with them than anyone else. We should feel free to let the coach know anything we think will affect our child's participation. This may include stress in his home life or school, the fact that he has chronic asthma, or that he is grieving over the death of a family pet or has to miss a game to attend a family wedding. We also should be able to expect that the coach will share any concerns with us about our child at any time.

As I know all too well from my conversations with parents and coaches over the years, there is nothing that worries and confuses parents more. It is simply astounding how many otherwise confident and competent mothers—successful trial lawyers, emergency room physicians, business executives, and stay-at-home moms—end up lying awake in the wee hours of the morning, worrying about this issue. The reason is that, unlike your child's teacher, her coach, in all probability, is not a professional educator trained to put the child's interest first at all times.

Since it simply isn't possible to shield our children completely from bad coaches, when we feel that we have something to say, no matter how unpopular, we should speak up. If your intuition is to speak, speak. There is no dishonor in voicing an opinion; there is no dishonor in trying to protect your child.

OPEN THE LINES OF COMMUNICATION EARLY

The mother from Georgia was facing an almost impossible task: to do something about an abusive coach in the middle of the season. Had the lines of communication been opened before the season started, had everyone—parents, athletes, coach, athletic director, and club—understood and agreed on what they expected of one another, maybe the coach would not have felt free to abuse his players.

My first piece of advice in talking with coaches is to open the lines of communication *as early as possible*. The most successful sports seasons are the ones that begin with a preseason meeting for parents and players. The meeting sets the stage for the season to come. The time and place of the meeting set the stage, too. Make sure there is time for Q&A. If there is a preseason meeting, be sure to attend. It is *never* a waste of time. If one isn't planned, ask for it.

At my first parent-coach meeting as a coach, there were some parents who seemed annoyed that a woman would be coaching their sons. One father questioned my qualifications and wanted to know how his son was going to be given equal playing time, especially since all three of my sons were on the team. I was initially agitated at his confrontational style, but when I realized that I could answer all of his questions easily, I relaxed (after all, his questions were legitimate and ones I would probably have asked).

By opening the lines of communication with parents from the start and by making it clear that I had a child-centered coaching philosophy, I set the parents' minds at ease and set a positive tone for the season.

What to Expect from a Good Preseason Meeting

In addition to opening the lines of communication early, a good preseason meeting provides:

❖ Parents an opportunity to find out the coach's style, philosophy, expectations, and goals for the upcoming season

❖ The coach a chance to tell parents what he expects in terms of sideline behavior, getting players to practices and games on time and in uniform, etc.

❖ Coaches and parents a chance to develop a team charter (see below)

The Advantages of a Team Charter

If you have ever attended an initial parents meeting, you know that parents and coaches don't always share the same expectations, attitudes, and philosophies about youth sports in general or the upcoming season in particular. Some parents have tight budgets; others don't. Some may expect the team to play in a lot of out-of-town tournaments; others may want less travel and more emphasis on skills development. There are the "play through pain" adherents and those who expect decisions on sitting a player out due to injury to be based on credible medical advice. Some coaches and parents may believe in equal development playing time; some are thinking "a championship this year or never," even if it means that some players will be spending a lot of time riding the bench. Some players joined the team for fun and camaraderie; others may have their sights set on record books and college careers.

It is usually easier for parents to talk to coaches about their child before or after a practice than after a game.

The problem is not that these different viewpoints exist, but that generally they do not surface until there is a crisis. By then, emotional intensity and crippled communication may have destroyed the opportunity to find reasonable solutions.

The solution: agree before the first practice to a team charter. That way your team can take some conflict-prevention measures that anticipate challenges and determine how to handle them. Working as a group, you can reach a common understanding of everyone's expectations, agree on principles that will build stability and confidences, and iron out differences before any actual problems arise. It's a simple document, but one that can be the backbone of a smoothly functioning youth sports team and the catalyst for a stress-free, enjoyable season.

According to my friend and MomsTeam colleague Jeannette Twomey, an attorney, trained mediator, and veteran sports mother, there are six steps to creating a charter that meets your team's specific needs:

1. **Select a facilitator.** The key to developing an effective team charter is informal, respectful group discussion moderated by a person who does not take sides. The facilitator explains the purpose of the discussion, gets it started, and keeps it on track. Look for someone who doesn't have a stake in the team and who has patience and organizational and communication skills. If you can't find the ideal outsider, select a parent or team supporter with these qualities who can remain neutral.

2. **Meet early.** If you don't create the team charter at the beginning, it's not going to work. Get parents and coaches together, with input from players, soon after the team is formed. An hour or two should be enough time. (A prototype charter can be found on the MomsTeam Web site.)

3. **Identify the what-ifs.** The facilitator asks the group to make a list of anticipated problem areas—where glitches in communication and decision making might arise. This entails identifying a series of what-if questions, such as "What if we have unex-

pected expenses?" "What if we can't get enough parents to share the driving?" "What if someone disagrees with the coach's approach to injury or the use of muscle-building supplements?" Anyone in the group can contribute, and no one judges another's entry.

*4. **Brainstorm solutions.** Members of the group suggest strategies for handling each what-if. Everyone gets an opportunity to be heard, and there's no evaluation or debate. All potential solutions are welcome. The atmosphere should be upbeat and proactive.*

*5. **Build consensus.** The facilitator revisits with the group the list of what-ifs and possible solutions. Agreed-upon solutions become part of the charter. Any disputed items are discussed and addressed by voting, modifying, or dropping from the charter.*

*6. **Give everyone a copy.** The result of the group's effort is a team charter, a copy of which is given to each parent, coach, and, if age appropriate, players. The finished product should be a useful guide for constructive behavior. Parents, coaches, and players are committed to following the charter because they have helped to create it.*

❖ Provides an opportunity to review the rules (parents sometimes forget that the rules aren't always the same as the pros use; knowing the rules can prevent misunderstandings during the season)

❖ Allows for an exchange of important information (e-mail addresses, phone numbers, etc.)

❖ Gives parents a chance to have their questions or concerns answered (for a list of possible questions, see sidebar)

❖ Gives parents a chance to become involved, such as by organizing a "water and orange" schedule, getting directions to away games to distribute to parents, organizing car pools, helping out at practices, or becoming the team administrator (see chapter 13)

~~~~~~

Twenty Questions to Consider Asking at the Preseason Meeting

1. How much coaching training do you have, and are you certified?

2. Will someone with up-to-date certification and training in first aid, CPR, and the use of an automatic external defibrillator (AED) be present at all practices and games?

3. Will there be an AED at the field or court?

4. Will someone with a cell phone be at all practices and games?

5. Who will be responsible for calling the EMTs if necessary?

6. What is the league's policy regarding playing time?

7. What is the coach's policy regarding playing time?

8. What should we do if we notice that our child is not getting the minimum playing time?

9. What tournaments are you planning for the team to attend?

10. Will you be in contact with parents during the season to give progress reports?

11. What is the best way to contact you?

12. What type of volunteer help do you need?

13. Who are the parent volunteers?

14. Do you follow a two-adult rule to eliminate the possibility of sexual abuse? (See chapter 8)

15. What rules have you established regarding contact with players? (See chapter 8)

Parents report that, by attending practices, they become much more knowledgeable about the skills that their child needs to practice to develop as a player.

16. If you cannot make a game, will you let us know who is going to be the coach?

17. What is your policy regarding missed practices or games?

18. Do you plan to emphasize having fun over winning, and if not, why not?

19. Will you agree to never angrily yell at players for making mistakes?

20. Will you agree to never angrily yell at officials for making what you believe to be bad calls?

~~~~~~

BEFORE YOU TALK

If you have an issue with your child's coach—whether about playing time, yelling at players, or anything else—before you talk to the coach, talk to your child to find out what he is feeling and thinking. His feelings may be very different from yours, and they deserve your respect. The conversation should be low-key. Ask open-ended questions like, "How are you getting along with Coach this year?" It is best not to bad-mouth the coach; use the issue you or your child is having with the coach as an opportunity to teach a life lesson.

Second, encourage your child to talk to the coach herself first. If you jump in every time your child has a problem, your child will soon get the message that she isn't capable of taking care of herself and will look to you to solve other problems she may be having in her life. For instance, if she is not getting enough playing time, she should ask, "Coach, what do I need to work on so that I can earn more playing time?"

Third, don't speak up until you see a pattern and after you have gathered all the facts with an open mind. Even if your child's feelings mirror your own, don't conclude that you *have* to talk to the coach. Consider the effect your talking to the coach may have on your child's relationships with his teammates and the coach. Sometimes, it may be better to bite your tongue until you have given the matter more thought and perhaps talked to other

Attending practice is an excellent way of letting your child know that you care about her participation in sports and that every aspect is important, not just the games, not just whether her team wins or loses, or how she performs.

parents to see if they have concerns similar to yours. If so, you may be better off going to the coach as a group or going over his head. Be patient.

And don't jump to conclusions. One time, just after the team I was coaching had finished playing its final game of the season, a player's mother and sister started questioning me for not playing him during the second half of the game. "You know the rules. Everyone plays. Why didn't he play?" they asked. They did not let me get a word in. Players and parents milled around in awkward silence. Finally, they paused long enough for me to speak. I told them that, had they talked to their son and brother, they would have learned that he had suffered an asthma attack and had *asked* me to keep him on the bench.

TALKING TO THE COACH: THE WHEN, WHERE, AND WHAT

If your child can't resolve the problem with the coach on her own, it is time for you to become your child's advocate and meet with the coach. Your child should be present (if he wants to be), even if you end up doing most, if not all, of the talking because it will help her learn how to speak for herself in the future with other coaches and authority figures.

❖ **Choose the right time and place.** If you want to have a heart-to-heart with your child's coach, absolutely the worst time is in the heat of the moment: right before, during or immediately after games or practices. The worst place to talk to a coach is front of players and other parents. Instead, contact the coach later that day, when you have calmed down and had a chance to develop some perspective, after you have had a chance to collect your thoughts. Or, better yet, put them down on paper. If a face-to-face meeting is warranted, set a time and place which is free of distractions, where you can talk and maintain good eye contact. Someplace where you can talk over a cup of coffee or grab a doughnut works well. If you are better at communicating in writing, consider sending an e-mail, but remember that they can be easily misinterpreted and come off as confrontational and can be read by, and forwarded to, anyone.

❖ **Don't apologize.** While there is no best way to give criticism, don't apologize or make excuses. According to Georgetown University professor and noted linguist Deborah Tannen, "women tend to say *I'm sorry* more frequently than men, and often they intend it . . . as a ritualized means of expressing concern." Men tend to view such ritual apologies as a sign of weakness and that the speaker lacks confidence.

❖ **Keep the message simple but direct.** As Barbara and Allan Pease note in *Why Men Don't Have a Clue and Women Always Need More Shoes*, when "a woman talks she often uses indirect speech. . . . When women use indirect speech with other women there is seldom a problem—women are sensitive to picking up the real meaning. It can, however, be disastrous when used on men [who] use direct speech and take words literally." Don't simply spew out all of your concerns at once. Focus on the ones that really matter, introducing one or two concerns, at most, simply, briefly, honestly, and directly. Be respectful. Don't exaggerate. Describe the situation in nonjudgmental terms. Explain how it affects you and your child, and then state a preference for how you believe it can best be resolved.

❖ **Watch your tone of voice.** Women have a different speaking style than men, one that often makes us seem less competent and self-assured than we actually are. I found that I was able to advocate more effectively for my child when talking to a coach if I lowered my voice so I didn't whine and didn't get emotional or angry (unfortunately, women who are angry and tense sound whiny). So before you talk to a coach, work on modulating your pitch. You want your voice to convey that you are serious about working toward a mutual resolution to a problem. Starting out the conversation by talking about something positive will help you use the correct tone of voice.

❖ **Check your body language.** Are your arms tightly folded across your chest, or are your hands loose and comfortable? Are you making direct eye contact and are your eyes open without the "evil eye" appearance that you may really want to be expressing?

❖ **Talk slowly.** Deep breathing helps to regulate and slow down your speaking.

❖ **Understand that men and women have different linguistic styles.** What is natural speech for most men is different from what's natural for most women, says Deborah Tannen. Girls tend to learn conversational styles that focus on the *relationship* aspect, while boys learn conversational styles that focus on the *status* dimension. "One of the rituals girls learn growing up," Tannen says, "is taking the 'one-down' position but assuming that the other person will recognize the ritual nature of the self-denigration and pull them back up." As a result, Tannen says, conversations between men and women can be like cross-cultural communication: you can't assume that the other person means what you would mean if you said the same thing in the same way.

❖ **Appreciate regional differences in speech.** While it would be perfectly natural for a southern coach to call you "hon" or "ma'am," it is foreign to someone born in New England, who may view such language as inappropriate. Children may experience communication glitches with their coaches and team members because they haven't adjusted to the different ways people speak in different areas of the country. Sarah wrote to me after she moved from New York City to northern Vermont. She said her son was having a difficult basketball season and experiencing problems that he never had in New York City. I suggested to Sarah that perhaps some of the problems he was experiencing were because the fast-paced and direct way he had learned to talk growing up in Manhattan came across as pushy or bossy. (Later in the season Sarah let me know that this was indeed the problem.)

❖ **Avoid words that block open communication.** What you say can make a big difference in how you are perceived. Here are seven little words that communications expert Susan Fee says to avoid:

1. *But.* If you qualify what you are saying with the word *but*, you give the impression that you are trying to have it both ways ("I think you are a great game coach *but* only a fair practice coach"). Use *and*

instead; that way both statements in the sentence become true ("I think you are a great game coach *and* only a fair practice coach").

2. *Try.* Don't ask the coach to "try" to do something. Ask him to commit to actually doing it. Asking him to try gives him a way out; he can just come back to you later and say, "I tried it, but it didn't work."

3. *Should.* Women are especially likely to be indirect when it comes to telling others what to do, so resisting the urge to tell a coach what he *should* do should be fairly easy.

4. *Have to.* As a mother you know that children don't like to be told what they have to do. The same holds true for adults. Instead of dictating the outcome ("Coach, you just *have to* give my daughter more playing time"), ask him what she needs to do to earn more playing time ("Coach, will you give my daughter more playing time if she improves her ball handling?").

5. *Always.* Invariably an exaggeration. Nothing is usually that black and white. Better to be more diplomatic by using less extreme words like *sometimes, occasionally,* or *usually*.

6. *Never.* The opposite of *always* and a word that, because it makes a blanket statement, invites disagreement. Replace it with *sometimes* or *occasionally*.

7. *Obviously.* Since we base our opinions on our own perceptions, what's obvious to you may not be true for others. Assuming so comes across as arrogant. Instead of making broad generalizations, own your message: "Based on what I've noticed, it appears to me . . ."

❖ **Be assertive, not aggressive.** Be firm but polite. You want the coach to hear you, believe you, and help resolve an important problem, not feel as if he is being attacked. Yet common communication techniques almost guarantee the opposite result, notes Jeannette Twomey. Too often, we lead with personal attacks, exaggerations, and prejudgments. Opening salvos such as "You told Allison that she would be the starting midfielder" or "Josh never would have played on this team if you'd told us how expensive it was going to be" are guaranteed conversation stoppers. They beg for debate and rebuttal, rather than inviting problem solving and empathy. Instead, send a powerful message that can get through the defensive walls because it focuses on the problem, not the person.

❖ **Practice active listening.** After the coach has stated her thoughts you should paraphrase what she has just said, such as by saying, "What I hear you saying is that . . ." It is actually quite powerful to look a coach in the eye and say, "What I understand you saying is that some of the girls will play the entire game and most will play only half the game or less." Try to see things from the coach's point of view. Adopting his frame of reference (what Tannen calls "empathic understanding") is likely to vastly improve the quality of the discussion.

❖ **Look for common ground.** Usually, we think we have the solution all figured out, before we know enough about the problem. For instance, a parent might tell the coach that "There's no way I'm paying for any more hockey equipment," when he wasn't aware that the team bus was flooded in a torrential rain and his payment would be refunded as soon as the insurance claim was processed. As Jeannette Twomey notes, making a single, nonnegotiable demand prevents discussion of other creative options and makes it harder to back down in favor of a better idea. A more constructive approach is to accept that there are many ways to solve a problem. Then generate as many options as possible that combine the coach's interests and your own. For example, "What if we get the insurance company to expedite the claim?" Or, "Maybe the sporting goods company will give us the equipment on credit."

CLIMBING THE LADDER

I am often asked by parents if going over a coach's head is a good idea. My answer is that there are some times when indeed it is necessary to go over the coach's head, either because you can't get anywhere with the coach or because he or she has acted in a way that is so egregious that it needs to be brought to the attention of higher authorities.

When you do, try to enlist the help of other parents. Being part of a group reduces the risk that you will be viewed as an overzealous parent and makes it more difficult for the higher authority (league director, athletic director, school principal, etc.) to ignore your complaints. Forming a parents group also makes it more difficult for the coach to retaliate against your child by reducing her playing time or otherwise singling her out for adverse treatment.

Pick one person to speak for the group, someone to ask the tough questions. Draft a complaint letter signed by all the parents documenting the specific concerns about the coach you all share. Invite the athletic director or club president to watch a game to see for himself what has gotten you and the other parents (and players) so upset about the coach. Finally, make sure to obtain a commitment from the AD to inform the coach that no retaliation against the players of those parents who complain will be tolerated.

END-OF-SEASON LETTERS

Good coaches appreciate being thanked at the end of the season if they have done a good job. My son Hunter's high school freshman soccer coach, Mr. Fuery, did a fabulous job. I made a point of sending him a letter praising his fairness (he gave every player roughly equal playing time), quality teaching skills, and knowledge about child development. Hunter had grown seven inches during the spring and summer prior to the season and was going through an awkward stage so typical of adolescent boys. I sent a copy of my letter to the athletic director, the principal, and the school committee.

On the other end of the spectrum was Spencer's freshman lacrosse coach, who had made life miserable for Spencer and his teammates by his constant yelling. I had sent him a letter (with copies to the AD, the principal, the school committee, and other parents), although that letter was not to thank him, of course.

If your criticisms are shared by the other parents, ask them to send similar letters to the coach, with copies to the AD. By being proactive, you just might save the kids who are a year behind yours from a bad experience.

GIVE YOURSELF CREDIT

I have yet to meet a mom who did not fret and fuss over the best way to talk to a coach about a potential or a real problem. It is not easy, but you are your child's best advocate and you should never second guess yourself. Keep in mind that other parents may have just had the exact same conversation with the coach and by speaking up you may have validated the other parents' concerns. Parents who effectively engage in their children's sports life can do more to make the experience more enjoyable than those who keep their heads down. Be proud of yourself for trying to keep your son or daughter happy and healthy. Know you are doing the best you know how.

Chapter Twelve

Can't We All Just Get Along?
Cooling Down Out-of-Control Parents

OUT-OF-CONTROL PARENTS

About one in seven parents in the 2005 Missouri, Minnesota, and Notre Dame study admitted to having angrily criticized their child's sports performance, leading more than one in five children in the survey to say they preferred that their parents stay at home rather than watch them compete. About one in seven parents also admitted to having yelled at a referee or sports official. The survey supports the view that the reports of misbehaving parents in the media are not isolated events.

Clearly, some parents are taking children's games far too seriously. The games are for our children, yet time and time again, we are witness to *parents* losing control. What lessons are our children learning when they see mothers and fathers yelling insults at referees, hands clenched, faces red with anger? What does a young player learn when an out-of-control father rushes onto a field and, in full view of scores of horrified spectators, assaults a player from an opposing team? Children can't be expected to develop healthy attitudes toward competition in such an environment.

As parents, we need to set an example for our children to follow. We need to keep our cool and keep youth sporting events in perspective. Parents cannot exhibit poor sportsmanship and then turn around and expect their children to be good sports, to lose our cool and expect them not to lose theirs, to harass refs and not expect them to do the same.

Bury the Hatchet At some point in your child's sports career you will find yourself in an uneasy situation where he may be on the same team with a child whose parents who are not setting a good example. This is a very uncomfortable situation and even more so if your child is aware of it.

There are a couple of things that you can do to try to ensure a comfortable season. Some psychologists suggest confronting the parent. This seems to work well for many men. Women wishing to be part of a community, especially a harmonious community, will many times turn their backs on people they don't care for. This "solution" can make for a very long season. Sometimes parents can stem the decline of civility on the sideline and get another parent to behave simply by giving that parent a look of consternation or disapproval or an icy glare.

Each time that I found myself in this situation, I tried to find a way to clear the air. Instead of confronting the person, I would try to bring the entire team of parents together by giving each a cup of freshly brewed coffee or bottle of soda. I can still remember the look in their eyes as I handed them a drink with a smile. It was almost like passing a peace pipe.

Lend an Ear Another way to deal with a difficult parent is to see if you can calmly engage them in a conversation to find out why they are so upset. The next time another parent in the stands or on the sidelines is exhibiting poor sportsmanship, listen to what they are saying. Watch their facial expressions and body language, at whom they are pointing.

Perhaps he is yelling out of frustration and really just wants someone to sympathize with his situation, whether it is a lack of playing time for his son, the incompetence of the coach, or a referee who either doesn't know the rules or is too tired to properly referee the game.

Approach the person and ask in a calm and sympathetic way what the problem is. Try to make sure the individual knows that you understand what he is saying or feeling. Volunteer to talk to the coach with him or the referee after the game *in private* if he will agree to calm down in the meantime.

Ain't Misbehaving It was an oppressively hot and humid Sunday in late June. The travel soccer team on which Hunter and Taylor were playing had made it to the league's postseason tournament. As the three o'clock start time for the game approached, parents began looking around for the referee. He was nowhere to be found, so technically we could not start the game. Finally, two minutes before the game was supposed to start, he arrived from having just refereed another game. Out of breath, his referee's jersey soaked with perspiration, he didn't look like he was in any shape to referee the game.

Once the game started, my fears were realized. The referee was barely able to run and was missing calls left and right. I am sure he was doing the best he could, but he clearly was tired.

Most of his calls were in our team's favor. Upset at the calls, parents from the opposing team and its coaches began to verbally harass the referee. Fifteen minutes into the game, he warned the coach to stop questioning his calls, but the second-guessing continued unabated.

Midway through the second half, with our team ahead, 3–0, neither the parents nor the coach had ceased the torrent of verbal abuse about his officiating. Finally, the ref snapped. He blew his whistle, walked over to the coach and informed him that he was declaring the game a forfeit and awarding our team the victory. This was an important lesson for all of us. The game may not have been out of control had the ref been fresh and in better shape and had the opposing team's parents and coach been less abusive.

A Survey Finds Spectator Abuse the Major Cause of the Referee Shortage

Nine out of ten high school sports associations need more referees, according to a 2001 survey by the National Association of Sports Officials (NASO). More than 75 percent of the survey respondents—the sixty governing bodies in charge of administering high school sports in the United States—listed poor sportsmanship on the part of the spectators as the reason, while 68 percent said poor sportsmanship on the part of the participants was the single biggest reason officials quit. According to the National Alliance for Youth Sports, 15 percent of youth games involve some sort of verbal or physical abuse from coaches and parents, up from 5 percent just five years earlier. NASO reports receiving two to three calls a week reporting physical threats or acts of violence against sports officials.

Many leagues and even state legislatures are making efforts to curb misconduct. In July 2004, Illinois governor Rod Blagojevich signed two sports officials' protection bills into law, making his state the 17th state to pass legislation specifically protecting referees and umpires. The new law increased the penalties for those who commit assault and/or battery against officials and makes it aggravated assault to attack a sports official or coach at any level in Illinois.

SYMPTOM OR DISEASE

It seems to be popular these days to blame the parents for their out-of-control behavior at youth sports events. There is probably no way to completely eliminate the emotional pressure a parent feels when attending a child's athletic event (pressure that naturally increases as the child moves up the competitive ladder), but are parents who act out a symptom of what is wrong with youth sports or the disease itself? I think it is a bit of both: part of the blame lies with the parents themselves, part can be blamed on the way youth sports is organized and run. There will always be adults who act inappropriately; however, if we can shift the focus from the current adult-centered philosophy to one that is child centered we will see the bulk of the bad behavior eliminated.

Part of the problem stems from parents who:

❖ **See winning as paramount.** For men, the male hormone testosterone magnifies the positive effect of winning and the negative effect of losing. Because the boost in testosterone men experience when they win creates a feeling of euphoria and exhilaration, men who compete and win, even if they are just coaching or watching (winning by proxy), have an incentive to compete not enjoyed by women, whose testosterone levels goes up most regularly if they feel they have *played well*, whether or not they have won. Whether as parent or coach, most men want to see that their team or child win. Because they are so intent on experiencing more emotional highs (and trying to avoid the emotional letdown when their child loses), such parents may let their emotions get the better of them, with just about any kind of behavior justified in their minds if it helps the child or child's team win. They imagine that they identify with their child, but in fact they end up ignoring their children's real feelings, goals, and dreams and focusing instead on their own.

❖ **Are unable to cope with the emotional ups and downs of youth sports.** It isn't easy being a parent of a child playing sports. The ups and downs of competition not only challenge a child's coping skills but a parent's as well. Some parents lack the skills to handle the emotional roller coaster and end up acting in inappropriate ways.

❖ **View youth sports as a zero-sum competition with other parents.** All parents want their children to be successful, but increasingly, many see parenting itself as a competitive sport in which success as a parent depends on their child winning and the children of other parents losing.

❖ **See the time and money spent on their child's youth sports as an investment.** Parents these days seem willing—indeed many

Listen to the comments you make at your child's game. Are you singling out your son for the touchdown run but forgetting to praise the guard who made the block that sprung him into the clear?

feel compelled—to make enormous sacrifices of time, money, and emotional energy to give their children the best chance of succeeding in an increasingly winner-take-all society. Notes Canadian sports journalist Jim Coyle, because youth sports demands the two things that most parents have in shortest supply—money and time—too many have come to view their sacrifices as investments which, like any investments, they want to monitor and to protect. When that investment is made in the name of the thing they cherish most, their child, and when that investment is made in a market (youth sports) that arouses strong emotions, and in the case of contact sports like hockey, soccer, basketball, and football is also intense, fast-paced, and inherently violent, the desire to protect the investment often causes parents to act in inappropriate ways.

❖ **Exhibit lower standards of behavior in youth sports.** Parents wouldn't yell out at a child's play, "Emily, you botched your lines again." Why do they feel they have the right to loudly criticize their child's sports performance? Research by sports psychologist Brenda Bredemeier and her colleagues at the Center for Sports, Character, and Culture at Notre Dame University shows that adults and children tend to suspend their normal level of moral reasoning when entering the sporting arena and adopt a form of "game reasoning" that allows them to be more willing to accept unethical and unsportsmanlike behavior simply because it is sport.

❖ **Have a hard time giving up control.** As Jim Coyle wrote recently, youth sports are "an arena . . . to which parents who are themselves competitive, ambitious and frequently controlling by nature are drawn. And, vexingly for them when they take to the stands, it is an arena in which control must be yielded: to the coach, to the kids on the ice, to the officials." Sometimes, such lack of control leads a parent to act inappropriately to try to get back the control they have lost.

Expressing Frustration But sometimes parents who act out at youth sports contests are simply expressing their frustration over larger, more *structural* problems in the youth sports experience itself, some of which can be fixed. Consider the following examples:

❖ A mother, seeing her child riding the bench, screams at her child's coach to give everyone, including her child, a chance to play. She might be screaming at the coach because he isn't following league rules regarding minimum playing time or because the coach failed to make clear to the parents that his philosophy is to play the "best" players. The problem could have been avoided had the issue of playing time been addressed at the preseason meeting so that the coach, players, and parents had the same expectations, or if the youth sports program had an equal playing time rule.

❖ A father yelling at the coach for poor decisions could be criticizing the coach because he wasn't adequately trained. The problem could have been avoided had the coach been properly trained.

❖ A mother admonishing the referee for making a bad call may be doing so because she is overly invested emotionally in the game's outcome or because she or the referee doesn't know the rules. I remember a mother of a player on one of my soccer teams who told the referee that he made a "stupid call" when he issued her son a yellow card for unintentionally head butting another boy as they were both going for a 50-50 ball. Had I gone over the rules at the preseason meeting, had she understood that it was a violation, unintentional or not, she would probably not have yelled at the referee.

In other words, some of the misbehavior by parents on the sidelines of youth sports contests could be avoided in the first place if expectations were set before the season started about playing time, if the coach had been adequately trained, if the parent had been educated about the rules, or if the program itself was more child-centered.

While parents' codes of conduct seem to be the answer, they are not necessarily effective, largely because they don't address the root of the problem (that it is adult- instead of child-centered). Setting expectations for parental behavior through the use of such codes, however, can't hurt. Another way to address the problem would be to ask a parent to serve as a kind of ombudsman to deal with misbehaving parents. Look for someone, such as a minister, social worker, or mental health professional, who has strong interpersonal skills, to serve as a "vibe watcher" and talk to a parent at the first sign that he or she is about to lose control and engage in abusive behavior.

Part 3 What Mothers Can Do to Reform Youth Sports

Chapter Thirteen

From the Stands to the Sidelines
Why Mothers Make Great Coaches and Administrators

The mother's heart is the child's schoolroom.

—HENRY WARD BEECHER

JOINING THE CLUB

Because I was raising three sons who were all the same age and in the same grade in school but with different teachers, I was able to make comparisons that other mothers couldn't make. If my sons were on different teams, I was able to observe and compare coaching styles and philosophies. I was afforded a unique opportunity to identify and distinguish between good coaches and bad, good communication and bad. It became a constant process of evaluation. I soon learned what coaching style I wanted for all three of my sons, and I eventually put that knowledge to work when I became a soccer coach myself.

NO-MOM'S-LAND

Youth sports organizations *say* they want more women involved, but the simple fact is that far fewer women coach youth sports then men. Of the 4.1 million youth sports coaches, only 654,000 are women. Even women who take the time to get their coaching licenses and want to coach are sometimes denied coaching positions.

The dearth of female coaches translates into fewer role models and mentors for female athletes and fewer future coaches. The problem is compounded by the fact that female athletes, having become used to being coached by men and having only rarely been coached by women, seem to favor male coaches and perceive them as more competent and authoritative, leading to a recruiting disadvantage for female coaches.

Old Habits Die Hard The reason for the relative lack of women coaches and administrators seems obvious. The absence of women coaches and administrators is the vestige of the sex-segregated sports system that existed before the passage of Title IX: The old-boy network in sports is still very much alive and well.

Anecdotal evidence suggests that some male athletic administrators, whether at the college, high school, or club level, continue to tend to hire, or in the case of youth sports, appoint, other men as administrators and coaches. Too many men still hew to the gender stereotype that males are more competent and authoritative.

WOMEN HAVE THE RIGHT VALUES FOR YOUTH SPORTS

Women also are reluctant to become coaches because they don't want to have to act like men in order to be successful in a male-dominated profession. They shouldn't have to.

There are a number of reasons women, particularly mothers, make excellent youth sports coaches:

❖ **Women are natural teachers.** As the NFL's youth football director Scott Lancaster observes, "women generally have a better over-

> *"We cannot do great things on this earth We can only do small things with great love."*
>
> —MOTHER TERESA

all capacity to be organized and prepared to provide a quality experience to all kids involved."

❖ **Women tend to be less authoritarian leaders.** Women tend to lead by consensus, a leadership style that even boys prefer, rather than employing a more authoritarian form of leadership. Women tend to connect by empathizing and establishing relationships. A mother's instinct to be a calming influence and peacemaker and to want to emphasize how every player is the same, not different, serve her well as a youth sports coach, where playing favorites or allowing teammates to bully and tease other teammates can create a hostile psychological climate.

❖ **Women are natural nurturers.** Science has proven that women are generally more adept than men at detecting mood from facial expression, body posture, and gestures, and thus knowing if a child is unhappy. Because they tend to be more emotionally open and have good communication skills, mothers are able to motivate and relate well to players, which is essential if a child is to have an enjoyable sports experience.

❖ **Women tend to want to find a balance between competition and cooperation**. A woman's focus is more on teamwork, arising out of her belief that the best result comes when everyone contributes and the most is gotten from everyone's individual talents. Women tend to reject the common supposition that competition *must* consist of winning and losing and of displays of power, dominance, and control, for better or worse. "What we need to be teaching our daughters and sons," says Alfie Kohn, author of *No Contest*, "is that it's possible to have a good time—a better time—without turning the playing field into a battlefield."

❖ **Women care about all children, not just their own.** In the *Motherhood Study, Fresh Insights on Mothers' Attitudes and Concerns*, a 2005 report commissioned by the Mothers' Council of the Institute for American Values, more than 9 out of 10 mothers agreed with the statement, "After I became a mother, I found myself caring more about the well-being of all children, not just my own." As Martha Farrell Erickson and Enola Aird, the co-authors of that study observed, mothers have a "special sense of responsibility for children in general."

❖ **Mothers want to protect children from the pressures of the adult world.** Nine out of ten mothers questioned in *The Motherhood Study* and most child psychologists agree that exposing kids too fast to the pressures of the adult world is a *bad thing*; that childhood should be a time when children are protected from, not intentionally exposed to large parts of the adult world. Many mothers are concerned about the "disappearance of childhood" as author, media critic, and NYU professor, the late Neil Postman, called it, and see themselves, in a sense, as what Postman called the "overseers" of children. As coaches, mothers tend to resist the concept, increasingly prevalent in today's youth sports, that intentionally exposing children to the harsh realities of the adult world (cutthroat competition, sorting out of winners and losers) at ever-earlier ages is somehow a good idea.

❖ **Women are safety conscious and risk adverse.** Studies show that serotonin levels in the brain are inversely related to risk-taking behavior. Evolutionary biologists believe that a woman's higher levels of serotonin, combined with her instinct to survive by avoiding risk, prompt women to be more careful about safety so as to avoid exposing their children to an unreasonable risk of injury.

❖ **Women are good at teaching boys healthy masculinity.** Female coaches can teach male athletes that they don't have to conform to society's male gender stereotype by hiding their emotions, pain, and injuries; that it's possible to be emotionally open and still be a man. Argues Canadian professor Alexis Peters, an expert on masculinity, violence, and ethics in sports, in a February 19, 2004 article in the *Calgary Herald*, "the root of the problem is not men, athletes or sport themselves . . . The issue is adults who forget what it is like to be a child and impose 'real man' values into youth sport." The presence of women as coaches of boys raises, as Ellen Staurowsky argues in the 1990 classic book, *Sport, Men, and the Gender Order: Critical Feminist Perspectives*, "profound questions about male supremacy and directly challenges the patriarchal notion that maleness is a key prerequisite for coaching and for leadership." In other words, more women coaching boys could, by changing the way men think about masculinity, help destroy the myth that women are somehow lacking the qualities to be leaders in society.

❖ **Women coaches are role models for girls and can teach them to celebrate being a female athlete.** Women coaches break down gender stereotypes by proving that women can be just as competent and tough as men. As Professor Staurowsky told me recently, the presence of women in large numbers as coaches at the youth sport level would help boys and girls see that "women *can* coach, thus affecting their vision of how sports systems operate."

More Time to Coach Nearly nine in ten mothers in *The Motherhood Study* say spending more time with their children is a high priority. Coaching their son's or daughter's team is one way to do that.

According to the U.S. Census Bureau, the number of stay-at-home moms (23 percent in the Motherhood Study) rose in the past decade, reversing three decades of decline. One out of five mothers works part-time. As more and more women work part-time or become stay-at-home moms, more are turning toward volunteerism. A recent article in the *Wall Street Journal* entitled "The 'Pick Me!' Parents" documented the fact that so many mothers are rushing to volunteer at schools that many schools are having to turn them away or hold lotteries and set volunteer quotas. As *The Motherhood Study* revealed, others are already involved in their communities in groups working to improve the lives of mothers, children, and families.

Yet there is, as of yet, no glut of mothers volunteering in youth sports. Mothers either don't volunteer, are told they aren't needed at all, or asked only to fill traditional roles, like team administrator. Any mother who wants to undertake the significant commitment of time and energy needed to be a youth sport coach should be able to coach. Stay-at-home mothers and those who work part-time who want to coach, but find it hard to balance the competing demands of family and coaching should be allowed to schedule practices right after school so they can be home in time to make dinner for the family and be provided with babysitting help. (Indeed, argues a 2003 article in *The Journal of Physical Education, Recreation & Dance*, "If the mother has older children on the team, the sports community needs to forge a welcoming culture so that she feels empowered to succeed as a coach without worrying about being perceived as a smothering parent.")

HOW TO GET INTO COACHING

If you want to coach, here's what you need to do:

Identify the sport you are interested in coaching. Chances are it will be the sport your son or daughter is playing, or thinking of playing, as is often the case. Most parents, at least when they begin coaching, do so because they have a child on the team (one study estimates that about 90 percent of the volunteer coaches in a given community are the parent of one or more team members).

If you want to coach your child's team, understand that doing so may present, as the author of a 2005 article on the parent coach–child athlete relationship in the *Research Quarterly for Exercise and Sport* observes, a conflict of interest for both you and your child. As the article notes, your child may feel "pressure from [you] and [his] coaches to perform well, and desire that [you] be [a] source of social support and leave skill and strategy instruction to the coach's domain." You also may find separating your role as parent from your role as a coach, a "fine line to tread." As one respondent indicated in focus group interviews for the article, "parents coaching their own children [may be] fine for lower skill levels, where the emphasis is on skill development and fun" and "where equal playing time is the norm" but at more advanced, competitive levels, "it's so hard to be the perfect, impartial, neutral coach, as if it wasn't your daughter no matter how hard you try."

> "Women who coach male teams are challenging the stereotype of coach as father figure, male protector, and male authority. For the first time there is an emerging feminine counterpart in the form of the coach as mother figure, female protector, and female authority. The issue, however, is not to establish coaching counterparts [but] for females and males in sport to work with conviction towards conceptualization of coaching and sport as human enterprises, inclusive of that which is valuably male and female."
>
> —ELLEN STAUROWSKY
> *WOMEN COACHING MALE ATHLETES: SPORT, MEN, AND THE GENDER ORDER*

Learn everything you can about the sport. Many women think they can't coach a sport because they don't know enough about it. Talk to other coaches, attend clinics, high school and college games, watch instructional videos, read up on the history of the sport, its rules, and its culture. The Internet, of course, is a great place to find information.

Take coaching classes. Find out on the Internet when coaching classes are being held in your area for the sport in which you're interested. Ask the coordinator of your town club whether they will pay for you to attend. For instance, the course for the lowest level soccer certification offered by the Massachusetts Youth Soccer Association (class G) costs $30.00 and takes four hours. As I found out, when you have a coaching certificate, it is much harder for the powers-that-be to turn you down for a coaching position.

Join a coaches' organization. This will keep you up to date on information after becoming a certified coach.

Become certified in first aid, CPR, and the use of an AED. Sign up for sports safety training for coaches offered by American Red Cross and the National Center for Sports Safety (www.sportssafety.org).

Become an assistant coach, co-coach, or team administrator first. Most of those who become long-term coaches start out as assistant coaches or have a mentor. Ask a veteran or retired coach if he will mentor you or, better yet, co-coach.

GETTING INVOLVED IN YOUTH SPORTS ADMINISTRATION

Colleen Superko is a senior partner in one of America's most prestigious and venerable law firms. The mother of three young hockey-playing sons and an athlete herself, Superko wanted to sit on the board of the local youth hockey organization, to make sure it was doing everything it could to make ice hockey safe for all the children in the program. After being turned down for several years, Superko finally was asked to join the board. In three years she rose to the elected position of league president.

Superko is a relative rarity in youth sports: a woman member of a board of directors. Of the 496 seats on the boards of 20 leading national youth sports organizations, only 54 are held by women, nearly one-fourth of those (13) on the board of a single organization (US Lacrosse) (see table on page 226). The same holds true for other national organizations that have been established in the interest of reforming youth sports.

Becoming a Team Administrator, aka Team Mom

Not only should mothers strive to become coaches and administrators, they should continue to fill the traditional roles they have always played in youth sports, such as that of team administrator (TA), the politically correct term for what used to be called team mom. Having a TA doing all the behind-the-scenes work allows the coach to focus on coaching. Finding a TA with strong organizational skills is a plus for any team.

Here are some of the major responsibilities of a TA:

1. Money manager. ❋ Administering the financial needs of the team can be a huge responsibility. The TA is often responsible for collecting money from parents for entrance fees for tournaments, equipment, clinics, end-of-season gifts for coaches, and the like. An updated financial statement should be distributed to each player's family on a monthly basis. The TA may also need to look into the need for team insurance. Most larger organizations and leagues require teams to carry such insurance in case of injury, and the team will have to show proof of this insurance for entry into some tournaments.

Money may not be the root of all evil, but it often causes problems for a youth sports team. I have seen hard feelings engendered between parents and coaches because of poorly managed records and unfair fee collection practices.

2. "Answer person." ❋ The TA is the go-to person on all questions regarding team activities, fund-raising, tournaments, housing, etc. The TA should know the schedule and where to find the tournament brackets, directions, etc., via the Internet.

> ". . . In order to create a new model of the champion we, as coaches and parents, must combine the best qualities of women with the best qualities of men. If we do, we'll come up with an incredible athlete like Judy Foudy, who is aggressive, tough, intense, assertive, fit and competitive and finds a way to win while being relational, empathetic, compassionate and nurturing."
>
> —TONY DICICCO AND COLLEEN HACKER
> *CATCHING THEM BEING GOOD*

Why is lacrosse
the fastest
growing sport?

It is no
coincidence that
US Lacrosse
has the
only national
governing board
with equal
representation of
men and women
on its board
of directors.

Who is Running the Show?
2006 Boards of Directors

SPORT	TOTAL NUMBER OF DIRECTORS	MEN	WOMEN
AAU Baseball & Amateur Softball Association	30	25	5
Little League Baseball and Softball	20	19	1
Babe Ruth League	18	16	2
PONY Baseball and Softball (Protecting Our Nations Youth)	25	24	1
Dixie	7	7	0
Dixie Boys Baseball (13–19)	43	42	1
Dixie Softball	32	29	3
Dixie Youth Baseball (5–12)	49	49	0
USSSA Baseball	13	13	0
USA Basketball	25	18	7
Pop Warner Little Scholars (Football and Cheer)	11	9	2
American Youth Football and Cheer	19	19	0
USA Football	14	13	1
USA Hockey	101	92	9
US Lacrosse	26	13	13
US Youth Soccer Association(USYSA)	9	8	1
American Youth Soccer Organization (AYSO)	11	10	1
Soccer Association for Youth (SAY)	13	12	1
USA Swimming	25	20	5
US Youth Volleyball League	5	4	1

Source: Brooke de Lench, May 2006

3. "Keeper of the list." ❖ A team contact list is an important tool to aid in communication and getting to know the team and family members. The contact list should include: player names and jersey numbers; parents' names; players' siblings' names; home addresses; parents' home and work phone numbers; cell phone numbers, and e-mail addresses. Keep in mind that if a player has more than one set of involved parents, all involved parents' info needs to be listed. Since e-mail is the easiest and preferred method of communication these days, the TA should create a group e-mail listing of all team members and use it regularly in communicating with all team members and their parents.

4. Preseason meeting coordinator. ❖ The TA plans the preseason meeting, which should be attended by at least one member from each family. At this meeting the coaching staff presents its goals and expectations for the upcoming season and answers questions about their coaching philosophy, and the TA can discuss fund-raising and financial matters. The TA should have each player and his or her parents fill out a prospective player and parents questionnaire during tryouts to obtain contact information and get a feel for the parents' expectations.

At the preseason meeting, the TA distributes:

❖ **Player-parent expectations sheet.** An information sheet to every parent and player so they know what is expected of them as a part of their new team. The information sheet should include (1) the background of the team, (2) club, player, and family expectations, (3) financial commitments, and (4) basic coach contact info.

❖ **Code of conduct.** Each team member, parent, and adult should be responsible for reading, understanding, and signing a code of conduct that the coaches, manager, and TA have come up with to outline what is expected of the players and the parents. When they sign this document, it shows that they understand the rules. The TA should be responsible for holding on to these documents for future reference.

❖ **"Hold harmless" waivers.** This document is something a team might want to consider having on file for each player in case of injury.

5. File clerk. ❖ The TA should have a copy of each player's birth certificate on hand in case there is a discrepancy. Some of the larger tournaments require a birth certificate with an official seal in order to register a team.

6. Fund-raising coordinator. ❖ Fund-raising can be a large part of being on a team. Many teams travel or enter large tournaments where fund-raising helps to offset the out-of-pocket costs for the parents. Teams can hold fund-raising events such as a trivia night, an auction, and they can solicit sponsorship from resources and businesses in the community. Many teams have banners made displaying the names and logos of their sponsors and hang them in the dugout during their games. This gives the sponsors visibility throughout the season.

7. Volunteer coordinator. ❖ Team administrators need to be able to delegate responsibilities to other parents. It is a big job being a TA, and that person has to be able to ask other parents for help when and if needed, such as with carpooling, bringing water and oranges to games, etc.

8. Webmaster. ❖ Having a team Web site is a great way to communicate to the team members and for the players to take ownership of their team in another way. Photos, stats, schedules, phone numbers, Web site links, etc., can be posted for easy team access. If you don't want to set up your own, there are several sites already set up for teams and you just plug in your information, though there does need to be a webmaster to control your site (MomsTeam.com is a good place to start your search).

9. Travel agent. ❖ Making travel arrangements is an important aspect of the TA's job. Researching the closest facility to the tournament fields, communicating to all the parents the booking requirements for each hotel, making sure each family has booked their rooms, keeping a master list of those booked and not booked, and canceling the bookings in case there is a problem are all important responsibilities of the TA.

10. Team patch/pin buyer. ✳ Some of the larger tournaments have a patch or pin trading aspect. The idea is that each team creates a unique lapel pin or patch, and each player is armed with enough to trade with all the other teams in the tournament. Ideally, each player will come home from the tournament with pins or patches from each opposing team. Not only does this create camaraderie amongst the teams, it is a fun way to meet the other teams' players and have a collection of souvenirs from the tournament. The TA organizes or delegates the job of designing the team pin/patch, finding manufacturers, soliciting bids, and ordering pins. This is actually a fun but time-consuming task and one best started months before the pins or patches are needed so you are not rushing at the end and have them in plenty of time before the start of the tournament.

APPLYING THE BRAKES

As Eli Newberger, MD, one of the country's most distinguished pediatricians and experts in child development recognizes in his book, *The Men They Will Become,* "It isn't females, predominantly, who have built the elaborately overorganized system of sports for boys [and girls] in the United States, mimicking professional sports with uniforms, leagues, intricate scheduling, commercial sponsors, media coverage, maintenance of performance records, selection of all-stars, seasons leading to playoffs, and enormous emphasis on competitiveness and winning. While both fathers and mothers engage in their sons' [and daughters'] competitions vicariously, it is mostly men who have imposed many of the extrinsic values of their occupations on what should be intrinsically pleasurable children's play, and who bear much of the responsibility for this invasion of childhood."

While we can't change the fact that, as Dr. Leonard Sax argues, "human nature is gendered to the core," this does not mean that youth sports necessarily have to reflect only *male* values and attitudes. That guys need to outperform other guys, or at least keep up with them, and that men tend to filter their worth through their performance *in the adult world*, does not translate well in the *world of children* where they can, and often do, end up doing a lot of damage.

Dr. James Dobson argues it best in his book *Bringing Up Boys*: "the sexes were carefully designed . . . to balance one another's weaknesses and meet one another's needs. Their differences didn't result from an evolutionary error . . . Each sex has a unique purpose in the great scheme of things . . . Their individual temperaments are designed to moderate each other . . . in almost every aspect of life." Dr. Dobson analogizes men and women to the accelerator pedal and brake of an automobile, both vital to its safe operation.

What mothers need to do, then, is to be the brake in youth sports: to balance and moderate the competitive nature of men, their need for control, their goal- and achievement-oriented tendency to sort out winners and losers, their risk taking, their need for adventure, their stoicism, their tendency to be unemotional, and their need for structure and rules with a women's empathy, compassion and interests in nurturing and relationships.

As the boys on my first soccer team learned, children will see that women are just as competent as men, just as knowledgeable about sports, just as able as men to motivate players and teams to do their best.

GUARDIANS OF CHILDREN AT PLAY

As mothers we have always been the guardians of children at play. As more women achieve positions of leadership in sports they can further their innate desire to protect all children against abuse of any kind—physical, psychological, emotional, or sexual. The result will be a safer youth sports experience for our children.

We need the new kind of female power described by Anne and Bill Moir in their book, *Why Men Don't Iron*: "something more subtle, a force that creates relationships, bind families and build societies." "Our job now," says Leonard Sax, "is to create a society that has the courage and the wisdom to cherish and celebrate the innate differences between the sexes while at the same time enabling equal opportunities for every child."

POTENTIAL FOR CHANGING THE YOUTH SPORTS CULTURE

Just as women are increasingly assuming leadership roles in business, politics, and the legal and medical professions, and as a result have begun to change their cultures, so too should women strive to assert themselves and achieve leadership positions at all levels of youth sports—from the boardrooms of the national organizations governing youth sports all the way down to the coach's box and the family dining table—so as to change its culture. Taking a more active leadership role in youth sports will also allow the increasing number of mothers who interrupt careers to raise children to simultaneously accomplish two important objectives that studies show most mothers want: to spend more time with their children during their formative, preadolescent years *and* keep their skills sharp for an eventual return to the workforce.

Perhaps Tony DiCicco and Colleen Hacker put it best in their book *Catching Them Being Good: Everything You Need to Know to Successfully Coach Girls*: "In the end, striking a balance by using the best characteristics of men and women makes for a better way to lead and a better way to influence and foster a higher level of performance. It's not really a questioning of abandoning the old model, it's simply a matter of infusing and applying the strength from both models to complement and support each other."

"Many sport organizations have yet to come to terms with simple liberal agendas and concepts like equality, let alone grapple with the implications of sharing power or transforming relations between men and women, adults and children, coaches and athletes. Women in sport are engaged in a cultural struggle, not just with men but with other women and their own assimilated traditions of 'power as domination.'. . . [W]omen's agency [can be] used to achieve personal, group and institutional change in sport. But however successful women's efforts are . . . they will not succeed in transforming the institution of sport . . . without the commitment and assistance of men in authority."

—CELIA BRACKENRIDGE
SPOILSPORTS:
UNDERSTANDING AND
PREVENTING SEXUAL
EXPLOITATION IN SPORT

Chapter Fourteen

The Controversy over Cutting

In ninth grade, I tried out for varsity field hockey. Although it was the first time in my life that I had participated in tryouts, I was already aware that it was a very intimidating process, as I had an older sister on the team.

On the first day, we were told there would be cuts. After the tryouts, I was selected for the junior varsity team. My friend Hilary, who was a talented athlete, was not so lucky. Suffering from heat exhaustion, she performed poorly. On the second day of the three-day tryout she got sick to her stomach. I remember going with her to the locker room. She was hurt, humiliated, and embarrassed by the tryout process. Sadly, she didn't come back for the third day of tryouts and was cut forever, never to return to a team to try out again.

Since that day I have always been against cuts.

THE CRUELEST CUT OF ALL

The practice of cutting athletes from middle or high school teams, while it has existed for at least fifty years, is arguably the most controversial practice in youth sports. While there are two sides to the argument, I believe the practice is outmoded and needs to be reexamined in light of twenty-first-century realities.

Cutting Damages a Child's Self-esteem Proponents of cutting often argue that cutting is necessary to prepare children for an adult world where there are winners and losers. The belief is that children are better off for having been cut because getting cut "toughens them up" and exposes them to the disappointments all of us experience in adulthood. They also argue, with considerable justification, that, since parents should be teaching their children not to base their sense of self on their identity as an athlete, a child with a healthy self-image will not unduly suffer from being cut, and will simply find another sport or extracurricular activity in which to excel.

While it is true that it is important for kids to learn the value of overcoming obstacles with hard work and how to grow through failure, the fact is, however, that being cut from a middle school or high school sports team is often one of the most upsetting and traumatic events in a teenager's life. (One high school sophomore described it like being punched in the stomach.) For many, being cut represents an assault on their self-esteem, and their first exposure to rejection. They feel the pain and embarrassment of being rejected, excluded from an activity in which they want to participate, and denied the important social connection sports allows athletes to make with their peers.

The goal in childhood should be to prepare children for adulthood by giving them a chance to develop coping skills and the self-confidence needed to succeed in the adult world in a safe and nurturing environment. Many say cutting children from athletic programs fosters an environment that hurts, rather than fosters, self-esteem.

Cutting Hurts the Children Who Need Sports the Most In a cruel irony, the children who are cut, as the least skilled and the ones with the least

The practice of cutting is arguably the most controversial practice in youth sports. No other topic sparks as much heated debate among sports parents.

self-confidence, are the very children who would benefit most from continued participation in an activity where they can learn such skills as a good work ethic and working cooperatively with a group of peers toward a common goal.

Cutting Is Exclusionary and Promotes Elitism It is especially important for teenagers to know that they belong, that they fit in. No wonder freshman handbooks of most high schools advise incoming students to participate in sports. Of the one hundred tips handbooks give freshmen, joining a sports team is always in the top five.

Cutting tells teenagers that they don't fit in, that they don't belong. This is the wrong message to send during adolescence, a time when teenagers are confused about their bodies and want the approval of their peers.

As the most prominent of all high school extracurricular activities, athletics continues to confer on its participants the highest levels of status and prestige in our teenage culture. The feeling by athletes that they are special tends to lead to disharmony, the creation of cliques, and to reinforcing the jock culture, not to promoting feelings of community, full inclusion, and cooperative learning that schools work so hard to instill.

It is particularly ironic that, unlike most private schools, which are by definition exclusive when it comes to admissions but generally extremely inclusive when it comes to sports (to the point of giving everyone who comes out for a team a roster spot and requiring participation in sports), public schools, which are by definition inclusive when it comes to academics, are exclusive when it comes to sports. They do not guarantee each child a place in the sports program who wants to participate and don't require participation in sports, much less provide alternatives to team sports such as intramurals, dance, yoga, etc.

Cutting Puts Kids at Risk of Antisocial Behavior The creation of separate classes of athletic haves and have-nots not only promotes elitism but, argues Katherine Newman in her book *Rampage: The Social Roots of School Shootings*, the jock culture it spawns "is responsible for a great deal of the damage done to the boys who cannot compete." A no-cut policy provides boys an outlet through sports for their aggression and need to connect socially with other boys.

A 2001 report to the surgeon general found that teenagers "who have weak social ties, that is, who are not involved in conventional social activities and are unpopular at school, are at high risk of becoming violent, as are adolescents with antisocial, delinquent peers. These two types of peer relationships often go together, since adolescents who are rejected by or unpopular with conventional peers may find acceptance only in antisocial or delinquent peer groups."

Another recent study found a positive association between playing interscholastic sports and an increase in the number of an athlete's friends who are academically oriented. The study also found that participation in sports "significantly increased social ties between students and parents, students and the school, parents and the school, and parents and parents." The same study found that intramural athletes do not reap the same benefits from participation as do interscholastic athletes. Again, the flip side is that cutting a teenager from an interscholastic sports program not only denies her the chance to participate, it is likely to adversely affect her connection with her parents, school, and peers and her academic performance.

Cutting Creates a Self-fulfilling Prophecy Cutting can start a downward spiral that can make further participation in the sport remote. Those who say that with hard work and effort a child who is cut from a middle or high school team has just as much chance as anyone else to make future teams are ignoring reality. Kids cut as freshmen often never try out again.

Those who cite Michael Jordan as an example of someone who was cut only to come back stronger forget that he was *never* cut. In fact, he tried out for varsity, did not make that team, but remained on the JV squad. The next year, still in the program, he moved up to varsity. In fact, the Michael Jordan example *proves* my point. If he been cut completely from the program, he might not have made the effort to make the team the following year, and the world might not have seen the extraordinary magic he displayed on the basketball court.

> "We have to give our children, especially Black boys, something to lose. Children make foolish choices when they have nothing to lose."
>
> —JAWANZA KUNJUFU
> AUTHOR

Cutting Sends a Mixed Message About the Value of Athletic Participation The current youth sports system promotes participation—at least at the younger ages—then, by cutting children at the middle and high school levels, limits their participation. It thus plants a seed in a young athlete's mind that, as much as she may love playing a sport, as she gets older, participation takes more and more of a backseat to winning.

Cutting Turns Kids Off to Exercise Those children who are cut from sports teams will not exercise as frequently as they would if they were playing sports; they will be likely to spend their afternoons watching television, becoming obese, and getting into trouble. According to the recommendations of an expert panel published in the June 2005 issue of the *Journal of Pediatrics,* the old saying "a healthy mind in a healthy body," from the Latin *mens sano in corpore sano,* is apt. Our youth are not nearly as physically fit as they should be. According to a February 2006 Gallup Youth Study, one in five teens is now overweight with only 21 percent of teens claiming to participate in sports or recreation five to six days a week and only 19 percent of our teens participating in vigorous sports or physical activity five to six days a week.

Cutting Reduces the Talent Pool The town where I grew up wins titles in boys' and girls' soccer and lacrosse year after year. A large part of the town's success is derived from having a no-cut policy. Some of its best players were not stars when they were eleven or twelve. Because they were not discouraged from continuing to play by being cut, they were still playing soccer and lacrosse when they reached high school, where they blossomed into varsity players. Thus, cutting kids from sports teams is like cutting a bud off a tree just because it hasn't bloomed as early as the rest.

This is especially true given the limited opportunity of coaches or whoever is doing the cutting to truly evaluate the potential of every athlete during tryouts. Coaches and other adults cannot predict with any degree of certainty after evaluating kids during one, two, three or even five days of tryouts that a particular child will or will not succeed at any sport he or she is motivated to play.

A teacher wouldn't give up on a child who is getting poor grades and say she was only going to spend her time teaching the ones she thought had the potential to go on to college. Childhood is the time to give all children a chance to grow and develop, not a time to stunt their athletic growth prematurely.

Cutting Isn't Necessary to Ensure Strong Athletic Programs The goals of school-based athletics are educational: to teach the athletes skills they can use as adults. Compromising the educational value of interscholastic athletics in order to emphasize winning has little justification, at least through middle school.

Implementing a no-cut policy is likely to increase the chances that school teams will enjoy success. Keeping late bloomers in the program long enough for them to actually bloom enlarges the talent pool, so ultimately it helps high schools field the best possible varsity teams, sometimes championship teams. I've always been amazed how many kids who end up being the tallest kids in their high school graduating class don't play high school basketball because they were cut from the middle school or high school freshman team and stop playing basketball before they attained their full height.

The National Association for Sport and Physical Education (NASPE) recommends a no-cut policy at the middle school level as "consistent with [their] overall philosophy" and because "middle school interscholastic programs should not attempt to emulate the highly structured interscholastic sports competition offered by high school." NASPE also recommends that intramural programs continue to be offered. A 1992 NASPE study shows that, between the two, participation rates of 90 percent can be achieved.

A rule against cutting should not be confused with an equal playing time rule. For instance, at the University of Chicago Laboratory Schools, the middle school's no-cut policy "refers to the opportunity to join a team." It merely guarantees all players who adhere to the coaches' training guidelines a chance to participate in competitions. Whether the players become successful is up to them, that is, how hard they are willing to work, and, of course, ultimately, to whether they have athletic ability and the necessary motivation to succeed.

The most skilled players are still likely to get the bulk of the playing time on middle and high school varsities, thus ensuring that schools will still be able to field the most competitive teams. High school football provides a classic example: most programs don't have cuts, and as a result, many players see little if any game time, yet the atmosphere is positive.

In addition, teenagers have a pretty good idea of their own ability or lack of ability. Those who are lesser skilled will usually recognize their lack of ability, sooner or later, and either self-cut or work extra hard to try to compensate. Since one of the main purposes of education is to teach children to be self-reliant and develop good decision-making skills, it should be up to the athletes themselves to decide if it makes sense to continue participating in a sport in which they come to realize they don't have enough ability or dedication to working harder to get playing time. Why make that decision for them?

Cutting and Budgetary Constraints After a tough hurricane season during the fall of 2005, school administrators from the Charlotte County, Florida, middle schools canceled interschool sports. They feared that fuel for the team buses would be scarce and expensive. Athletic directors decided to include all children who wanted to play in a new intramural program. After running the numbers, it was announced that it cost the district the same amount of money to run either program. At Port Charlotte Middle School, ninety girls were now able to participate in after-school volleyball instead of the twelve who traditionally made the cut.

As Port Charlotte Middle School discovered, budget savings from cutting are usually insignificant. Whether a school continues to cut or eliminates the practice is usually just a matter of how it sets its priorities. In most instances, no request for extra funds to avoid cutting has ever been made, so no one knows whether the funds are available or not. If the community is sufficiently motivated to eliminate the practice of cutting, the high school athletic booster club or an ad hoc group of parents may be able to raise the extra funds needed (as I did for my son's middle school football program).

Other schools are realizing that it makes more sense to earmark scarce financial resources for an inclusive intramural program than for an exclusive competitive program. As one athletic director said, "If you want more bang for your buck, more kids out of trouble after school, intramurals is the way to go."

The current public high school model—one first-year team, one varsity, one subvarsity—might have made sense at the time it was adopted in 1924, when the number of roster spots was roughly equal to the number of those who wanted to play. But it makes no sense today, when the number of those who want to continue playing sports in middle and high school far exceeds the finite number of spots available under such a system. Whenever there is excess demand, schools should add additional teams to accommodate that need, even if it means adding two or three additional teams. Some schools have successfully updated their programs to offer a place for all subvarsity athletes, sometimes with as many as three JV teams, with players only in good academic standing and no disciplinary problems qualifying to play in games against other schools.

DEALING WITH CUTS

The best solution to the problem of cuts in middle and high school interscholastic athletic programs (not by privately run sports programs, where cutting would still be permitted) is to eliminate the practice.

If this is an issue about which you are passionate, recognize that change will probably not come easily. You will be going against the grain of years of the professionalization of youth sports. But keep in mind that if sixty kids try out for fifteen spots, there are going to be forty-five sets of upset parents. In other words, they are going to be the *majority*, and your voice may just be the additional one needed to provide the critical mass necessary to persuade school authorities to change the policy.

If you can't eliminate the practice altogether, try to make sure the selection process is fair, objective, and nonpolitical as possible. If you feel

Given the obesity epidemic in this country, we should do everything possible to keep kids active and foster a love of sports and physical activity.

the politics in your town are out of control, it might not be in your child's best interests to try out in the first place. Trust your intuition.

If your child is going through the tryout process, here are some tips:

❖ Before the tryouts, prepare your child for the possibility that she won't make the team. Be realistic about her chances. Find the balance between optimism and pessimism. Being overly optimistic puts extra pressure on kids to make the team; being too pessimistic about her chances will discourage her from trying her best. Let her know that not making the team won't be the end of the world.

❖ If she does get cut:

  ❖ Offer unconditional love and support.

  ❖ Avoid an immediate overreaction. While you may not be happy with the outcome, let her know that you are happy she did her best.

  ❖ Empathize with your child. Validate her feelings, don't play them down. Let her vent and have her feeling heard; give her a chance to share her pain and disappointment. Don't paint her as the victim—it will only make her more disappointed.

  ❖ Educate your child on the thought process of how coaches determine who makes the team and who doesn't. With my years of interest in the cutting phenomenon I am aware that coaches will always choose the strongest players with the rest of the group being a subjective choice. Ask your child, "Were there some kids on the team who were better than you?" Next ask, "Were you better than some of the kids?" If your child feels that he was better than some, explain that he is an average player. Not the best. Not the worst. But in the middle. Tell him, coaches choose kids based on what they can add to make a team strong. Some may be good jumpers, some have quickness. So, in order to be sure you are selected you need to be one of the best.

  ❖ Develop a game plan for the future: Some children will be motivated by being cut to redouble their efforts to improve so they make the team next year. If so, volunteer to work with her to get better (but remember, don't push—her motivation has to come from within). Consider talking with the coach in a nonconfrontational way to find out why your child was not selected and what she needs to improve to make the team next year. Be aware that some kids may view being cut as the end of the road for their participation in a particular sport. They may recognize that they don't have the skill to play the sport at the next level. If you agree, you should suggest that she try another sport: This is especially good advice for children under twelve. They should be experimenting with a number of sports before settling on one in which to specialize (or finding some activity they can enjoy and feel passionate about).

By the Numbers:
* *Percentage of high school sophomores advising incoming freshmen to play sports in high school: 99*
* *Percentage of high school students trying out for sports teams who are cut: 62*

Chapter Fifteen

Why All Politics Are Local
What Mothers Can Do to Improve
Youth Sports Programs
in Their Communities

*Sport is a universal language. At its best it can bring
people together, no matter what their origin, background,
religious beliefs or economic status.*

UNITED NATIONS SECRETARY-GENERAL KOFI ANNAN

BUSINESS AS USUAL

It has now been several years since the beating death of youth hockey
coach and father Michael Costin at the hands of Thomas Junta after
their children's adult-"supervised" pickup hockey game in Reading, Massachusetts. It was a beating so brutal, so senseless, so shocking that it
was supposed to become a turning point for prompting parents, coaches,
and administrators to finally take steps to reform youth sports to make
them safer, saner, less stressful, and more inclusive.

On July 2, 2005, five years to the week after Michael Costin's death,
the anniversary was marked, not by editorials noting progress but,
ironically, by the death of another father, Robert Abrams, killed during
a brawl at a baseball tournament in Springfield, Ohio, and yet another

in a seemingly endless stream of stories on the "ugly state of youth sports."

Groups have popped up all around the country to address the issue, drafting comprehensive parent codes of conduct, forming parent education and research-based organizations, and conducting character, leadership, and sportsmanship conferences and seminars. Cities, towns (the Village of Scarsdale, New York, being a prominent example), and states (most notably Maine, with its Sports Done Right™ initiative) have held youth sports summits and created task forces to draw up guidelines for reforming youth sports and how to run sports programs. Groups have drawn attention to the problem by issuing "national report cards" on parental behavior.

Sadly, the problems continue, it seems, because the focus in the media continues to be on the parents and coaches, when the real problem is the culture of youth sports itself. Because parents come and go, because change at the national level is unlikely, the path to fundamental change in that culture will only be accomplished at the grassroots, community level. It is here that concerned mothers—and fathers—can make youth sports about having fun, make sports safer for our children, and include every child who wants a chance to play.

Listen to what children want. Studies repeatedly show that the vast majority of boys and girls, when asked what they would like to see changed about youth sports, say they would like to see less emphasis on winning. We need to start *listening* to what our children tell us they want.

Have the courage to speak up. Most parents in this country want a youth sports system that serves the interests of children. They represent a vast silent majority who just need the courage to stand up and band together to fight those who want to preserve a status quo serving the interests of adults. Perhaps the Wisconsin Interscholastic Athletic Association said it best: "Carrying the torch for less pressure and more perspective in youth programs may not be a popular position. Those who demand more games, more wins, more trophies, more travel, and more of everything can talk the loudest and sound convincing. It's up to all of us to have the courage to be just as passionate on the side of balance."

"Except for the most extreme violence or abuse in youth sports, the coaches and parents who create trouble for our children are not bad people. They are caught up in, and sometimes corrupted by, youth sports systems that have gone astray. Such systems allow misdirected principles and priorities to take over. These are not bad people in charge; these are flawed systems in control. . . . If we do not reform the youth sports systems themselves, we're just putting a muzzle on a dog that still wants to bite."

—BOB BIGELOW, TOM MORONEY AND LINDA HALL
JUST LET THE KIDS PLAY

Push to reform school athletic programs. As John Gerdy writes in his book *Sports in School*, "our sports programs are elitist and exclusionary, neither designed nor conducted with the health benefits of participants in mind." He argues that "If we were interested in deriving the greatest health return on dollars spent on athletics, more resources would be spent on broad-based, participatory intramural, club and physical education programs than on the current programs designed to cater to a small population of elite athletes."

Fundamentally altering the outmoded model that most schools follow for interscholastic sports will be a monumental undertaking. It will require the effort of a large and vocal group of committed parents. But it can be done. First, try to eliminate cutting at levels below high school varsity.

Second, accommodate the interests of those students not playing competitive team sports but who want to continue to engage in some form of physical exercise or sports in a noncompetitive setting, by developing and funding after-school programs offering aerobics, dance, exercise walking, self-defense, yoga, Pilates, strength training, flag/touch football, and Ultimate Frisbee.

Third, ask schools to consider returning to same-sex PE. Co-ed physical education, while it has obvious advantages, also has some significant downsides for both boys and girls. A study of South Carolina middle and high school girls reported in the September 2005 issue of the *American Journal of Public Health* found that girls taking girls-only PE exercised substantially more than girls in co-ed programs.

Establish noncompetitive programs like that set by Jim Piatelli, the owner of the Pond, an indoor sports facility and ice hockey rink in Norwood, Massachusetts, who developed a program of no-check, no-scorekeeping, attitude-free hockey for all age groups and levels of play, from pee wee through adult, to provide fun for skaters and spectators alike. The Pond continues to offer competitive hockey, but the program provides parents with an opportunity to have their kids play and improve their basic skills in an atmosphere that emphasizes basic sportsmanship.

Mothers at the Pond told me they now feel a "sense of calm while watching their sons focus on their skills instead of their physical strength."

Redefine winning at the pre-high school level. It should be based on how much effort the participants put in, not the outcome. Borrow a feature from the pickup games of yesteryear, when kids divvied up players in such a way as to achieve equally balanced sides; if one side got way ahead, the game was stopped and new teams picked or the game simply ended. By choosing the teams so that they are balanced, the games won't be lopsided affairs.

Seek to abolish tryouts that result in excluding or cutting children prior to sixth grade. One way to accomplish this goal is deny the use of public facilities by any tryout-based teams with children younger than sixth-graders, as was recently done in Scarsdale, New York, where eight out of ten parents overall and three out of four parents involved in tryout-based programs believed there should be no tryouts and cutting before fifth grade. Organize as many teams as there are children wanting to play. If there aren't rules to ensure equal, or at least significant, playing time, make them and enforce them (nine out of ten Scarsdale parents were strongly in favor of a policy requiring significant playing time for all kids; among the recommendations of its youth sports task force was the creation of a consistent and fair policy on playing time as a prerequisite for use of public facilities by an independent youth sports organization). Not only will this help develop all players, but it will prevent the benchwarmers, who might be terrific athletes when they grow up, from becoming so discouraged and bored that they quit.

Ask that teams be selected by independent evaluators, not parent coaches. Parents who responded to a survey in Scarsdale were nearly unanimous that tryouts run by parent coaches are unacceptable. As the authors of a 2004 Report on Youth Sports issued by the Scarsdale task force noted, "very powerful concerns [were expressed] throughout the community about the fairness, politics and behavior associated with the selection of children for teams. . . . reflect[ing] a deep cynicism about the fairness of the selection process."

"Moral cowardice that keeps us from speaking our minds is as dangerous to this country as irresponsible talk. The right way is not always the popular and easy way. Standing for right when it is unpopular is a true test of moral character."

—MARGARET CHASE SMITH

Push for teams comprised of kids of the same age, from the same neighborhood, and of mixed abilities before fifth grade. All too often, a player whom the powers-that-be consider exceptionally precocious will be asked to "play up" on a team of older kids. All this does is deny a roster spot to a player in the older age group, throw the younger child in with kids he or she doesn't know and aren't his or her classmates in school. In response to those who say that the more "talented" players shouldn't be "forced" to play with players perceived as less talented, point out that asking them to play with kids their own ages and of mixed abilities won't dilute the competition, hold them back, or prevent them from being a high school, college, or pro star. Ask them what is more important: winning or ensuring that the kids have fun, get a chance to develop their skills and exercise? Play teams from other towns that are equally committed as your program to including every kid who wants to play.

Restore an appropriate balance between sports and family life. Push for limits at the pre–high school level on the number of hours of practice each week and the number of games per week and per season. Playoffs and championships should not take place before high school. Holidays, both religious and nonreligious, school vacations, and Sundays should be off limits for sports. Kids should not be penalized for missing games or practices because of religious or family obligations. The number of tournaments should be sharply curtailed. In the Scarsdale model, sports programs that operate in more than one season are being asked to limit their activities to a single season through fifth grade. For those programs that decide to still offer multiseason programs, a multiseason commitment is not a condition for participation.

To those who say that such steps won't work, that more training, more tournaments, and more travel are necessary to turn out competitive athletes, consider the example of the high school football program in Wyzata, Minnesota, which has sent a team to the state championship game more than half a dozen times in the past twenty years. Its players honed their skills in a recreation league following the steps just outlined. If a group of parents were to get together and speak with one voice on these issues, you may be surprised what can be accomplished.

Push for youth sports safety reforms. In addition to the things you can do as a parent to make the sports experience safer for your own child, there are a number of other steps you can take, along with other like-minded parents, to make the experience safer for all children in your community:

First, push school, community-based, and private programs to adopt comprehensive risk-management programs. If concern is expressed that implementing such a program could end up increasing the exposure to lawsuits because any deficiency or oversight in meeting self-imposed safety requirements could provide the basis for a negligence lawsuit, help the club or school board understand that such fear shouldn't be an impediment to implementation. The alternative is worse: without such safety programs, more kids are likely to get hurt.

Second, call for community-, private-, and school-based sports organizations to view youth sports safety from a children's rights perspective (see sidebar), recognize that children playing sports are owed a duty of care, identify best practices, and implement child protection programs to combat physical, emotional, and sexual abuse in youth sports as has been done in the United Kingdom. Because such programs implement standards that apply to everyone, not just parents but coaches, players, officials, and other adults who work with children in sports, they won't reduce just the number of out-of-control parents, but the number of out-of-control, abusive coaches, team bullies, spectators, and volunteers as well.

"Instead of promoting mass participation, most leagues focus on a talented few . . . and ignore the needs of the rest. Such programs turn young people away from sports in huge numbers. If adults stop organizing these programs on the basis of their own needs, great changes are possible."

—SHANE MURPHY, PHD

Abuse in Youth Sports: Depriving Basic Human Rights?

The human rights of children and the standards to which all governments must aspire in realizing these rights for all children are most concisely and fully articulated in the United Nations Convention on the Rights of the Child (CRC). The CRC spells out the basic human rights that children everywhere should enjoy, among them the right to survival, to develop to the fullest, to protection from harmful influences, abuse, and exploitation; and to participate fully in family, cultural, and

social life. The convention protects children's rights by setting stan-
dards in health care, education, and legal, civil, and social services.
These standards are benchmarks against which progress can be as-
sessed. Countries that have ratified the CRC—including every country
in the world except the United States and Somalia—are obliged to
develop and undertake all actions and policies in the light of the best
interests of the child.

UN Convention on the Rights of the Child:
Key obligations for parents with regard to young athletes

SITUATION	RELEVANT PROVISION(S) OF THE CONVENTION
Never force children to participate in sports	Articles 2, 3, 6 and 12
Show proper attention and interest with regard to children's sporting activities and provide appropriate guidance. Be properly informed about the people caring for children during their sporting activities.	Article 5
Always listen to children's opinions and take them duly into account for their own empowerment and protection	Article 12
Empower children progressively in order to provide them with the tools for their own empowerment and protection	Articles 12 to 17
Respect children's privacy	Article 16
Ensure that children are not forced to train excessively and that they are not pushed into illicit unhealthy behavior (such as doping)	Articles 3, 6, 19 and 24
Behave with fair play and respect toward others, such as opponents and sports officials	Articles 5 and 29
Ensure that children's right to education is not overshadowed by considerations concerning a sporting career	Articles 3 and 28
Encourage sound skill development	Article 29
Playing is a right!	Article 31
Protect children from any form of economic exploitation	Article 32

Third, take a public stand against bullying and hazing and push for adoption by your child's school of a strict antihazing policy to be emphasized in preseason meetings and written materials distributed to every team member, and above all, enforced.

Require accountability and transparency by youth sports organizations. There is a troubling lack of accountability in youth sports. While the worst offenders seem to be the unregulated so-called travel ball programs (which, one commentator recently analogized to the Wild West, with "relatively no laws and no sheriffs"), even local youth sports organizations affiliated with national organizations such as Little League Baseball or U.S. Youth Soccer are not as accountable as they should be to the parents and children they supposedly serve.

Identify decision makers. In order to hold those who run the show accountable for the "product" they produce, challenge the way they do business, and identify problem organizations, begin by finding out about the structure of the organization, says Barbara Jones, a partner in the law firm of Kirkpatrick & Lockhart who specializes in business and corporate law. Does the group operate as a profit or not-for-profit business? Does it have a governing body? Who is accountable or responsible for the decisions made or actions taken? Is it a corporation or a partnership? By going to the Web site of your state's secretary of state, you can obtain annual reports of profit and not-for-profit corporations, both those incorporated in your state and "foreign" corporations (those registered to do business in your state but incorporated elsewhere) as well as the names of officers and directors. Not-for-profits are also required to register with the state's attorney general, typically in a division relating to charities, and to file annual reports on their finances and fund-raising activities.

Parent input. At the local level most youth sports organizations are run like small—and, in some cases, not-so-small—businesses, with officers, boards of directors, bylaws, and annual meetings. Yet most operate with virtually no oversight beyond their volunteer boards of directors. Push for the formation of a parent advisory group (PAG) consisting of representative parents with children currently playing in the program to provide the board of directors with feedback (both negative and positive) from other parents; the input helps to insure that the board's decisions are reflective of and responsive to a broad cross-section of the youth sports community. Run for a seat on the board. Attend meetings.

Open meetings. Ask that the mission statement of a youth sports program, its bylaws, and the names, phone numbers, and e-mail addresses of board members and other officers be publicly available, and that the time and place of board meetings be advertised and open to any parent or concerned individual (even if only to observe). All coaches, including the middle school and high school coaches, should be encouraged to attend at least one meeting a year.

Term limits. Like our political leaders, directors, administrators, and coaches who become entrenched in a program for years on end tend to put the "blinders" on and may become too comfortable with the status quo. New blood can keep a program fresh and strong. Longtime board members can be given emeritus or ex officio status.

Financial accountability. A recent investigation by the *Toronto Star* into complaints by parents wanting to know where millions of dollars in player fees were going forced minor league hockey clubs in Canada to implement public financial disclosure measures.

Benchmarking. The first step in implementing a public health approach to violence and abuse prevention in youth sports is surveillance: creating a consistent, comparable, and accurate data system that can track the performance of youth sports organizations, their progress in eliminating abuse and toward full inclusion, and how they compare with one another. A particularly effective benchmarking tool is the Justplay Behavior Management Program designed by Elaine Raakman, a Canadian mother of two sports-active children. Game officials are asked to complete a report card after every game rating the overall behavior of the coaches, players, and spectators of each team on a five-point scale (1 = very good to 5 = very poor), and the official's own personal satisfaction level within the context of the game. The report cards help identify and quantify the variables that contribute to problem behavior in the team sport environment and determine other common elements that might contribute to problem behavior.

Ask for more training of coaches and mandatory evaluations. The United States is the only country in the major sporting world that does not have a national coaching education program. Of the 4.1 million coaches in the United States only 74,000 have received any formal training. Twenty-three states do not require any type of certification for interscholastic coaches. Only one state—New Jersey—requires coaches to attend a safety orientation and training skills program.

With all the money being poured into youth sports, it is simply astounding that the smallest investment is in coaches, even though they usually have the most impact on kids and keeping them safe. National and local youth sports organizations need to make coaching education a top priority.

Ask for parent training. Parents who have been trained are better able to handle the stress of watching their child compete without losing their cool. They are more likely to understand the advantages of mission statements and team charters, and how they can not only prevent conflicts from developing among parents, coaches, and youth sports officials, but restore the balance between winning and skill development. When everyone involved understands in advance that one of the rules of a particular program is equal playing time, parents won't need to scream at the coach to put their child in the game and the coach won't be under pressure to play only the "best" players.

Use the power of the purse. Women are responsible for 90 percent of a family's primary shopping and write 80 percent of the checks. Support companies and programs that reflect your values. Shop at stores that carry sports apparel for girls and companies that sponsor women's sports. Buy products from companies that underwrite youth sports reform initiatives. It can make a difference. As Sports Authority CEO Martin Hanaka told *Forbes* after a comprehensive survey of Sports Authority stores and shoppers found that women ages twenty-five to forty-five contributed 70 cents of every dollar spent, whether the purchase was footwear, fishing equipment, or Little League gear, "Mom is pivotal."

Reexamine Title IX. As a number of recent books argue, Title IX, as it is presently interpreted, isn't working. True, an amazing amount of good has come to girls from the passage of Title IX. However, the law has increased athletic opportunities for women at the college level by *eliminating* opportunities for men. Something is wrong when colleges have a difficult time finding female athletes to fill teams while many men (especially wrestlers) are being deprived of the opportunity to continue playing college sports in the name of gender equity. The law also has appeared to have given female high school athletes an unfair advantage in the college admissions process. Although a full discussion of the inadequacies and inequities of Title IX are beyond the scope of this book, this is an issue that is not going to go away. As Jessica Gavora argues in her book, *Tilting the Playing Field: Schools, Sports, Sex, and Title IX,* if boys and girls are hardwired differently, "it is time to take a serious look at a federal anti-discrimination law that has come to assume exactly the opposite."

Establish a youth sports council. One of the most effective ways to start a community-wide dialog about reforming youth sports is to establish a youth sports council. The council can hold a series of meetings to which representatives from a broad cross section of the community (parks, recreation, and conservation departments; elementary, middle school, and high school physical education teachers and principals; athletic directors; school board members; superintendents of schools; municipal officials; civic and business leaders; child development specialists; mental health providers; independent youth sports organizations; coaches; sports officials; parents; PTOs; and middle- and high school athletes) are invited to discuss such issues as early specialization, the appropriate age for cutting and competitive tryouts, the best way to recruit and train paid and/or volunteer coaches, the stratification of children based on their perceived abilities, background checks, and how permits are handed out to use city-owned facilities. The objective of the meetings should be to develop an independent Youth Sports Council and a youth sports charter for adoption by the town or municipality governing the use of publicly owned facilities. By utilizing the power of the venue permits, a municipality can reform youth sports by exercising public oversight over the use of taxpayer-funded fields, diamonds, tracks, pools, and courts, denying permits to programs that fail to abide by the charter on equal opportunity, playing time, conduct by coaches, players and parents, minimum age or grade for select/travel teams, etc.

~~~~~~

Improving Youth Sports: A Checklist

✓ *Balance female and male coaches and administrators*

✓ *Include minority views*

✓ *Below high school varsity: no cutting, equal or significant playing time, winning = trying one's best, no playoffs or championships*

✓ *After-school exercise and/or sports programs for nonvarsity athletes within the school setting*

✓ *Same-sex physical education*

✓ *Establish a youth sports council*

✓ *More fun-based sports programs*

✓ *Teams comprised of kids the same age and mixed abilities*

✓ *Limits on number of hours of practice and games per week*

✓ *Games and practices off-limits on holidays, Sundays, and during school vacations (other than summer)*

✓ *Fewer tournaments*

✓ *No penalty for missing games or practices because of religious or family obligations*

✓ *Adoption of comprehensive risk-management and child protection programs*

✓ *Increased safety training for coaches and officials*

✓ *Adoption and enforcement of antihazing policies*

✓ *Accountability and transparency for youth sports organizations*

✓ *Benchmarking*

✓ *Increased coaching education*

✓ *Parent training*

✓ *Reexamine Title IX*

〜〜〜〜〜〜〜〜〜〜〜〜〜〜〜〜

Chapter Sixteen

Expansion Teams
How to Start a New Youth Sports Program

STARTS AND STOPS

Several years ago, I started a travel soccer club after my sons and many of their friends, who had been on an *successful* U12 (under twelve) travel soccer team, were not offered the chance to continue playing travel soccer when they moved up to U14. Stunned and saddened for all the children who had no place to play with others of a similar age and skill level, my immediate goal in starting a new travel soccer club was to give them, and the eighty other boys who were also cut from the existing program, a chance to keep playing travel soccer and to continue to develop their skills during the fall season. My ultimate goal was to bring about changes in the existing club so that all of the kids playing in the new program I created would be offered spots on the existing club's teams the following spring season, at which point we would discontinue operation of a separate club.

Fortunately, as things turned out, *every* player on all of the new teams (all of which had successful seasons and more than held their own, even against teams from the established club), was offered a spot in the existing club's program that spring after they adopted a more inclusive model, so we were pleased to discontinue operations. Some of the players, deemed by the existing club as not being good enough to be on a team, later went on to make their high school varsity soccer team (see discussion of late bloomers in chapter 2).

DEDICATION AND DETERMINATION

As with team sports, success in starting a new youth sports program takes teamwork, determination, and a willingness to do one's best to reach a common goal.

You will need a team of dedicated individuals to head the effort and the support of parents who share your passion for providing a place for all children to play. You and your team will have to be able to put everything aside because often you will be under severe time constraints. There is nothing like a good adrenaline rush to help complete a monumental task.

Be prepared for the possibility that the existing club will pull as many strings as possible to prevent your club from getting off the ground. But know that if you do your homework, if you understand all the hurdles that you are likely to face, you will be better able to clear them.

Starting a new youth sports program has three phases:

Before you start. Before you set up a new league, create a "value" checklist of the reasons that you are starting a new club or program:

1. Exhaustion of remedies ❖ It is vital that you do everything in your power to reform the existing youth sports program before you make the decision to start a new one. If you can document the meetings you attended and your written request for a more inclusive program, it will be easier to explain the reasons you have been forced to start a new one.

2. Lack of inclusiveness ❋ The number one reason why people start a new program is to give kids a chance to play who would otherwise not play. It is also the best reason, the one easiest to justify, and the one most likely to garner the political support you are likely to need from the local officials who control the fields, diamonds, or courts. Putting officials in a position where they will be viewed as engaging in discrimination if they deny your request for facilities makes it less likely that they will block your requests. It will also make it very difficult for third parties to support what you should be able to cast as an elitist program.

3. Lack of accountability ❋ It is far easier to start a new club if the existing club is not affiliated with a national youth sport organization or is run by a group of adults on an entrenched board of directors who doesn't conduct open board meetings or have term limits. Where the board feels it is not accountable to anyone but itself, it can lose sight of its responsibility to serve the best interests of its constituents: the children.

4. Adult-centered ❋ If the existing club is run with a child-centered philosophy, there most likely won't be any need for a new club, but an adult-centered program—one whose missions and goals really serve the interests of parents looking to give their children an advantage by excluding late bloomers from the program (see chapter 2 on the advantages enjoyed by early bloomers)—is pretty much a great reason for starting a new organization.

Research. This is the phase in which you will need to do a lot of the research necessary to organize a new club and get it off the ground. Among the questions you will need to answer are:

> *"Whatever course you decide upon, there is always someone to tell you that you are wrong. There are always difficulties arising which tempt you to believe that your critics are right. To map out a course of action and follow it to an end requires courage."*
>
> —RALPH WALDO EMERSON

❖ Are there enough interested children?

❖ Where will the children play?

❖ Who controls the permits?

❖ What national organization will your new club join, if any?

❖ Who will handle the money?

❖ Who will officiate the games?

Facilities inventory Because it is the rare town that has recreational facilities that aren't already being fully utilized, you will probably have to be creative in finding the space you need for your teams to play. Start off by conducting a facility inventory. If you are trying to start a new soccer club, for example, make a list of every soccer field (or potential soccer field) in town. Look at the community fields, the school fields (both private and public), and fields that aren't even fields (for instance, many large businesses have expansive fields that can be turned into soccer fields).

Permits Once you complete the field inventory, determine who is responsible for giving out the permits for each field. Figure out how many venues (fields, courts, diamonds, etc.) are needed for your new club, best case and worst case.

The next mission is to secure permits for practice and game fields. Usually the Parks and Recreation department in a city or a town keeps a master list of fields and facilities and gives out the permits. For school fields, you will need to get permits from the school's athletic directors; for businesses, you will need to talk to the facility manager.

Securing permits may be the most challenging hurdle to clear. You are likely to discover that just finding enough space for existing clubs is already an issue. If the person who is in charge of permits is overworked or shorthanded, the challenge will be even greater. In speaking with parents from around the country, I've learned that most of those who are responsible for issuing permits are used to working with the established youth sports organizations and may view a newcomer with skepticism, not as a solution to the larger challenge of finding a place for every child to play. You may be given multiple reasons why you cannot have permits. If this happens you will have to take the matter up the chain of authority.

I have often found in working with parents, however, that where there is a will, there is a way, and that if you are very creative you can come up with a solution to the facility shortage. Ask to see the existing schedule. At the very least, you will have a better understanding and appreciation of the challenges the permiting authority faces. At worst, you will see that the existing program is hogging the venues (like tying up a field five days a week when it plays games on only two) and have to "rent" fields from them. Hopefully, by using a scheduling software program, you will be able to free up the necessary fields. If there truly are no fields available, you may reach a dead end (this is why this step is in the beginning of phase two).

Find out if there are any laws restricting municipalities or recreation departments in your state from handing out permits for public fields in a discriminatory manner. Even if there aren't, you may be able to convince your elected officials that allowing private clubs which cut children before a certain age shouldn't be allowed to use public facilities to which everyone should be given equal access. In the case of the club I started, the recreation director had given the existing club essentially unfettered access to all of the town's fields, so I appealed to the town manager.

When I didn't get anywhere with the town manager, and with time running short, I approached the athletic director at each of the town's schools. As it was July, most were on vacation, not to return until August. The AD at the high school told me he had no available fields. Because I had actually walked around the high school, I knew that there was one run-down soccer field up a hill in the middle of the woods that nobody used (it was in dire need of reseeding). He noted the poor condition of the field ("too many holes," etc.). When I told him our club would clean up the field and that the school department had to cut the grass anyway, he agreed to let us use the field. But we needed more. Ultimately, after lots of hard and creative work, we were able to cobble together enough game and practice fields to accommodate five teams from about ninety boys who would not have had a place to play soccer in the fall.

What organization to join Look at all your options. In the case of soccer, there are a number of national organizations, including U.S. Youth Soccer, AYSO (American Youth Soccer), and SAYS (Soccer Association for Youth) with which your new club could become affiliated (the Moms Team.com Web site has a full listing of national organizations and contact information for each sport).

Once you have decided on the national organization to join (if any), identify the persons to contact at the state, county, or regional level to find out how to become a member and enter teams. You will probably end up speaking with the registrar at the regional or county level, who will tell you what you need to do, most likely including completing a variety of insurance and other forms and then appearing at a meeting of the league's board of directors to obtain approval to enter teams. Be prepared at the board meeting for representatives from the existing club to argue against the admission of your club to the league.

If the league in which you want to play has a rule against more than one club from a town being a member, don't let it be a roadblock: just see if you can get your club under the umbrella of another national organization. In the meantime you may need to find teams your kids can play against if the existing organization will not let you join. During the first season you may need to resort to playing scrimmage games against the teams from towns in the existing league. This can actually be a fun way to keep the children playing for the season without being overly concerned about league standings.

Board of directors In order to affiliate, many national organizations will require that your group create a nonprofit corporation headed by a board of directors. At the very least, they will want to know who is running the club (president), who is handling the money (treasurer), and who is keeping the records (clerk), and will require that you provide a driver's license and Social Security number for each. Of the three, the treasurer is the most critical person to select first. A person with a financial background (ideally, an accountant) willing to be treasurer can make things a lot less confusing.

Money matters Money will need to be collected from parents to cover such costs as registration fees, officials fees, uniforms, and field permits. It is best to identify a person in the group who will serve as the treasurer early on, as handling the money can be rather daunting job. With no money in the bank and without a large pool of players, you may need to ask for help from a local business in exchange for printing its name on the uniforms.

The treasurer will need to set up a bank account, and the board will need to declare the type of organization you are to become. Even if you incorporate as a nonprofit corporation it will take time before you can obtain 501(c)(3) status from the Internal Revenue Service so you can accept tax-deductible contributions.

Clerk The clerk will need to check with the league to get a list of all the paperwork necessary to enter a team or teams in the league. Keep in mind that some organizations will not offer much in the way of help, and this is where you will need to use a woman's instincts as a detective to anticipate what will be needed. This part of entering a team is critical. In most cases, a miss is as good as a mile: if you fail to furnish *every* piece of the required information in the proper format your application to enter teams may be summarily rejected.

The following are some of the basic requirements:

❖ Rosters (the minimum number of teams in most leagues is two or three)

❖ Birth certificates (copies) for every player

❖ Coach and co-coach names, proof of identification, and Social Security numbers. Hopefully, the league in which you hope to enter teams requires background checks on coaches and any other adult

If you get knocked down, pick yourself up, dust yourself off, and keep the children in your focus.

volunteers. Your local police department should be able to provide you and the coaches with a clearance letter that should be sufficient for the league. You will need to find out what the league will accept. Even if they do not require this information, you will want to keep a record to let parents know that you are looking out for their children's safety in selecting coaches.

Field permits Some organizations will not allow you to enter teams until you provide proof that you actually have venues where the kids can play. Remember that the league will be scheduling you to play with many other towns or teams, and they do not want to schedule home games for your teams if you have no place to play.

Game officials In most instances it will be your responsibility to line up licensed officials for your home games, and you may be asked to submit the names of the game officials as part of the registration process. Locating officials can be very tricky as most of the time the list is maintained by the existing organization. When it comes down to actually hiring referees, you may need to motivate them to officiate at your games by paying them more than the going rate. Look for younger referees at the high school level, since they usually have no allegiance to an existing club. This is an excellent time to think about taking a referee course yourself and encouraging other mothers and older siblings of players to become certified. Not only can they earn extra money, but they will learn to appreciate just how hard a job it is to officiate a youth sports contest and understand why there should be zero tolerance for yelling at referees.

Membership You will need to collect extra fees to cover the cost of membership in the national organization for each coach and player, as they will be required to present their membership cards before each game as proof of age and qualification. Be sure that each coach laminates the cards, punches them, and keeps them on a large key ring so they can be taken off quickly and handed to the players when they line up to meet the referees. Lamination keeps the signature from blurring, which might eliminate a player.

Coaches You will need to select the coaches very carefully. If you have time to draft your own list of requirements and ask each potential coach to sign an agreement, it will make everyone's life easier. Remember that the reason you are starting your own club is because of the problems with the existing league or club, and most times it is because of poor coaches and administration. Since you are writing on a clean slate, this is an excellent time to approach mothers to ask if they will coach, as they are more apt to become involved if they know they are wanted, needed, and will not be joining a club which may have a preexisting bias against women as coaches.

You also need to make sure that whoever volunteers to coach appreciates the time commitment that will be required. Too many times a parent will volunteer not knowing that she will have to run two practices a week, and clear a three-hour chunk of time for a game on Saturday or Sunday. If you are coaching baseball or softball, it is possible you will practice or play a game three weekday nights, and will also play one weekend game. If a coaching candidate cannot commit to the time needed to do the very best job, he or she should step aside and let someone who has the time step forward. If volunteers are scarce, consider creating co-coaching teams (ideally, a man and a woman), and then make sure that parents and players know up front that co-coaching is necessary because the coaches' other commitments will conflict with some of the practices and games.

Players In order to have a successful club you must stock each team with enough players to avoid forfeits. It is also important to have enough players so you can give each a free game pass, which can be used to miss a game during the season without being penalized (as long, of course, as they tell the coach in advance).

Volunteers As you are starting a new club, find out what each player's family is willing to do to help make it successful. Put together a list of ways they can help, distribute the list to each family, and ask parents to volunteer as they see fit. You will usually find that parents are so thankful that their child or children are being given a chance to play that they are willing to do just about anything that is needed. When parents are part of the team and feel appreciated, stress levels go down all around and the harmony is contagious. It is similar to hosting a potluck supper: giving everyone a small task makes them vested in the outcome and reduces the stress for everyone, most especially the coach.

Implementing

Uniforms and equipment After you have succeeded in establishing your new organization, it will be time to purchase uniforms and equipment. Pay a visit to some of the sporting goods stores in your area, and speak to the manager. Many sporting goods stores do screen-printing of uniforms and will be very happy to help a new club get off the ground, as they will also benefit as you grow.

Equipment needs may be expensive unless you are willing to ask for donations from local businesses or buy from used sporting goods stores. If you know the person in charge of equipment for the existing club, see if he has any spare equipment you could use. This approach will keep you in the loop with some of the folks connected with the existing program who share the mission and values of your new club.

Insurance Most leagues now require that clubs purchase liability insurance and accident and medical insurance covering players, managers, coaches, scorekeepers, and volunteer officials.

Public relations After you have worked out all the details, you will want to make sure that all children and families know about the registration dates and the ability to play for the new club. Because you may not have a list of the children cut from the existing program, it will be important to get the message out by any means possible. Talk to the sports editor of your local paper, and send information to local radio stations and the cable access channel. If you are lucky, the sports editor will write a story about what you are trying to accomplish. At the very least, the newspaper will run notices about registering for your club. Be aware, however, that as soon as your organization and the reasons for starting a new club are made public the critics may come out of the woodwork.

Newspaper articles may be great PR for our new organization, but very poor PR for the board running the existing club, which may be cast as entrenched and out of touch with the needs of the community. Trust in yourself and remember: If you are an organization in which the needs of the children come first, it doesn't matter what the naysayers may say. Hold your head up high and turn the other cheek, knowing that you are doing something that benefits the children.

Conclusion

There came a moment quite suddenly a mother realized that a child was no longer hers. . . . without bothering to ask or even give notice, her daughter had just grown up.

—ALICE HOFFMAN

The solution to the youth sports crisis isn't simply to require parents to sign a code of conduct and be banned from the sidelines if they misbehave. It is to recognize that *everyone* with a stake in youth sports—parents, spectators, players, coaches, trainers, athletic directors, school administrators, members of club boards of directors, referees, umpires, sponsors, and the citizens in the local community—has played a part in creating the crisis in youth sports, and that the only way we are going to solve it, to make youth sports safer, saner, less stressful, and more inclusive is for *everyone*, not just parents, to agree to and then actually implement fundamental changes in the way we *all* view youth sports. In other words, to understand that we are all part of the same *team*, and that, like any other team, its success depends on teamwork and on putting the goals of the team—to put the youth back in youth sports and to make it the best possible experience for our children—above individual, parochial concerns.

School administrators, parents, and coaches must enter into an ongoing partnership to make sure youth sports programs are character-based. While parents are the prime educators of character, all adults associated with an athletic program should embody and reflect the moral authority that we have bestowed on them.

The ethical climate in sports will inevitably change for the better when more women take an active role in youth sports and roll up our sleeves to work for change. From my work deep in the trenches of youth sports, I know that there is a solution-oriented community of mothers in this country ready and eager to take a much more active role in youth sports.

How, of course, will be the challenge. It won't be easy. It won't happen overnight. But we can do it! We owe it to our kids. We owe it to ourselves. We owe it to future generations of kids yet to fall in love with sports.

If this book was helpful to you, please consider giving a copy as a gift to another person interested in improving the culture of youth sports. Together we can make a difference in the lives of all children.

—Brooke de Lench
Concord, Massachusetts
June 2006

FURTHER READING

For further information on any of the topics from this book, to receive a *free* monthly newsletter, and to participate in on going discussions and surveys, please visit: MomsTeam (www.MomsTeam.com).

For a list of speaking engagements or to contact the author, please send an e-mail to: info@brookedelench.com

Bigelow, Bob, Tom Moroney, and Linda Hall. *Just Let the Kids Play: How to Stop Other Adults from Ruining Your Child's Fun and Success in Youth Sports.* Deerfield Beach, FL: Health Communications, 2001.

Blumenthal, Karen. *Let Me Play: The Story of Title IX.* New York: Atheneum Books for Young Readers, 2005.

Brackenridge, Celia H. *Spoilsports: Understanding and Preventing Sexual Exploitation in Sport.* New York: Routledge, 2001.

Buren, Jodi. *Superwomen.* New York: Bulfinch Press, 2004.

David, Paulo. *Human Rights in Youth Sport: A Critical Review of Children's Rights in Competitive Sports.* New York: Routledge, 2004.

DiCicco, Tony, and Colleen Hacker. *Catch Them Being Good: Everything You Need to Know to Successfully Coach Girls.* New York: Penguin, 2002.

Doe, Mimi. *Busy but Balanced: Practical and Inspirational Ways to Create a Calmer, Closer Family.* New York: St. Martin's Griffin, 2001.

Dorrance, Anson, and Gloria Averbuch. *The Vision of a Champion: Advice and Inspiration from the World's Most Successful Women's Soccer Coach.* Chelsea, MI: Sleeping Bear Press, 2002.

Elliott, Steve. *The Grassfire Effect: How One Small Spark Can Change Your World*. Nashville: Broadman & Holman, 2005.

Engel, Susan L. *Real Kids: Creating Meaning in Everyday Life*. Cambridge: Harvard University Press, 2005.

Franklin, Tony. *Victor's Victory*. Lexington, KY: Tony Franklin Companies, 2005.

Gavora, Jessica. *Tilting the Playing Field: Schools, Sports, Sex, and Title IX*. San Francisco: Encounter Books, 2001.

Greenberg, Doreen, and Michael Greenberg. *A Drive to Win: The Story of Nancy Lieberman-Cline* Anything You Can Do . . . New Sports Heroes for Girls, Vol. 1. Terre Haute, IN: Wish Publishing, 2000.

———. *Fast Lane to Victory: The Story of Jenny Thompson*. Anything You Can Do . . . New Sports Heroes for Girls, Vol. 3. Terre Haute, IN: Wish Publishing, 2001.

———. *Sword of a Champion: The Story of Sharon Monplaisir* Anything You Can Do . . . New Sports Heroes for Girls, Vol. 2. Terre Haute, IN: Wish Publishing, 2000.

Gurian, Michael, and Kathy Stevens. *The Minds of Boys: Saving Our Sons from Falling Behind in School and Life*. San Francisco: Jossey-Bass, 2005.

Janda, David H. *The Awakening of a Surgeon: One Doctor's Journey to Fight the System and Empower Your Community*. Chelsea, MI: Sleeping Bear Press, 2001.

Kindlon, Dan, and Michael Thompson. *Raising Cain: Protecting the Emotional Life of Boys*. New York: Ballantine Books, 1999.

Klug, Chris, and Steve Jackson. *To the Edge and Back: My Story from Organ Transplant Survivor to Olympic Snowboarder*. New York: Carroll & Graf, 2004.

Kohn, Alfie. *No Contest: The Case Against Competition*, rev. ed. New York: Houghton Mifflin, 1992.

Kuchenbecker, Shari Young. *Raising Winners: A Parent's Guide to Helping Kids Succeed On and Off the Playing Field*. New York: Times Books, 2000.

Lake, Celinda, and Kellyanne Conway. *What Women Really Want: How American Women Are Quietly Erasing Political, Racial, Class, and Religious Lines to Change the Way We Live*. New York: Free Press, 2005.

Lancaster, Scott B. *Fair Play: Making Organized Sports a Great Experience for Your Kids*. New York: Prentice Hall Press, 2002.

Murphy, Shane. *The Cheers and the Tears: A Healthy Alternative to the Dark Side of Youth Sports Today*. San Francisco: Jossey-Bass, 1999.

Newberger, Eli H. *The Men They Will Become: The Nature and Nurture of Male Character*. Cambridge: Perseus Publishing, 1999.

Pease, Barbara, and Allan Pease. *Why Men Don't Have a Clue and Women Always Need More Shoes*. New York: Broadway Books, 2004.

Peskowitz, Miriam. *The Truth Behind the Mommy Wars: Who Decides What Makes a Good Mother?* Emeryville, CA: Seal Press, 2005.

Pollack, William. *Real Boys: Rescuing Our Sons from the Myths of Boyhood*. New York: Henry Holt, 1998.

Rhoads, Steven E. *Taking Sex Differences Seriously*. San Francisco: Encounter Books, 2004.

Rosenfeld, Alvin, and Nicole Wise. *The Over-Scheduled Child: Avoiding the Hyper-Parenting Trap*. New York: St. Martin's Griffin, 2000.

Roy, Travis, and E. M. Swift. *Eleven Seconds: A Story of Tragedy, Courage, and Triumph*. New York: Warner Books, 1998.

Ruggiero, Angela. *Breaking the Ice*. East Bridgwater, MA: Drummond, 2005.

Sax, Leonard. *Why Gender Matters: What Parents and Teachers Need to Know About the Emerging Science of Sex Differences*. New York: Doubleday, 2005.

Schulz, Mona Lisa. *The New Feminine Brain*. New York: Free Press, 2005.

Senay, Emily. *From Boys to Men: A Woman's Guide to the Health of Husbands, Partners, Sons, Fathers, and Brothers*. New York: Scribner, 2004.

Storm, Hannah. *Go Girl!: Raising Healthy, Confident and Successful Girls Through Sports*. Naperville, IL: Sourcebooks, 2002.

Suggs, Welch. *A Place on the Team: The Triumph and Tragedy of Title IX*. Princeton: Princeton University Press, 2005.

Sullivan, J. Andy, and Steven J. Anderson, eds. *Care of the Young Athlete*. American Academy of Orthopaedic Surgeons and American Academy of Pediatricians, 2000.

Thompson, Jim. *The Double-Goal Coach: Positive Coaching Tools for Parents and Coaches to Honor the Game and Develop Winners in Sports and Life*. New York: HarperResource, 2003.

———. *Positive Coaching: Building Character and Self-Esteem Through Sports*. Portola Valley, CA: Warde Publishers, 1995.

Tofler, Ian MD, and Theresa Foy DiGeronimo. *Keeping Your Kids Out Front Without Kicking Them From Behind: How to Nurture High-Achieving Athletes, Scholars, and Performing Artists*. Jossey-Bass, 2000.

Wolff, Rick. *The Sports Parenting Edge*. Philadelphia: Running Press, 2003.

BIBLIOGRAPHY

Chapter One

Erickson, Martha Farrell, and Enola G. Aird. "The Motherhood Study: Fresh Insights on Mother's Attitudes and Concerns." University of Minnesota, University of Connecticut, and New York: Institute for American Values 2004. Available online at www.motherhoodproject.org.

Lancaster, Scott B. *Fair Play: Making Organized Sports a Great Experience for Your Kids*. New York: Prentice Hall Press, 2002.

Chapter Two

Advisory Council on Youth Sports, Scarsdale (NY). *Report on Youth Sports*. September 22, 2004. http://www.scarsdale.com/Recreation/sports_survey.asp.

Alley, Thomas, and Catherine M. Hicks. "Peer Attitudes Towards Adolescent Participants in Male- and Female-Oriented Sports." *Adolescence* 40, no. 158 (2005): 273–280.

American Academy of Pediatrics: Committee on Sports Medicine and Fitness. "Intensive Training and Sports Specialization in Young Athletes." *Pediatrics* 106, no. 1 (2000): 154–157.

Bayrinan, I. I., and S. M. Vaitsekhovskii. "The Aftermath of Early Sports Specialization for Highly Qualified Swimmers." *Fitness Sports Review International* (August 1992): 132–133. Cited in *Research in Youth Sports: Critical Issues Status*, Ryan Hedstrom and Daniel Gould. Institute for the Study of Youth Sports, Michigan State University, November 1, 2004.

Bloom, B. S., ed. *Developing Talent in Young People*. New York: Ballantine Books, 1985. Cited in *Research in Youth Sports: Critical Issues Status*,

Ryan Hedstrom and Daniel Gould. Institute for the Study of Youth Sports, Michigan State University, November 1, 2004.

Bompa, T. *From Childhood to Champion Athlete*. Toronto: Veritas, 1995. Cited in *Research in Youth Sports: Critical Issues Status*, Ryan Hedstrom and Daniel Gould. Institute for the Study of Youth Sports, Michigan State University, November 1, 2004.

Brady, Frank. "Children's Organized Sports: A Developmental Perspective." *Journal of Physical Education, Recreation & Dance* 75, no. 2 (2004): 35–38.

Butcher, Janice, Koenraad J. Lindner, and David Johns. "Withdrawal from Competitive Youth Sport: A Retrospective Ten-Year Study." *Journal of Sport Behavior* 25, no. 2 (2002): 145–163.

Coakley, Jay. "When Should Children Be Competing: A Sociological Perspective." In *Sport for Children and Youths*, Edited by M. R. Weiss and D. Gould. Champaign, IL: Human Kinetics, 1986. Cited in "Children's Organized Sports: A Developmental Perspective" by Frank Brady. *Journal of Physical Education, Recreation & Dance* 75, no. 2 (February 2004): 35–38.

Cook, Gareth. "Thought for Thinkers: 'Follow Your Gut,' Study Advises on Big Decisions." *Boston Globe*, February 17, 2006.

Csikszentmihalyi, Mihaly, Kevin Rathunde, and Samuel Whalen. *Talented Teenagers: The Roots of Success and Failure*. New York: Cambridge University Press, 1993. Cited in Ryan Hedstrom and Daniel Gould. "Research in Youth Sports: Critical Issues Status," Institute for the Study of Youth Sports, Michigan State University, November 1, 2004.

David, Paulo. *Human Rights in Youth Sport: A Critical Review of Children's Rights in Competitive Sports*. New York: Routledge, 2004.

Donnelly, Peter. "Problems Associated with Young Involvement in High-Performance Sport." In *Intensive Participation in Children's Sports*, edited by B. R. Cahill and A. J. Pearl. Champaign, IL: Human Kinetics, 1993.

Donnelly, Peter, and Leanne Petherick. "Workers' Playtime? Child Labour at the Extremes of the Sporting Spectrum." *Sport in Society* 7, no. 3 (2004): 301–321.

Eder, Donna, and Stephen Parker. "The Cultural Production and Reproduction of Gender: The Effect of Extracurricular Activities on Peer-Group Culture." *Sociology of Education* 60, no. 3 (1987): 200–213.

"Excessive Physical Training in Children and Adolescents." Position statement International Federation of Sports Medicine, November 1990.

Fish, Joel. *101 Ways to Be a Terrific Sports Parent*. New York: Fireside Press, 2003.

Frankl, Daniel. "Should Elementary School Children Take Part in Inter-School Sports Competition." column, January 2003. *The New P.E. & Sports Dimension*, www.sports-media.org/sportapolisnewsletter16.htm.

Glamser, Francis, and John Vincent. "The Relative Age Effect Among Elite American Youth Soccer Players." *Journal of Sports Behavior* 27, no. 1 (March 2004): 31–38

Gould, Daniel. "Personal Motivation Gone Awry: Burnout in Competitive Athletes." *Quest* 48 no. 3 (1996): 275–289.

Gould, Daniel, and Sarah Carson. "Fun and Games? Myths Surrounding the Role of Youth Sports in Developing Olympic Champions." *Youth Studies Australia* 23, no. 1 (2004): 27–34.

Grenfell, C., and R. Rinehart. "Skating On Thin Ice." *International Review for the Sociology of Sport* 38, Vol. 1 (2003): 79–97.

Hedstrom, Ryan, and Daniel Gould. "Research in Youth Sports: Critical Issues Status." Institute for the Study of Youth Sports, Michigan State University, November 1, 2004.

Josephson Institute of Ethics. "Sportsmanship Survey 2004." http://www.charactercounts.org/sports/survey2004/ (accessed December 11, 2005).

Kantrowitz, Barbara, Holly Peterson, and Pat Wingert. "When Women Lead." *Newsweek*, October 24, 2005.

Murphy, Shane. *The Cheers and the Tears: A Healthy Alternative to the Dark Side of Youth Sports Today*. San Francisco: Jossey-Bass, 1999.

———. "When Is Your Child Old Enough for *You* to Get Involved in Youth Sports," October 28, 2002. http://www.momsteam.com/alpha/features/cheersandtears/old-enough.shtml.

"Mysteries of the Teen Years: An Essential Guide for Parents." *U.S. News & World Report*, 2005.

Rhoads, Steven E. *Taking Sex Differences Seriously*. San Francisco: Encounter Books, 2004.

Rowland, T. "Predicting Athletic Brilliancy, or the Futility of Training Till the Salchows Come Home." *Pediatric Exercise Science* 10 (1998): 197–201.

Suggs, Welch. *A Place on the Team: The Triumph and Tragedy of Title IX*. Princeton: Princeton University Press, 2005.

Susanj, David, and Craig Stewart. "Specialization in Sport: How Early . . . How necessary?" http://www.coachesinfo.com/article7 (accessed June 25, 2005).

Tofler, Ian, and Theresa Foy DiGeronimo. *Keeping Your Kids Out Front Without*

Kicking Them from Behind: How to Nurture High-Achieving Athletes, Scholars, and Performing Artists. San Francisco: Jossey-Bass, 2000.

Wiersma, L. D. "Risks and Benefits of Youth Sports Specialization: Perspectives and Recommendations." *Pediatric Exercise Science* 12 (2000): 13–22. Cited in "Fun and Games? Myths Surrounding the Role of Youth Sports in Developing Olympic Champions," Daniel Gould and Sarah Carson. *Youth Studies Australia* 23, no. 1 (2004): 27–34.

Chapter Three

de Lench, Brooke, "Equal Playing Time: Should It Be the Rule, Not the Exception?" http://www.momsteam.com/alpha/features/lessonslearned/equal_playing_time.shtml (accessed September 30, 2005).

———. "Not to Win but to Take Part." http://www.momsteam.com/alpha/features/editorial/to_take_part.shtml (accessed October 23, 2005).

Ewing, M. E., and V. Seefeldt. "American Youth and Sports Participation: A Study of 10,000 Students and Their Feelings About Sport." Athletic Footwear Association, North Palm Beach, FL, 1990.

Fleming, David. "The Unlikely Hero: After Resisting the Urge to Quit, Chris Cardone Led Toms River to Victory." *Sports Illustrated*, September 7, 1998.

Kids First Soccer. "Little League and Varsity Sports Parenting." www.kidsfirstsoccer.com/sport_parent.htm (accessed May 9, 2006).

Shields, David, Nicole LaVoi, and F. Clark Power. "The Sport Behavior of Youth, Parents, and Coaches: The Good, the Bad, and the Ugly." *Journal of Research in Character Education* 3, no. 1 (2005): 43–59.

Chapter Four

Buren, Jodi. *Superwomen: 100 Women, 100 Sports.* New York: Bulfinch Press, 2004.

Butcher, Janice, Koenraad J. Lindner, and David Johns. "Withdrawal from Competitive Youth Sport: A Retrospective Ten-Year Study." *Journal of Sport Behavior* 25, no. 2 (2002): 145–163.

DiCicco, Tony, and Colleen Hacker. *Catch Them Being Good: Everything You Need to Know to Successfully Coach Girls.* New York: Penguin, 2002.

Driscoll, Anne. "Girls Are Playing Their Own Kind of Game." *Boston Sunday Globe*, February 6, 2000, G-1.

———. *Girl to Girl: Sports and You!*: Element Books, 2000.

Eastman, Susan, and Andrew Billings. "Sportscasting and Sports Reporting: The Power of Gender Bias." *Journal of Sport and Social Issues* 24, no. 2 (May 2000): 192–213.

Eblert, Bob. "Give Girls a Competitive Edge." *Better Homes and Gardens*, November 1999.

Gavora, Jessica. *Tilting the Playing Field: Schools, Sports, Sex, and Title IX*. San Francisco: Encounter Books, 2001.

Geary, David, Jennifer Byrd-Craven, Mary Hoard, Jacob Vigil, and Chattavee Numtee. "Evolution and Development of Boys' Social Behavior." *Developmental Review* 23, no. 4 (2003): 413–498.

Greenberg, Doreen. "The Importance of 'Sheroes.'" www.MomsTeam.com (accessed November 26, 2005).

———. "When Your Daughter Wants to Play on the Boys Team," www.MomsTeam.com (accessed November 26, 2005).

Hanson, Sandra, and Rebecca Kraus. "Women, Sports, and Science: Do Female Athletes Have an Advantage?" *Sociology of Education* 71, no. 2 (1998): 93–110.

Josephson Institute of Ethics. "Sportsmanship Survey 2004." http://www.charactercounts.org/sports/survey2004/ (accessed December 11, 2005).

"Keeping Score: Girls' Participation in High School Athletics in Massachusetts." Joint Report by the National Women's Law Center and Harvard Prevention Research Center on Nutrition and Physical Activity, Harvard School of Public Health, February 2004. www.nwlc.org/pdf/KeepingScoreGirlsHSAthleticsInMA2004.pdf.

Massachusetts Mutual Financial Group. "New Nationwide Research Finds: Successful Women Business Executives Don't Just Talk a Good Game . . . They Play(ed) One." Press release, February 4, 2002.

"Mysteries of the Teen Years: An Essential Guide for Parents." *U.S. News & World Report*, 2005.

Nelson, Mariah. *Embracing Victory: Life Lessons in Competition and Compassion*. New York: Morrow, 1998.

Pipher, Mary. *Reviving Ophelia: Saving the Selves of Adolescent Girls*. New York: Ballantine Books, 1995.

Sax, Leonard. *Why Gender Matters: What Parents and Teachers Need to Know About the Emerging Science of Sex Differences*. New York: Doubleday 2005.

Shakib, Sohaila, and Michele Dunbar. "How High School Athletes Talk About Maternal and Paternal Sporting Experiences." *International Review for the Sociology of Sport* 39, no. 3 (2004): 275–299.

Shields, David, Nicole LaVoi, and F. Clark Power. "The Sport Behavior of Youth, Parents, and Coaches: The Good, the Bad, and the Ugly." *Journal of Research in Character Education* 3, no. 1 (2005): 43–59.

Wiseman, Rosalind. *Queen Bees and Wannabes: Helping Your Daughter Survive Cliques, Gossip, Boyfriends and Other Realities of Adolescence*. New York: Three Rivers Press, 2002.

Women's Sports Foundation. "Her Life Depends on It: Executive Summary." May 20, 2004. http://womenssportsfoundation.org/cgi-bin/iowa/issues/body/article.html?record=991 (accessed May 9, 2006).

Chapter Five

Adams, Lorraine, and Dale Russakof. "Dissecting Columbine's Cult of the Athlete: In Search for Answers, Community Examines One Source of Killer's Rage." *Washington Post*, June 12, 1999, A01.

Chamberlain, Tony. "Lessons in Grandfathering." *Boston Globe*, October 14, 2005.

Kindlon, Dan, and Michael Thompson. *Raising Cain: Protecting the Emotional Life of Boys*. New York: Ballantine Books, 1999.

Newberger, Eli H. *The Men They Will Become: The Nature and Nurture of Male Character*. Cambridge: Perseus Publishing, 1999.

Pollack, William. *Real Boys: Rescuing Our Sons from the Myths of Boyhood*. New York: Henry Holt, 1998.

Pope, Harrison G., Katherine A. Phillips, and Roberto Olivardia. *The Adonis Complex: The Secret Crisis of Male Body Obsession*. New York: Free Press, 2000.

Pride, Mike. "Code of Silence." *Brill's Content*, February 2000.

Rhoads, Steven E. *Taking Sex Differences Seriously*. San Francisco: Encounter Books, 2004.

Sax, Leonard. *Why Gender Matters: What Parents and Teachers Need to Know About the Emerging Science of Sex Differences*. New York: Doubleday, 2005.

Senay, Emily. *From Boys to Men: A Woman's Guide to the Health of Husbands, Partners, Sons, Fathers, and Brothers*. New York: Scribner, 2004.

Sorgman, Vanessa. "Boys' Coaches Need to Learn Compassion." *Santa Barbara News-Press* (August 9, 1999), http://www.ayso.syv.com/Tournament/Common/Young_Voices.htm (accessed April 25, 2000).

Staurowsky, Ellen. "Women Coaching Male Athletes." In *Sport, Men, and the Gender Order: Critical Feminist Perspectives*, edited by Michael Messner and Donald Sabo. Champaign, IL: Human Kinetics, 1990.

Wilson, Shelly. "She's Your Coach?" *Athletic Management* 14.2 (February/March 2002). http://www.momentummedia.com/articles/am/am1402/shecoach.htm (accessed May 9, 2006).

Chapter Six

Paul, Marilyn. *It's Hard to Make a Difference When You Can't Find Your Keys: The Seven Step Path to Becoming Truly Organized.* New York: Penguin, 2003.

Steen, Suzanne. "Food On the Go: Strategies for Parents Feeding Athletes Away from Home." http://www.momsteam.com/alpha/features/nutrition/food_on_the_go.shtml (accessed August 27, 2005).

Chapter Seven

Coyle, Jim. "Kids' Hockey Can Make You Crazy: Understanding Parents' Rink Rage." *Toronto Star*, January 20, 2005.

Doe, Mimi. *Busy but Balanced: Practical and Inspirational Ways to Create a Calmer, Closer Family.* New York: St. Martin's Griffins, 2001.

Douglas, Susan J., and Meredith W. Michaels. *The Mommy Myth: The Idealization of Motherhood and How It Has Undermined Women.* New York: Free Press, 2004.

Engel, Susan L. *Real Kids: Creating Meaning in Everyday Life.* Cambridge: Harvard University Press, 2005.

Erickson, Martha Farrell, and Enola G. Aird. "The Motherhood Study: Fresh Insights on Mother's Attitudes and Concerns." University of Minnesota, University of Connecticut, and Institute for American Values (New York 2004), available online at www.motherhoodproject.org.

Kantrowitz, Barbara, Holly Peterson, and Pat Wingert. "When Women Lead." *Newsweek*, October 24, 2005.

Kids First Soccer. "Little League and Varsity Sports Parenting." www.kidsfirstsoccer.com/sport_parent.htm (accessed May 9, 2006).

Kuchenbecker, Shari Young. *Raising Winners: A Parent's Guide to Helping Kids Succeed On and Off the Playing Field.* New York: Times Books, 2000.

Lake, Celinda, and Kellyanne Conway. *What Women Really Want: How American Women Are Quietly Erasing Political, Racial, Class, and Religious Lines to Change the Way We Live.* New York: Free Press, 2005.

Owens, Judy A., and Jodi A. Mindell. *Take Charge of Your Child's Sleep: The All-In-One Resource for Solving Sleep Problems in Kids and Teens.* New York: Marlowe & Company, 2005.

Rosenfeld, Alvin. "Harvard, Soccer, Over-Scheduled Families." Keynote address, International Youth Sports Conference, Atlanta, GA, September 13, 2003.

———. "The Hyper-Parenting Trap." 2005 *Parents League Review.*

Rosenfeld, Alvin, and Nicole Wise. *The Over-Scheduled Child: Avoiding the Hyper-Parenting Trap.* New York: St. Martin's Griffin, 2000.

Smith M. L. "Wanted: A Day of Rest for Youth Sports," *The Minneapolis Star-Tribune,* October 2, 2005.

Warner, Judith. *Perfect Madness: Motherhood in the Age of Anxiety.* New York: Riverhead Books, 2005.

Chapter Eight

American Academy of Child and Adolescent Psychiatry. "Child Abuse—The Hidden Bruises." Facts for Families #5 (October 1992, updated July 2004), www.aacap.org/publications/factsFam/chldabus.htm (accessed October 4, 2005).

Barton, Lindsay. "Abuse, Harassment, and Neglect: The Pain of Emotional Injuries." www.MomsTeam.com (accessed September 12, 2005).

———. "Abuse, Harassment, and Neglect: The Pain of Emotional Injuries." http://www.momsteam.com/alpha/features/health_safety/abuse_harassment.shtml (accessed October 21, 2005).

———. "Preventing Abuse and Harassment in Youth Sports: What to Say at Home." http://www.momsteam.com/alpha/features/health_safety/preventing_abuse.shtml (accessed October 22, 2005).

———. "Preventing Harassment and Abuse in Youth Sports:What Parents Can Do." http://www.momsteam.com/alpha/features/health_safety/preventing_harassment_and_abuse.shtml (accessed October 21, 2005).

———. "Recognizing the Warning Signs of Sexual Abuse." http://www.momsteam.com/alpha/features/health_safety/warning_signs_sexual_abuse.shtml (accessed October 21, 2005).

———. "What You Should Do If Your Child Reports Harassment/Abuse/Neglect." http://www.momsteam.com/alpha/features/health_safety/child_reports_harassment.shtml (accessed October 21, 2005).

Blue Cross and Blue Shield of Minnesota. "Parents Strongly Against Out-of-Control Behavior at Child Sports Events." http://www.bluecrossmn.com/bc/wcs/idcplg?IdcService=GET_DYNAMIC_CONVERSION&RevisionSelectionMethod=Latest&dDocName=POST71A_015528 (accessed November 11, 2005).

Brackenridge, Celia. "Women and Children First? Child Abuse and Child Protection in Sport." *Sport in Society* 7, no. 3 (2004): 322–337.

Brackenridge, Celia, and Kari Fasting. "The Grooming Process in Sport: Narratives of Sexual Harassment and Abuse." *Auto/Biography* 13 (2005): 1–20.

"California Teen Accused of Killing Friend in Bat Attack After Baseball Game." *Associated Press*, April 14, 2005.

Coakley, Jay. "Ethics in Coaching: Child Development or Child Abuse?" *Coaching Volleyball* (Dec/Jan 1994): 18–23.

de Lench, Brooke. "Yelling at Your Kid from the Sideline: The Damage Done," http://www.momsteam.com/alpha/features/health_safety/yelling_at_kids.shtml (accessed December 2, 2005).

Elling, Steve. "What Price Success?" *Golf World*, January 21, 2005.

Fasting, Kari, Celia Brackenridge, and Jorunn Sundgot-Borgen. "Prevalence of Sexual Harassment Among Norwegian Female Elite Athletes in Relation to Sport Type." *International Review for the Sociology of Sport* 39, no. 4 (2004): 373–386.

Gervis, Misia, and Nicola Dunn. "The Emotional Abuse of Elite Child Athletes by Their Coaches." *Child Abuse Review* 13 (2004): 215–223.

Greenfell, Christopher, and Robert Rinehart. "Skating on Thin Ice: Human Rights in Youth Figure Skating." *International Review for the Sociology of Sport* 38, no. 1 (2003): 79–97.

Nack, William, and Don Yaeger. "Who's Coaching Your Kid? The Frightening Truth About Child Molestation in Youth Sports." *Sports Illustrated*, September 13, 1999.

"Police investigate hockey coach accused of ordering kids to fight." *Landsing State Journal*, http://www.lansingstatejournal.com/apps/pbcs.dll/article?AID=/20051018/COLUMNISTS09/510180329 (accessed June 4, 2006).

Rocha, Alexandria, and Bill D'Agostino. "Abuse of Power: Recent Coach, Teacher Misconduct No Surprise to Experts." *Palo Alto (CA) Weekly*, September 28, 2005, www.paloaltoonline.com/weekly/morgue/2005/2005_09_28.coach28.shtml (accessed September 27, 2005).

Shields, David, Nicole LaVoi, and F. Clark Power. "The Sport Behavior of Youth, Parents, and Coaches: The Good, the Bad, and the Ugly." *Journal of Research in Character Education* 3, no. 1 (2005): 43–59.

"Soccer player's mom charged after teams brawl." *The Associated Press State and Local Wire*. May 4, 2004.

StopHazing.org (www.stophazing.org/definition.html) (accessed September 24, 2005).

Webbe, Frank, and Jeffrey Barth. "Short-Term and Long-Term Outcome of Athletic Closed Head Injuries." *Clinical Sports Medicine* 22 (2003): 577–592.

Webbe, Frank, and Shelley Ochs. "Recency and Frequency of Soccer Heading Interact to Decrease Neurocognitive Performance." *Applied Neuropsychology* 10, no. 1 (2003): 31–41.

Wilson, Keith. "Hazing: A Ritual Undermining Performance." http://www.momsteam.com/alpha/features/parenting/hazing.shtml (accessed December 14, 2005).

Witol, Adrienne, and Frank Webbe. "Soccer Heading Frequency Predicts Neuropsychological Deficits." *Archives of Clinical Neuropsychology* 18 (2003): 397–417.

"Youth Coach Accused of Breaking Boy's Arms." ABCNews.com (accessed September 21, 2005).

"Youth Football Coach Resigns in Wake of Hazing Incident." *Associated Press*, August 28, 2004.

Chapter Nine

American Academy of Orthopaedic Surgeons. "National Athletic Trainers' Association and American Academy of Orthopaedic Surgeons Team Up on Youth Sports Injuries Public Service Campaign." News release, March 1, 2005.

American Academy of Pediatrics and American Academy of Ophthalmology. "Protective Eyewear for Young Athletes." Policy statement. *Pediatrics* 113, no. 3 (2004): 619–622.

American Heart Association "2005 American Heart Association (AHA) Guidelines for Cardiopulmonary Resuscitation (CPR) and Emergency Cardiovascular Care (ECC) of Pediatric and Neonatal Patients: Pediatric Basic Life Support" *Pediatrics*, Vol. 117 No. 5 May 2006, pp. e989–e1004.

ATLAS (Athletes Training and Learning to Avoid Steroids). http://modelprograms.samhsa.gov/print.cfm?pkProgramid=6 (accessed August 30, 2005).

Barton, Lindsay. "Antibiotic-Resistant Skin Infections in Athletes on the Rise, Officials Say." http://www.momsteam.com/alpha/features/health_safety/skin_infections_in_athletes.shtml (accessed November 7, 2005).

———. "Preventing Mouth Injuries: The Importance of Mouthguards," http://www.momsteam.com/alpha/features/health_safety/mouth_guards.shtml (accessed November 17, 2005).

Boden, Barry. "Direct Catastrophic Injury." *Journal of the American Academy of Orthopaedic Surgeons* 13 (2005): 445–454.

Boden, Barry, Letha Griffin, and William E. Garrett Jr. "Etiology and Prevention of Noncontact ACL Injury." *The Physician and Sportsmedicine* 28, no. 4 (2000). www.physsportsmed.com/issues/2000/04_00/boden.htm (accessed May 9, 2006).

"CA-MRSA & Youth Activities: Information for Participants, Parents, and Leaders of Organized Sports and Youth Activities," http://www.caercook.com/orsa/youthactivities.html (accessed April 19, 2005).

Cantu, Robert. "Concussions: Advice for Parents of Youth Athletes," http://www.momsteam.com/alpha/features/health_safety/concussion_advice.shtml (accessed November 7, 2005).

———. "Second-Impact Syndrome: Reason to Be Cautious with Even Mild Concussions," http://www.momsteam.com/alpha/features/health_safety/sis_cautious.shtml (accessed November 7, 2005).

———. "Second-Impact Syndrome: What Is It?" http://www.momsteam.com/alpha/features/health_safety/second_impact_syndrome.shtml (accessed November 14, 2005).

Casa, D., et al. "National Athletic Trainers' Association Position Statement: Fluid Replacement for Athletes." *Journal of Athletic Training* 35, no. 2 (2000): 212–224.

Ceto, C. K. "Preparticipation Cardiovascular Screening." *Clinics in Sports Medicine* 22, no. 1 (2003): 23–35.

"Climatic Heat Stress and the Exercising Child and Adolescent: American Academy of Pediatrics Policy Statement." *Pediatrics* 106, no. 1 (2000): 158–159.

Collins, Mickey, et. al. "Examining Concussion Rates and Return to Play in High School Football Players Wearing New Helmet Technology: A Three-Year Prospective Cohort Study." *Neurosurgery*, 58(2): 275–286, February 2006.

Corrado, Domenico, et al. "Cardiovascular Pre-participation Screening of Young Competitive Athletes for Prevention of Sudden Death: Proposal for a Common European Protocol." *European Heart Journal* 26 (2005): 516–524.

Drezner, Jonathan. "Sudden Cardiac Death in Young Athletes." *Postgraduate Medicine* 108, no. 5 (2000): 37–50.

Dye, Dave. "Surgery Throws Young Pitchers a Curveball." http://www.detnews.com/2005/health/0507/18/A01-251329.htm (accessed July 18, 2005).

Elliot, Diane, Linn Goldberg, Esther Moe, Carol DeFrancesco, Melissa Durham, and Hollie Hix-Small. "Preventing Substance Use and Disordered Eating." *Archives of Pediatric Adolescent Medicine* 158 (November 2004): 1043–1049.

Glazer, James. "Management of Heatstroke and Heat Exhaustion." *RedNova News*, http://www.rednova.com/modules/news/tools.php?tool=print&id=156416 (accessed June 18, 2005).

Grinspoon, Steven, and Ellen Seeley. "Is Adolescent Steroid Abuse/Misuse Rampant?" *Endocrine News* (April 2006): 12–16.

Guskiewicz K. M., et al. "Association between recurrent concussion and late-life cognitive impairment in retired professional football players." *Neurosurgery*, 57(4):719–26, October 2005.

Harmon, Kimberly. "Evaluating and Treating Exercise-Related Menstrual Irregularities." *The Physician and Sportsmedicine* 30, no. 3 (March 2002). http://www.physsportsmed.com/issues/2002/03_02/harmon.htm (accessed May 9, 2006).

Hazinski, Mary, et al. "Emergency Cardiovascular Care Committee: Policy Statement, American Heart Association." *Pediatrics* 113, no. 1 (2004): 155–168.

Horowitz, Stephen. "ACL Injuries in Female Athletes." http://www.momsteam.com/alpha/features/health_safety/acl_injuries_in_female_athletes.shtml (accessed January 4, 2006).

International Federation of Sports Medicine. "The Female Athlete Triad." Position statement, June 2000.

———. "Recommendations for Medical Evaluation and Sports Participation in Athletes with a Family History of Sudden Cardiac Death." FIMS position statement, June 2000.

Langburt et al. "Incidence of Concussion in High School Football Players of Ohio and Pennsylvania" *Journal of Child Neurology* 16, no. 2, February, 2001.

Mandelbaum, Bert, et al. "Effectiveness of a Neuromuscular and Proprioceptive Training Program in Preventing the Incidence of Anterior Cruciate Ligament Injuries in Female Athletes." *American Journal of Sports Medicine* 33, no. 7 (2005): 1–8.

Maron, B. J., L. C. Poliac, J. A. Kaplan, and F. O. Mueller. "Blunt Impact to the Chest Leading to Sudden Death from Cardiac Arrest during Sports Activities," *New England Journal Of Medicine* (August 10, 1995): 333:337–342.

Maron B. J., "Sudden Death in Young Athletes," *New England Journal of Medicine* (September 11, 2003): 349:1064–1075.

McCrea et al., "Unreported concussion in high school football players: implications for prevention" *Clinical Journal of Sports Medicine* 14, no. 1 (January 2004): 13–17.

McCrory, Paul, et al. "Summary and Agreement Statement of the 2nd International Conference on Concussion in Sport, Prague 2004." *Clinical Journal of Sport Medicine* 15, no. 2 (2005): 48–55.

Metzl, Jordan, "Concussion in the Young Athlete," *Pediatrics* 117(5): 1813, May 2006.

MomsTeam. "The Importance of Wearing Protective Eyewear for Young Athletes." http://www.momsteam.com/alpha/features/health_safety/imp_ protective_eyewear.shtml (accessed December 19, 2005).

———. "Safety Youth Football Recommendations Announced." http://www. momsteam.com/alpha/features/health_safety/football_info.shtml (accessed August 14, 2005).

Moser, Rosemarie Scolaro Ph.D., et al. "Prolonged Effects of Concussion in High School Athletes." *Neurosurgery*, 57(2):300–306, August 2005.

"MRSA Infections: Physicians Expect to See More Cases in Athletes." *The Physician and Sportsmedicine* 32, no. 10 (October 2004). http://www.physsportsmed. com/issues/2004/1004/news1004.htm (accessed May 9, 2006).

National Institutes of Health. "New Drug Prevention Program Helps Student Athletes Avoid Steroids Use." News release. November 19, 1996.

O'Connor, Francis, John, Kugler, and Ralph, Oriscello. "Sudden Death in Young Athletes: Screening for the Needle in a Haystack." *American Family Physician* 57, no. 11 (1998).

Preparticipation Physical Evaluation. 3d ed. New York: The Physician and Sportsmedicine, 2005.

Prevent Blindness America. "Recommended Sports Eye Protectors." www. preventblindess.org (accessed February 28, 2006).

Romano, Russ, et al. "Outbreak of Community-Acquired Methicillin-Resistant *Staphylococcus aureus* Skin Infections Among a Collegiate Football Team." *Journal of Athletic Training*, May 2006.

Steen, Suzanne. "Fluid Guidelines for Young Athletes." http://www.momsteam. com/alpha/features/nutrition/fluid_replacement_guidelines.shtml (accessed August 22, 2005).

———. "Heat Illnesses: Symptoms and Treatment." http://www.momsteam. com/alpha/features/nutrition/heat_illnesses_symptoms_and_treatment. shtml (accessed August 23, 2005).

———. "How to Ensure That Your Child Gets Adequate Fluids While Playing Sports." http://www.momsteam.com/alpha/features/nutrition/ensuring_ adequate_fluids.shtml (accessed August 23, 2005).

———. "The Warning Signs of Dehydration." http://www.momsteam.com/alpha/ features/nutrition/signs_of_dehydration.shtml (accessed August 23, 2005).

"Suggested Safety Items Parents Should Look for in a High School Athletic Program." National Athletic Trainers' Association, www.nata.org/publications/ press_releases/suggestedsafetyitems.htm (accessed August 31, 2005).

United States Department of Health & Human Services. "U.S. Surgeon General's Family History Initiative." www.hhs.gov/familyhistory/.

United States Department of Health & Human Services, Substance Abuse and Mental Health Services Administration, Center for Substance Abuse Prevention. "ATLAS (Athletes Training and Learning to Avoid Steroids)."

Weinstock, J., B. J. Maron, C. Song, P. P. Mane, N. A. Estes 3rd, M. S. Link, "Failure of commercially available chest wall protectors to prevent sudden cardiac death induced by chest will blows in an experimental model of commotio cordis" *Pediatrics* vol. 117, no. 4 (April 2006): e656–e662.

Withnall, et al. "Effectiveness of Headgear in Football." *British Journal of Sports Medicine* (2005): i40–i48.

"Youth Football: Heat Stress and Injury Risk; American College of Sports Medicine. Roundtable Consensus Statement." *Medicine & Science in Sports & Exercise* 37, no. 8 (August 2005): 1421–1430.

Chapter Ten

Bredemeier, B., and Shields, D. "Divergence in Moral Reasoning about Sport and Life." *Sociology of Sport Journal*, no. 1 (1984): 348–357.

———. "Values and Violence in Sport." *Psychology Today,* 19 (October 1985): 22–32.

———. "Moral Reasoning in the Context of Sport." http://tigger.uic.edu/~Inucci/MoralEd/articles/shieldssport.html (accessed September 6, 2005).

DiCicco, Tony, and Colleen Hacker. *Catch Them Being Good: Everything You Need to Know to Successfully Coach Girls.* New York: Penguin Books, 2002.

Josephson Institute of Ethics. "Sportsmanship Survey 2004." http://www.charactercounts.org/sports/survey2004/ (accessed December 11, 2005).

Sax, Leonard. *Why Gender Matters: What Parents and Teachers Need to Know About the Emerging Science of Sex Differences.* New York: Doubleday, 2005.

Shields, D., Bredemeier, B., "Character Development and Children's Sport." In *Children and Youth Sport: A Biopsychosocial Perspective,* edited by F. L. Smoll and R. E. Smith. Kendall/Hunt, 2002.

Shields, David, Nicole LaVoi, and F. Clark Power. "The Sport Behavior of Youth, Parents, and Coaches: The Good, the Bad, and the Ugly." *Journal of Research in Character Education* 3, no. 1 (2005): 43–59.

Weiss, Maureen R., and Susan D. Fretwell. "The Parent-Coach/Child-Athlete Relationship in Youth Sport: Cordial, Contentious, or Conundrum?" *Research Quarterly for Exercise and Sport* 76, no. 3 (2005): 286–305.

Chapter Eleven

Fee, Susan. "Seven Words to Avoid." www.susanfee.com/coaching/tips/SevenDeadlyWords.htm (accessed December 8, 2005).

Pease, Barbara, and Allan Pease. *Why Men Don't Have a Clue and Women Always Need More Shoes*. New York: Broadway Books, 2004.

Tannen, Deborah. "The Power of Talk: Who Gets Heard and Why." *Harvard Business Review* (September–October 1995).

———. *You Just Don't Understand: Women and Men in Conversation*. New York: Random House, 1990.

Twomey, Jeannette. "The Team Charter—Blueprint for a Hassle-Free Season." http://www.momsteam.com/alpha/features/teambuilders/build-team-relationships.shtml (accessed November 15, 2005).

———. "How to Talk to a Coach." http://www.momsteam.com/alpha/features/teambuilders/talk-to-the-coach.shtml (accessed November 15, 2005).

Chapter Twelve

Bigelow, Bob, Tom Moroney, and Linda Hall. *Just Let the Kids Play: How to Stop Other Adults from Ruining Your Child's Fun and Success in Youth Sports*. Deerfield Beach, FL: Health Communications, 2001.

Bredemeier, B., and Shields, D. "Divergence in Moral Reasoning about Sport and Life." *Sociology of Sport Journal*, no. 1 (1984): 348–357.

———. "Values and Violence in Sport," *Psychology Today,* 19 (October 1985): 22–32.

———. "Moral Reasoning in the Context of Sport." http://tigger.uic.edu/~Inucci/MoralEd/articles/shieldssport.html (accessed September 6, 2005).

Coyle, Jim. "Kids' Hockey Can Make You Crazy: Understanding Parents' Rink Rage." *Toronto Star*, January 20, 2005.

Shields, D., and Bredemeier, B., "Character Development and Children's Sport." In *Children and Youth in Sport: A Biopsychosocial Perspective,* edited by F. L. Smoll and R. E. Smith: Kendall/Hunt, 2002.

Young, Randy. "Parenting Parents." *Chapel Hill (NC) News*, August 30, 2005. www.chapelhillnews.com/sports/v-printer/story/277116p-9209886c.html (accessed September 6, 2005).

Chapter Thirteen

Brackenridge, Celia. *Spoilsports: Understanding and Preventing Sexual Exploitation in Sport*. New York: Routledge, 2001.

Carpenter, Linda, and R. Vivian Acosta. "Women in Intercollegiate Sport: A Longitudinal, National Study Twenty-Seven-Year Update 1977–2004."

———."Women in Intercollegiate Sport: A Longitudinal, National Study Twenty-Nine Year Update 1977–2006."

Character Counts! "New Survey Shows High School Sports Filled with Cheating, Improper Gamesmanship and Confusion About Sportsmanship." Press release, September 13, 2004. http://www.charactercounts.org/sports/survey2004/ (accessed December 1, 2005).

"Crisis in Female Coaches Shortchanges Women, Athletes." *Women in Higher Education*. http://www.wihe.com/$spindb.query.showwhat2.wihe.44 (accessed November 28, 2005).

DiCicco, Tony, and Colleen Hacker. *Catch Them Being Good: Everything You Need to Know to Successfully Coach Girls*. New York: Penguin, 2002.

Dobson, James. *Bringing Up Boys: Practical Advice and Encouragement for Those Shaping the Next Generation of Men*. Wheaton, IL: Tyndale House, 2001.

Eagly, Alice. "The Science and Politics of Comparing Women and Men." *American Psychologist* 50, no. 3: 145–58, Quoted in Rhoads, Steven, *Taking Sex Differences Seriously*. San Francisco: Encounter Books, 2004.

Erickson, Martha Farrell, and Enola G. Aird. "The Motherhood Study: Fresh Insights on Mother's Attitudes and Concerns." (University of Minnesota, University of Connecticut, and Institute for American Values (New York, 2004), Available online at www.motherhoodproject.org.

Geary, David C. *Male, Female: The Evolution of Human Sex Differences*. Washington, D.C.: American Psychological Association, 1998.

Geary, David, Jennifer Byrd-Craven, Mary Hoard, Jacob Vigil, and Chattavee Numtee. "Evolution and Development of Boys' Social Behavior." *Developmental Review* (2003).

Goodman, Ellen. "The Testosterone Bowl." *Boston Sunday Globe*, January 31, 1999.

Gray, John. *Men Are from Mars, Women Are from Venus*. New York: HarperCollins 1992.

Keates, Nancy. "The 'Pick Me!' Parents: Moms and Dads Are More Involved Than Ever in Many Classrooms—and That's Creating New Challenges at School." *Wall Street Journal*, September 2, 2005.

Kimura, Doreen. *Sex and Cognition*. Cambridge: MIT Press, 1999.

Kohn, Alfie. "Fun and Fitness Without Competition," *Women's Sports & Fitness* (July/August 1990), www.alfiekohn.org (accessed March 5, 2006).

———. *No Contest: The Case Against Competition*, rev. ed. New York: Houghton Mifflin, 1992.

Lake, Celinda, and Kellyanne Conway. *What Women Really Want: How American Women Are Quietly Erasing Political, Racial, Class and Religious Lines to Change the Way We Live*. New York: Free Press, 2005.

Lancaster, Scott B. *Fair Play: Making Organized Sports a Great Experience for Your Kids*. New York: Prentice Hall Press, 2002.

Maccoby, Eleanor E. *The Two Sexes*. Cambridge: Belknap Press, 1999.

Moir, Anne, and BillMoir. *Why Men Don't Iron*. New York: Citadel Press, 1999.

Newberger, Eli H. *The Men They Will Become: The Nature and Nurture of Male Character*. Cambridge: Perseus Publishing, 1999.

Pease, Barbara, and Allan Peas. *Why Men Don't Have a Clue and Women Always Need More Shoes*. New York: Broadway Books, 2004.

Peters, Alexis. "Gorillas in Our Midst: North American Sport Is Mucho Macho." *Calgary Herald*, February 19, 2004.

Postman, Neil. *The Disappearance of Childhood*. New York: Delacorte, 1982.

Rhoads, Steven E. *Taking Sex Differences Seriously*. San Francisco: Encounter Books, 2004.

Sax, Leonard. *Why Gender Matters: What Parents and Teachers Need to Know About the Emerging Science of Sex Differences*. New York: Doubleday, 2005.

Singleton, Ellen. "Rules? Relationships? A Feminist Analysis of Competition and Fair Play in Physical Education." *Quest* 55 (2003): 193–209.

Staurowsky, Ellen. "Taking Up the Call: Encouraging Women to Coach"

———. "Women Coaching Male Athletes." In *Sport, Men, and the Gender Order: Critical Feminist Perspectives*, edited by Michael Messner, and Donald Sabo. Champaign, IL: Human Kinetics, 1990.

"What Can Physical Educators Do to Encourage Participation of Mothers as Coaches in Youth Sports?" (Issues). *Journal of Physical Education, Recreation & Dance* 74, no. 8 (October 2003): 102(2).

Weiss, Maureen R., and Susan D. Fretwell. "The Parent-Coach/Child-Athlete Relationship in Youth Sport: Cordial, Contentious, or Conundrum?" *Research Quarterly for Exercise and Sport* 76, no. 3 (2005): 286–305.

Wilson, Shelly. "She's Your Coach?" *Athletic Management* 14.2 (February/March 2002). http://www.momentummedia.com/articles/am/am1402/shecoach.htm (accessed May 9, 2006).

Chapter Fourteen

Broh, Beckett A. "Linking Extracurricular Programming to Academic Achievement: Who Benefits and Why?" *Sociology of Education* 75, no. 1 (2002): 69–95.

Council on Sports Medicine and Fitness and Council on School Health "Active Healthy Living: Prevention of Childhood Obesity Through Increased Physical Activity" *Pediatrics* vol. 117, no. 5 (May 2006): 1834–1842.

de Lench, Brooke. "The Effects of 'Cutting' Athletes From Middle School Athletic Programs: One Parent's Perspective." http://www.momsteam.com/alpha/ departments/endlessseason/middleschool_no_cut.shtml (accessed September 2, 2005).

Eder, Donna, and Stephen Parker. "The Cultural Production and Reproduction of Gender: The Effect of Extracurricular Activities on Peer-Group Culture." *Sociology of Education* 60, no. 3 (1987): 200–213.

Erickson, Martha Farrell, and Enola G. Aird. "The Motherhood Study: Fresh Insights on Mother's Attitudes and Concerns." University of Minnesota, University of Connecticut, and Institute for American Values (New York 2004), available online at www.motherhoodproject.org.

Gallup poll, 2006 Youth Study. "Nearly One in Five Teens Is Overweight." http://poll.gallup.com/content/default.aspx?ci=21409 (accessed February 15, 2006).

Jeffries, Steven. "No-Cut Policies: Fancies and Facts." http://www.cwu.edu/ %7Ejefferis/framea.html (accessed May 9, 2006).

Lipsyte, Robert. "Varsity Syndrome: The Unkindest Cut." *Annals of the American Academy of Political and Social Science* 445 (1979): 15–23.

McNeal, Ralph. "Participation in High School Extracurricular Activities: Investigating School Effects." *Social Science Quarterly* 80 (1997): 291.

Nayor, Ella. "District to Revisit Middle School Sports Policy in Spring." http:// www.sun-herald.com/NewsArchive2/112005/tp1ch14.htm?date=112005&st ory=tp1ch14.htm (accessed May 9, 2006).

Newman, Katherine S. *Rampage: The Social Roots of School Shootings*. New York: Basic Books, 2004.

Suggs, Welch. *A Place on the Team: The Triumph and Tragedy of Title IX*. Princeton: Princeton University Press, 2005.

United States Surgeon General. "Youth Violence: A Report of the Surgeon General." http://www.surgeongeneral.gov/library/youthviolence/chapter4/sec3 .html (accessed December 31, 2005).

University of Chicago Laboratory Schools: Middle School Athletics Policies, http://www.ucls.uchicago.edu/students/activities/sports/mspolicy.shtml (accessed June 15, 2005).

Wilson, Keith. "Being Cut from a Youth Sports Team." www.MomsTeam.com (accessed October 1, 2005).

Chapter Fifteen

Advisory Council on Youth Sports, Scarsdale (NY). *Report on Youth Sports.* September 22, 2004. http://www.scarsdale.com/Recreation/sports_survey.asp.

Bigelow, Bob, Tom Moroney, and Linda Hall. *Just Let the Kids Play: How to Stop Other Adults from Ruining Your Child's Fun and Success in Youth Sports.* Deerfield Beach, FL: Health Communications, 2001.

Brady, Frank. "Children's Organized Sports: A Developmental Perspective." *Journal of Physical Education, Recreation & Dance* 75, no. 2 (February 2004): 35(8).

Brown, Dennis K. "Researcher Seeks to Improve Youth Sports Experiences." *Lumen* (March 2005). http://lumen.nd.edu/2005_03/YouthSports.shtml (accessed September 19, 2005).

Clay, Rebecca. "From Science to Service: Making a Model Program." http://alt.samhsa.gov/samhsa_news/VolumeXI_1/article6.htm (accessed August 30, 2005).

Convention on the Rights of the Child (1990), www.unhcr.ch/html.menu3/b/k2crc.htm (accessed September 17, 2005).

David, Paulo. *Human Rights in Youth Sport: A Critical Review of Children's Rights in Competitive Sports.* New York: Routledge, 2004.

Donnelly, Peter, and Leanne Petherick. "Worker' Playtime? Child Labour at the Extremes of the Sporting Spectrum," *Sport in Society* 7, no. 3 (2004): 301–321.

Gavora, Jessica. *Tilting the Playing Field: Schools, Sports, Sex and Title IX.* San Francisco: Encounter Books, 2001.

Gerdy, John R., *Sports in School: The Future of an Institution.* New York: Teachers College Press, 2000.

Greenfell, Christopher, and Report Rinehart. "Skating on Thin Ice: Human Rights in Youth Figure Skating." *International Review for the Sociology of Sport* 38, no. 1 (2003): 79–97.

Hood, J. "Many Children's Leagues Possess Bank Accounts That Startle Contributors." *Modesto Bee,* April 25, 2004.

Kientzler, Alesha. "Fifth- and Seventh-Grade Girls' Decisions About Participation in Physical Activity." *Elementary School Journal* 99, no. 5 (1999): 391–414.

Lake, Celinda, and Kellyanne Conway. *What Women Really Want: How American Women Are Quietly Erasing Political, Racial, Class, and Religious Lines to Change the Way We Live.* New York: Free Press, 2005.

Minnesota Coalition of Organizations for Sex Equity in Education. "Title IX: Providing Equal Opportunities for Girls." (pamphlet)

Sax, Leonard. *Why Gender Matters: What Parents and Teachers Need to Know About the Emerging Science of Sex Differences.* New York: Doubleday, 2005.

Sport England (Child Protection in Sport Unit) "Standards for Safeguarding and Protecting Children in Sport." (January 2003) www.thecpsu.org.uk (accessed 9/8/05).

Sports Done Right. A Call to Action On Behalf of Maine's Student-Athletes. The University of Maine Sport and Coaching Initiative. www.sportsdoneright.org

Chapter Sixteen

Advisory Council on Youth Sports, Scarsdale (NY). *Report on Youth Sports.* September 22, 2004. http://www.scarsdale.com/Recreation/sports_survey.asp.

PERMISSIONS

INDEX